AF305130

"Having spent over 20 years speaking with senior HR and business executives about what it really takes to build healthy, high-performing organizations, this book felt incredibly timely. *Rapid Reculturing* is a thoughtful and refreshing take on culture, not as a buzzword but as the real engine behind performance, connection, and long-term success. Alex Bailey and Kerri O'Neill bring both humanity and practical insight to a topic that has never mattered more."

—Chris Rainey,
CEO and cofounder,
HR Leaders and Atlas Copilot

"Every leader in every kind of organization needs a fresh perspective and empowering set of tools on how to create or transform culture to be the keystone for human thriving and organizational effectiveness. *Rapid Reculturing* provides practical guidance and inspiring stories for how to shape and steward culture to become the blueprint and engine for sustained excellence. The book details the key drivers and transformative skills needed to make culture the dynamic living infrastructure that rehumanizes and reinvigorates workplaces. The book is readable, relevant, and immediately actionable, making it a critical resource for all of today's leaders."

—Jane Dutton,
professor emerita of management and organizations,
University of Michigan

"In the age of transformation, the concept of rapid recapturing provides the opportunity to consider how cultures are reshaped.

This book provides a valuable practical approach to changing elements of organizational cultures to cope with the complexity, chaos, and messiness of change. Kerri and Alex share their experience of how reculturing can optimize assets, drive productivity and performance, and strengthen innovation. It is a concept well worth exploring and a book worth dipping into to learn more."

—Julie Hodges,
professor of organizational change,
Durham University Business School,
Durham University, England

"A long overdue wake-up call. As a top-level executive coach, I have worked alongside some of the finest leaders, and I have sat in enough boardrooms to know when someone is telling the truth about what is truly going on inside organizations. Alex and Kerri are telling that truth.

I have known both authors for years and have watched them each, in their own distinct ways, refuse to accept the comfortable platitudes that pass for culture thinking in most businesses. That intellectual restlessness is all over this book, and it is what makes it worth your time.

What strikes me most is the honesty of the diagnosis. The picture they paint of organizations quietly hollowing out, values gathering dust on intranet pages, leaders weary and uncertain, is not comfortable reading. But it is accurate. The data they draw on is compelling, and the pattern it describes will be familiar to anyone paying close attention to the state of working life right now.

The rewilding analogy captures something important: that we have over-engineered the human side of our organizations to the point where the natural connective tissue that once held people together has been smothered. The instinct to simplify, to reintroduce rather than redesign, is both smart and practical.

My one counsel to readers is to resist the urge to skim. The Introduction alone contains more genuinely useful provocation than most leadership books manage across their entirety.

This book is an important, science-informed argument for doing the hard work that matters. Given where most organizations find themselves right now, I would say the timing is rather good.

Highly recommended."

—John Ainley,
chair and partner, The Alexander Partnership

"Culture requires leadership. A CEO sets the horizon, sets the tone, and chooses the people. That is the work.

Rapid Reculturing treats this as a real, personal journey—not a formula—and focuses on what actually works. Culture lives only when people follow.

I endorse the work, and recommend you don't try to treat it as a recipe book but as something to inform you."

—Ben Veermeyen,
general partner, Keen Venture Partners

"As chairs, we are custodians of long-term value. We are responsible for ensuring our organizations are fit for the future, not just compliant in the present. This book by Kerri and Alex makes the case, persuasively and urgently, that culture is now the defining strategic priority. If we fail to invest in it with intention and speed, we risk drifting to a place from which it will be difficult to return. A powerful blueprint for leaders who know culture can't wait. Read it, act on it, and reculture with intent."

—Shaun Meadows,
chairman, First Central Insurance Management;
senior independent director,
First Central Group

"Bold, human, and beautifully practical.

This book brings a rare blend of humanity and practical wisdom to the work of culture. It offers bold new thinking, grounded in science and lived experience, yet always keeps people at the center. With tools that are both intuitive and actionable, including how to navigate AI with integrity and grace, Reculturing shows leaders how to evolve their organizations with intention, integrity, and tools that keep people at the heart of every choice. A timely, generous guide for anyone committed to cultures where people can truly thrive."

—Marie Sigsworth,
executive coach and advisor; NED, trustee

"This book, which is academically robust, is written in a voice that makes you want to read on and learn. Through the passion of the authors, it is clear that they want to encourage and lead to reader to seek out their own organizational solution. The style and content reflects not only the authors' expertise but also their commitment to shaping something meaningful through reculturing an organization.

There is clarity of thought, a preparedness to get behind assumptions, and an honesty to set out a how-to vision with precision and hope. It is not another book about "culture." By developing their thinking, letting the reader reflect on issues, and using the checklists, any organization can move forward.

Their ideas will resonate with readers, open up new conversations and opportunities for listening, and inspire further exploration. To the Alex and Kerri, congratulations. You have produced a work of real substance and lasting value.

May this book find its way onto the desk of CEOs and their top team and that they take time to understand how this fits with the future needs of their organization and its people."

—Michael Maher,
former public limited company chair and group HR director

"This book is for all leaders looking to unlock long term growth and performance. It's clear that AI is rapidly upending our blueprint for business success and with it our established mechanisms of effect; control, scale, and consistency, replacing them with those that are deeply human: community, relationships, and connected capability. It's no longer power over but more about power with. For Kerri and Alex, culture is our superpower for organizational success, the fertile ground for how people grow, but to unlock its power we need to reculture and rewild our organizations and restore our natural ecosystems. This is a highly practical guide and toolkit for how to do this and rapidly! They have turned a brilliant concept and made it practical, achievable, and, most importantly, exciting to do! The future belongs to the brave: are you brave enough?"

—Sue Brooks,
CEO Imagine

"Highly reflective, detailed, insightful analysis, and challenging observations. This book could shift organizational thinking about culture—for everyone's benefit."

—Charlie Warshawski,
founder, Love Your Coaching

"Kerri and Alex elegantly reframe and refresh culture change thinking through the powerful metaphor of rewilding: stop over-engineering, restore the conditions for health, and let the system regenerate. In an AI-accelerated world—where culture increasingly plays out across a human–nonhuman continuum—*Rapid Reculturing* offers brilliantly practical steps to rehumanize the workplace and spark a phoenix-like renewal of energy and connection in our ever more complex world."

—Vivienne Meredith,
owner, V Meredith consulting;
former Financial Times Stock Exchange group HR director

RAPID
RECULTURING

ALEX BAILEY · KERRI O'NEILL

RAPID RECULTURING

Transforming **Organizations** at **Pace** and **Scale**

WILEY

Library of Congress Cataloging-in-Publication Data is Available:

ISBN 9781394409556 (Cloth)
ISBN 9781394409570 (ePDF)
ISBN 9781394409563 (ePub)

Cover Design: Wiley
Cover Image: © Mikhail Bogdanov/Getty Images
Author Photos: Courtesy of the Authors

*With gratitude to the hundreds of thousands of humans
I'm honored to have worked with and learned from, and to my
family for their unwavering support. And to Kerri: "We did it!"
Loved every second. Thank you.*

—Alex Bailey

*To Evie and Ryan O'Neill, my daily inspiration. To my
treasured friends, family, colleagues, and peers. To my fellow chief
people officers and organizational development specialists, this is
for you, and of course to the people whose lives we touch through
the organizations we create. Finally of course to Alex: such an
inspiration and friend over the decades.*

—Kerri O'Neill

Contents

PART III   How to Reculture at Pace and Scale   **153**

Foreword

Someone once said to me that good leaders are always "up to something." If you'd met Alex Bailey and Kerri O'Neill, as I first did during their time at Aviva, you'd know exactly what that means. Even then, long before their paths diverged into Bailey & French and Ipsos, they carried a rare combination of curiosity, imagination and rigor. They were the kind of leaders who didn't just observe the world—they studied it and tried to make it better. It's no surprise that now, 20 years on, Alex and Kerri are still shaping conversations about how people thrive at work.

What has always set Alex and Kerri apart is the way they blend humanity with evidence. Alex brings a deep commitment to strengths-based leadership and positive organizational psychology, always searching for what enables people to flourish. Kerri brings a sharp, research-driven lens, grounded in behavioral science and a profound understanding of how organizations really function beneath the surface. Together, they have spent decades working across industries, cultures, and contexts, helping leaders navigate complexity with clarity and compassion.

Rapid Reculturing is the culmination of that shared journey—a thoughtful, practical, and deeply human guide for leaders who are steering their organizations through the fog of a hazy and uncertain future. Their evidence-based approach distils their reflections, their research, and their lived experience into something both accessible and transformative. For senior leaders, and especially for chief people officers (CPOs) or those responsible for shaping culture and leading change, this book is a timely and essential guide. It offers a perspective on culture that feels grounded, hopeful, and profoundly needed in the world of work today.

A Perfect Accompaniment for an Artificial Intelligence (AI)-Integrated Workplace

Kerri and Alex make a compelling case for creating adaptable cultures to meet the challenges of the day. In my own profession, human resources (HR), CPOs are operating in a landscape defined by rapid transformation, and the pressure on the role has never been more intense. They're expected to navigate a labor market where skills are evolving at a significant pace, while AI is reshaping job design, capability needs, and the future of organizations. This creates a dual challenge: inspiring performance and growth while simultaneously reskilling the existing workforce at pace. The pressure is amplified by shifting employee expectations about flexibility, purpose, and well-being, all of which, as set out in *Rapid Reculturing*, demand a more sophisticated and human-centered people strategy. There has never been a more perfect time to examine culture within organizations.

At the same time, CPOs are under growing scrutiny to deliver measurable business impact. Boards and CEOs expect HR to be a strategic engine, not a support function, which means demonstrating clear return on investment on people initiatives, improving productivity, and ensuring the organization's culture actively drives performance. Culture itself has become a design challenge rather than a set of values on a wall. CPOs are expected to protect well-being, prevent burnout, and maintain engagement in an environment where work is faster, more digital, and more demanding than ever. For many leaders, the new expectation is shaping the future of work while keeping the organization competitive, and culturally healthy. Alex and Kerri make the argument that *Rapid Reculturing* offers a chance for organizations to renew their cultures to meet the demands of the future in a sustainable, human-centered way.

Making Sense of Culture in Organizations

Organizational culture can feel abstract when you try to pin it down, but we make sense of it by paying attention to the everyday patterns that shape how work really gets done. As set out in *Rapid Reculturing*, culture is reflected in the lived experience of people navigating decisions, pressures, and relationships. We understand it by observing the unwritten rules: who gets listened to, how conflict is handled, what behaviors are rewarded, and what people quietly avoid. These subtle signals tell us far more about a culture than any formal statement ever could.

Alex and Kerri encourage "courageous observation" to help build an awareness of the culture within your organization, preempting what might be ready for evolution. I've seen countless examples across my career of leaders making sense of culture by listening to the stories people tell. When you hear people describe "how things work around here," they're giving you a window into the emotional logic of the organization—the norms that shape belonging, trust, and psychological safety. Stories help us understand not just what people do but also why they do it. As Alex and Kerri set out, culture is not static but instead it's a living system shaped by people, power, and purpose. Making sense of it means paying attention to the human signals that sit beneath the surface of strategy and structure.

What's on the Other Side of Rapid Reculturing?

When an organization gets its culture right, the gains are far-reaching. At the most fundamental level, a strong culture creates a form of clarity. People know what good looks like, how decisions get made, and what behaviors are expected of them. That sense of shared understanding helps to reduce conflict, speeds up collaboration, and gives colleagues the confidence to act with empowerment. In fast-moving environments, that clarity becomes a competitive advantage because it enables colleagues to act with purpose instead of hesitation.

Finally, getting culture right creates a strong, magnetic organizational focus. It attracts the right talent, aligns leaders on shared ideas, and builds trust. Culture becomes an important signal of what the organization stands for, shaping how it shows up in the world. *Rapid Reculturing* shows how a renewed culture creates a workforce that feels energized rather than depleted. When culture works, it becomes the engine that powers performance.

Summary

Rapid Reculturing offers leaders an evidence-based approach to revitalizing workplace cultures through connection and courage. It provides a meaningful framework for humanizing the world of work in the age of AI, and the four drivers of reculturing offer a pragmatic and inspirational method where people are invited to cocreate the future and reconnect to their purpose.

Sarah Gregory
Deputy Chief People Officer, BBC

Introduction

Is business culture as we know it dead?

In boardrooms and virtual meeting spaces around the world, quiet discomfort is brewing. It's not about missing key performance indicators or underperforming products. It's something deeper, harder to measure, but impossible to ignore: culture. Organizational culture transformation has been a high priority for decades. Culture is where the human element of strategy comes to life. We regularly hear the statement, attributed to famous author and management consultant Peter Drucker, that "culture eats strategy for breakfast," demonstrating the unrivaled power of culture to shape organizational success. Yet with the volume and pace of change, the march of artificial intelligence (AI) and workplace agents in our workforce, and deep uncertainty in the direction of global affairs, taking a human approach to change and innovation feels like a brave thing to do. We find ourselves in a time where today's typical corporate culture no longer creates the solutions we need, and in many cases is diminishing or even lost entirely.

What Is Culture?

Culture is one of the most talked about but least understood aspects of organizational life. Despite decades of research exploring the importance of culture to an organization's success, it still feels like a hard-to-put-your-finger-on ethereal concept. Culture is vital to business effectiveness because it's the fertile ground in which people in our organizations grow. It defines the space between people. It's the arena of our work. Where there are people, there is culture. It's a distinctive, universal human trait shaped by social membership (Tyler, 1871). It's the hidden bridging force that shapes whether our organization succeeds or not. You have a culture whether you like it or not, shape it or not. Our cultures powerfully work on us to define the collective identity of a group or society. It has the power to unify and to divide. It gets honed by the shared beliefs, customs, traditions, values, language, power cues, and expression. It can get shocked, but it can also be remarkably resilient. And crucially it can evolve.

Because culture sets the conditions for how people connect, communicate, and organize their working lives, creating both meaning and a sense of belonging, it is a uniquely important aspect of organizational life. Cultural norms tell us what is considered acceptable, admirable, or meaningful within the organization and so it is important for people as they navigate achieving results, developing careers and attracting people, customers, and investors.

Meetings, greetings, and what happens when the pressure is on, and off, are all tells of the culture you have. It shapes what you look out for, what gets noticed, and ultimately whose voices are heard. Some say you can tell a culture by the worst behavior it tolerates. As we think about performance and success for our firms, there are three strategic questions relating to the culture that any board or C-suite can ask itself:

- What is the culture we really have?
- What is the culture we need to achieve our goals?
- If there is a gap, how do we fill it?

Yet despite the seeming simplicity of the questions, most companies struggle to answer with the same confidence they would on other areas linked to strategy or technology.

The reason we collectively struggle to answer these pertinent, important questions is because culture largely sits in our subconscious, our symbols, in our nonverbal communication, some even question whether it is real. We try to use levers that used to work, but we now can't operate in the complexity of the Digital Era.

We still don't know how to consistently define it, measure it, and crucially align it to where the organization needs to head.

As a result, many organizations today find themselves in a strange and painful limbo. They're still operating, still delivering, still showing up but something feels off. The sense of belonging that once defined team dynamics has eroded. The clarity of purpose that once galvanized action is now a distant echo. The norms of business that didn't need to be spoken have shifted.

In short, they've lost or are in danger of losing their grasp of culture. And with it, they've stumbled into a profound quandary: How do you rebuild something that was once organic but now feels artificial to re-create?

The State of Organizations Today

The growing issues of culture slowly diminishing play out in ways both subtle and stark:

- Disengagement quietly spreads as people go through the motions.
- Collaboration gives way to silos as trust diminishes and relationships wither.
- Values become platitudes on posters, no longer felt or lived or even seen in a hybrid world.
- Turnover rises, especially among those who care deeply about purpose and belonging.
- Burnout festers in the absence of emotional safety or collective meaning.

In an age when machines and AI can do almost anything, this is a dangerous and otherworldly place for our organizations to be in.

At its core, the culture quandary is about being stuck between urgency and uncertainty. Leaders know something must be done, but they're unsure what will work and afraid that whatever they do may feel hollow or forced. They often try to fix culture through top-down initiatives: another survey, a new set of values or employee value proposition, a rebranded mission statement, a new leadership development program. But these actions rarely touch the deeper roots of culture, because culture isn't a document; it's a living, breathing system of relationships, and shared mindsets.

What makes this even more challenging is the speed of change in the world outside. Hybrid work, AI, agentic workforces, global crises, climate change, generational shifts—everything is evolving. And with it, our expectations of what work should feel like are shifting, too. The very people who drive organizational success, the curious, creative, connected, values-driven individuals, now expect more than just a job. They want to belong. To grow. To contribute to something meaningful, they can tell the difference between authentic culture and performative gestures. It is striking to us how many people have developed side hustles linked to how they want to contribute to give them the engagement and resilience they need to withstand today's corporate cultures. Added to this, various values and behavioral expectations produced over the last few decades to help align people's actions, behavior, and attitudes have largely fallen short for the times we find ourselves in.

Despite spending billions on workplace support, we know our organizations fail to give people the satisfaction they could have at work. According to Gallup's 2025 annual "State of the Global Workforce" report, only 21% of workers report feeling is involved in and enthusiastic about their work (Gallup, 2025). This level of engagement has dropped for the first time since 2009 during the Global Financial Crisis when we faced a stark lesson that something was amiss in our businesses. Engagement is no longer as helpful in creating stickiness in our workforces; engagement initiatives can feel more akin to consumer brand marketing than emotional connection to our work, and as a result we see strange things occurring, such as a recent UK study said that 40% of call center staff expect to leave their job due to well-being concerns, despite high levels of engagement (Bashford, 2025).

Furthermore, strikes and tribunals against companies are only growing. In December 2024 in the United Kingdom the employment tribunal system recorded an open caseload increase of 31% over the same period in 2023 (Ministry of Justice, 2025). We also know the damaging effects of our industrial era practices on our planet, despite the rise of sustainability governance and expertise. We've invested billions in technology and yet organizations haven't taught people the skills required to power it. Estimates vary but up to half of today's workers will need to be reskilled in the next few years. The economic cost of the skills shortage we have is estimated to be $8.5 trillion, and research by McKinsey suggests that in the United States alone, there is an imbalance of 20 job openings for every one net new employee in skilled trade roles (Greenberg, 2024). Organizations are not doing enough, fast enough, to ensure the workforce, which now spans five generations, evolves ready for the new age. And trust has gone. In the 2025 Edelman Trust Barometer, nearly two-thirds of respondents said that the pandemic made them feel a greater sense of grievance against business, government, and the wealthy (Edelman, 2025) and this is affecting length of service within organizations. The median number of years that wage and salary workers had been with their current employer was 3.9 years in January 2024, down from 4.1 years in January 2022, and the lowest since January 2002, the US Bureau of Labor Statistics reported in September 2024 (Bureau of Labor Statistics, 2024).

Values programs have been at the bedrock of culture management for the past five decades and have often been the immediate default for organizational culture refresh. We know organizations and the people within them evolve, taking the best of what they have and adapting to the new context they are in, but values programs themselves rarely evolve. We tend to stubbornly make the context fit the value, rather than the other way round. One of the earliest and most influential writings on company values comes from Thomas J. Watson Jr., the second CEO of IBM. In 1963, he wrote a book titled *A Business and Its Beliefs* (Watson, 1962), which codified IBM's core principles and values. This book became the prevailing text for understanding corporate culture and the importance of values in guiding a company's actions and decisions. Values have undoubtedly helped us to get businesses this far but without regular reflection, realignment, and iteration, values can quickly become irrelevant or, worse, feel like they belong to a past or highly idealized and a fake news version of the organization.

Organizations worldwide invest heavily in training and development, to the tune of $403 billion (Training Industry, 2024), in the hope this will translate into strategy execution and culture. Companies allocate significant budgets to programs, executive coaching, and skill-building initiatives to cultivate effective leaders to drive results and shape culture. According to McKinsey's studies (Gurdjian, 2014), most leadership development programs often fail due to a lack of contextual relevance, ineffective evaluation methods, and misalignment with organizational needs. Research highlights that many programs adopt a one-size-fits-all approach, ignoring the specific challenges and culture of the organization. Additionally, companies frequently measure success based on participant satisfaction rather than tangible improvements in leadership effectiveness. Another common issue is the failure to integrate leadership training into daily work, leading to minimal long-term impact. Without clear objectives, ongoing support, and evidence-based methodologies, leadership development efforts struggle to produce meaningful results.

The lack of cultural cohesion in our organizations mirrors what we are experiencing in society at large. With ever growing divisions, unpredictable trends and dysfunctional leadership everywhere we increasingly see rising tension and a deep and worrying inertia in politics, economics, and in business. The trend toward individualism in our societies and on our screens means there is less binding more of us than ever. Large global organizations have tried to move first against the rising tides of losing culture and have significantly retracted remote working and called their workforce back into the office, with the main aim to refind the culture and rebuild collaboration and innovation (Amazon, Meta, Goldman Sachs, NASA, Lloyds, and many more). With hybrid and remote working creating barriers to physical connectedness we rely on remote connection. This reliance has grown and replaces the previous absorbing of culture through osmosis being in the same physical space. We will imminently see the research and data come through on the impact of this on productivity and performance, but how much will we then be able to measure culture? Not only with the pandemic disruptions causing everyone to work differently, but with the rapid amount of movement between organizations we are questioning whether it is possible to maintain any cultural norms at all? We hear that organizations, leaders, and people don't even realize that it's diminishing with the slow but steady individualized and siloed focus we have let become the norm over the past five years.

The Time Is Now to Reculture

Despite the current picture feeling the most challenging it has ever been, we are optimistic. It is now time for organizations to do the inner work required to fix for the future ahead. The lives of 3.4 billion workers worldwide rely on it. Culture sets the boundaries of potential success and failure. We must work out how we rapidly support people to bring culture back to the forefront of their attention in private organizations, nongovernmental organizations, schools, hospitals, and governments. All places of work.

We believe we can help bring greater awareness, knowledge, and skills to more people on how to evolve their culture at pace. We can demystify what to focus on, what not to focus on, and where to pay attention. This means culture can be molded. The shaping and stewarding of culture is how we have managed group dynamics since the dawn of time. It is vitally important that we continue to use this part of our human ability honed over so many years. Because what will happen to us if we steadily lose this? Will we evolve to have fewer social skills, and will that have an increase in conflict with more miscommunication and misunderstanding? For example, the way we perceive authority, approach teamwork, or even our attitudes toward time can be deeply rooted in the cultural norms we've absorbed subconsciously. The way our subconscious mind influences our daily interactions is both intricate and impactful.

What Led to This Book

This book started when Alex and Kerri reconnected for dinner in the aftermath of the punishing lockdowns of the 2020 global pandemic. We reconnected as friends but spent the whole time talking about the fact that now, more than any time in our living memory, our organizations are in crisis and disarray. Performance and growth feel challenged in most industries. We first started working together in the early 2000s shaping the global people agenda for FTSE 100 insurer Aviva, then called Norwich Union, and have stayed in close touch since. Both of us have forged successful C-suite career paths, Alex as founder and chief executive officer of a highly successful global business and learning consultancy, and one of the world's leading experts on humanizing workplaces, and Kerri as an award-winning transformation-focused chief people officer, qualified executive coach, and nonexecutive director for several leading global organizations.

We discussed at length the cry for help that organizations regularly brought to us and that we advise on. Organizations on the surface seemed to have coped well with the pandemic but there was a bigger sense it was hiding something broader and more worrying goings-on in organizations. We discussed that organizations didn't seem to know how to systematically evolve their cultures at pace and scale to achieve growth or meet the times we are in. That models felt out-of-date. That everything culture-related felt either too complex or far too simple. Important advances in human science and knowledge have been overlooked as we stick stubbornly to what we learnt in a different era. Human resources itself is confused and being misdirected on the evidence in key areas such as performance, leadership development, cultural evolution, well-being, and inclusion. Instead of leaning in, organizations are retreating and convincing themselves that budgets are needed elsewhere currently.

These discussions extended into a concern about the painful, growing split in views on diversity and inclusion, technology and sustainability, all of which have been bedrocks of huge culture change efforts now for over 20 years. In some organizations the only recent discussion on culture has been diversity and inclusion related. And at a time when we needed to come together, we seemed more likely to be falling apart. Our work is underpinned by the field of organizational effectiveness and rooted in organizational psychology, both evidence-based and science-backed disciplines. We both have daughters, and we discussed our worry about the future for them. That was early 2022 and now we are in 2026 and predictions and worries we discussed that summer's evening have largely played out.

We are seeing now that jobs are being lost to AI. Phenomenal leaders have retired, given up and stepped out of corporate life as they are burnt out. Young people entering the workforce have given up on wanting to progress as they don't see the point of navigating what they see as an unfair system of bias. Every time we connect we feel an even greater sense of urgency. Organizations are lost. Leaders are lost. Complex solutions are not going to help. We need to get back to what makes organizations tick and relearn how to evolve our cultures, learning from what we know now from neuroscience, social sciences, and experience and leave behind those interventions that no longer work for the world and era we live in.

Reculturing occurred to us when we were exploring our cultural understandings over the years as observers, influencers, and leaders of culture in organizations. We were frustrated that some key science that had emerged in recent years is being overlooked and underused. Ideas and skills that could help us evolve at breakthrough levels of pace and scale and would make a difference have not been spread as effectively as they could be. We've seen the knowledge of how to view culture, pick impactful interventions, and create change that sticks is in low supply. Our attentions have been elsewhere for a long time, and organizations have been distracted. We have not joined the dots on new scientific research fast enough. We are seeing people stubbornly holding onto ideas that have long now proven to not really work or can't match today's world.

Doing the inner work required in organizations to reach new heights of performance breakthrough isn't easy. We felt a strong pull from other leaders to make sense of this quandary, to rethink what's been an accepted norm, and to have greater impact on the world of work and the impact of that on our planet. The fact we are both driven to do more and better for our world for future generations, including our own children, meant that we naturally align to approaches that feel natural, feel human, feel intuitively right and simple, as well as balancing data-driven ideas.

What Is Reculturing?

Reculturing in organizational terms simply means "to culture again or anew." To reculture means getting to grips once again with culture. Relearning its hidden powers, respecting it, and putting it back at the center of our strategic tool kit. It's deeper than giving it a refresh. It's the act of intentionally investing in and reshaping organizations for people to do their best work in service of achieving results, both in the long and short term. Organizations that choose to take a reculturing approach are signaling that the deep fabric of working lives is important, intentional, systematic, and aligned with strategy. Going on this journey means getting clear and honest about the culture we have, the culture we need for future success, and investment in the strategies to close the gap. Doing so will help us to make the real choices we need to make right now to ensure the organization is a success in the tumultuous Digital Age. It is our strong belief this needs to be done rapidly before we reach somewhere we will struggle to come back from.

Rewilding has become a surprising source of inspiration for us as we developed our thinking. This smart nature-led, conservation approach is focused on the restoring of natural ecosystems using a combination of both modern and ancient knowledge of the land, with the goal being to return land to its natural and self-sustaining state. We were both aware of rewilding from the examples at Knepp Estate and Sharpham Trust in the United Kingdom, Yellowstone National Park in the United States, and Gardens by the Bay in Singapore. The impact of rewilding has the allure of letting go of control and identifying key interventions that help return something to its natural state. When you speak to leaders of this movement, they speak to knowledge having been forgotten and great techniques and ideas being overlooked. They talk to harnessing the innate power of nature to do what it does to thrive. Power with and not power over. Hence when considering the incredible impact that rewilding has had and the association of sustainability (i.e. long-term thriving) we landed on our approach to solve this crisis. Reculturing captures a similar essence of trying to refind something important that can be overcomplicated and overworked to its ruin. We have overengineered much of what is going on in organizations. We are under so much weight of processes, practices, and nonsensical advice on how to manage people that we can barely breathe. Reculturing is about focusing only on what really matters at the core, on important reintroductions of proven human strategies at specific times and in specific ways that strategically bring about the living core. Rewilding is about creating a simplicity and wholeness that often feels refreshing. Reculturing will do the same.

Are you ready to reculture?

How to Use This Book

To get culture firmly back on track and at the heart of the thriving organization and society, we must face some fundamental truths. It also means letting go of some ideas that have now long permeated organizations over the decades. We honor these practices, and the practitioners who have dedicated careers to them, but for right now, for this next phase, they are just making the backpack too heavy. We need to free ourselves from the burden of them. We must stop ignoring the very ideas that could move the needle, unlearning and being curious as to how to get culture back and businesses facing forward again.

We can make sense of what we know now about how culture forms, what humans need from work, and put back what is missing.

And let's not forget: The biggest focus required for leaders over the next few years will be the culture we create and sustain to combine humans, the planet, and AI to thrive.

This book is organized into three parts.

Part I: Why Rapid Reculturing? discusses what reculturing is and why it's needed. We explore the tumultuous times we live in, with AI and the climate crisis affecting everyone, and see now as a chance to reset the dial on culture as a source of energy and flourishing for billions of people. We introduce a new lens for efforts to reculture as to rewild, so we are correctly orientated and attuned to what's coming at us. Reculturing is both a philosophy and a practical method, a science-backed approach. We share how it will help us to optimize our assets, deliver performance, strengthen innovation, grasp opportunity, and reduce risk. This new lens focuses on an approach that will harness, not exploit, what is already there for us.

Part II: Rapid Reculturing Explained, covers the three culture identification zones and the four drivers of reculturing we have discovered through our work. The zones help us identify if our organization's culture is lost, thriving, or cult, and helps us navigate where we are. These zones also help us activate the four human-centered drivers we have found, which, if paid attention to, will scale change rapidly and meaningfully. Working on the drivers will help organizations and their leaders regain the bravery and confidence they need to act.

Our work on culture has shown us other areas we need to rethink, namely, the old change management approach. The industry seems broken. The tools don't work. We must get back to the idea that a human problem needs a human solution. Our intention and attention alone are overlooked and powerful muscles that we can use to rebuild our culture leading to drivers that resonate with the new era we are in. We can't easily throw away years and even decades of culture-building activities and habits, so we highlight how to integrate both, and retire what no longer serves.

Part III: How to Reculture at Pace and Scale? covers five cultural evolution skills organizations can master to evolve culture at pace and scale.

In this part, we aim to share how we can evolve organizations at pace centering the well-being of the change leaders and without requiring lots of exhausting interventions and artificial programs. We share a new, simpler, more intuitive approach to support culture change based on five core cultural evolution skills. We introduce and share these skills that have worked for us both across many large organizations and are recognized by others through our research as the framework some are already subconsciously using. Bringing these to the forefront of our attention is what makes the difference to both pace and scale of change.

The three identifying zones, four drivers, and five skills make up our suggested reculture toolkit.

The Promise of Reculturing

Reculturing is not a temporary fix. It gives us permission to let go of culture-shaping activities that no longer serve. It is the shift that lets everything else align. This alignment is what enables lasting cultural shifts, not temporary engagement spikes.

It supports these factors:

- Human-centric AI adoption that augments rather than alienates
- Sustainability as a lived value, not a branded message
- Universal inclusion as a systemic design principle, not a siloed program

When culture supports this alignment, flourishing is not a side effect; it is the standard.

It operates through three human leadership principles:

- Clarity with our human switched on:
  - People need to know why they matter, what they're working toward, and how they connect to the bigger picture.
  - Clear direction fuels cognitive safety, strategic alignment, and meaningful autonomy. It enables you to move faster.

- Courage to embrace AI:
    - Fear is natural, but avoidance is costly.
    - Culturally, we must shift from resisting AI to shaping how we integrate it with ethics, empathy, and human creativity at the core. We need to be clear-eyed about what it can and can't do for us and, importantly, not pretend it is human.
- Compassion for our future and our planet:
    - Culture must model care for the natural world, for each other, and for future generations. Once these areas are forever gone, we cannot contemplate what life on earth will be like.
    - This care shows up in sustainable decisions, regenerative practices, and social responsibility woven into everyday work, again not as a side program or department.
    - These principles give reculturing its practical edge. They enable leaders and teams to act with confidence and cohesion, even amid change.
    - The promise of reculturing is that we can build futures worth working for and live through the transition with clarity, compassion, and courage.

With the right approach, companies can shape their cultures in new ways at pace and scale and supercharge themselves to new heights of growth. This energy can help to overcome the inevitable and wrenching challenges of the day. We argue that organizations need to quickly evaluate not just their strategies but their culture and ensure it will survive the next few decades. This is urgent and essential. It's not something else to do in an ever-growing list of what must be done. It's the rethinking of the guiding approach, decision-making model, sensemaking filter, and cultural underpinning of our organizations that we need to save us.

Who Is This For?

This book is for all those who lead or govern organizations, particularly in the realm of culture, as well as those who simply want to see their organization take a different path toward the future.

This book will challenge engrained norms and outdated practices. We will reframe what culture truly demands in today's AI-assisted, resource-stretched world, and equips strategic leaders with the tools to lead cultural evolution at pace and scale. By letting go of legacy thinking and embracing fresh foundations, purpose, mindset, energy, and connection, organizations can unlock agility, resilience, and relevance.

The future belongs to those brave enough to reculture.

Why Rapid Reculturing?

"Truth is like the sun. You can shut it out for a time, but it ain't goin' away."

—Elvis Presley

In this section we look very honestly at the state of our organizations today—challenging, yes, but also full of possibility. Just as leaders are stepping back and reassessing strategy in light of artificial intelligence (AI), geopolitical instability, and shifting markets, we must do the same with culture. The world that shaped our old cultural norms has changed, and by acknowledging this openly, we create the space to rebuild something stronger, more human, and more future fit.

Part I explores this cultural crossroads: what has been lost, what is emerging, and why now is the moment to reculture with intention and pace.

Cultures That No Longer Fits the World Around It

Organizations everywhere are sensing the same discomfort. The familiar markers of culture—shared rituals, in-person connection, the "way we do things around here"—no longer hold the same power. Hybrid and remote work have dissolved the everyday interactions through which culture once flowed effortlessly. People are more dispersed, more digitally connected, and more exposed to external influences than ever before. The result is fragmentation: teams operating in different realities, subcultures forming based on identity or geography, and leaders unsure how to bring coherence back.

But this fragmentation is not a failure. It is a signal. It tells us that the world has shifted, and culture must shift with it.

Culture in a Digital, Always-On Environment

We explore how culture now lives across a constellation of digital spaces—Teams, Slack, WhatsApp, Instagram, LinkedIn—each shaping how people communicate, belong, and express themselves. Social media accelerates movements, amplifies emotion, and blurs the boundaries between personal and professional identity. Organizations saw this vividly during the global response to the murder of George Floyd, when public pressure drove rapid commitments that later proved difficult to sustain. These moments reveal a deeper truth: Culture is no longer contained within office walls. It is porous, visible, and influenced by forces far beyond the organization.

When leaders recognize this, they can stop trying to control culture and instead learn how to guide it.

Why Traditional Culture Tools Are No Longer Enough

We share that for decades, organizations have relied on values statements, leadership cascades, engagement surveys and behavioral frameworks to shape culture. These tools were built for a slower, more predictable era. They assume we have time to fix what we see and that issues can be declared, and the solutions simply rolled out, and reinforced through programs. But culture is not static. It is dynamic, emotional, and deeply human. It lives in mindsets, assumptions, and relationships, not in posters or slide decks. And we don't have time to wait five years for change to show up.

The chapters highlight several outdated assumptions:

- Culture is lived, not stated.
- Values are meaningful only when they are experienced.
- Behaviors cannot be mandated; they must be modeled.
- Change is not linear; it is emergent.

Traditional change models were designed for industrial era organizations. They assume predictability, hierarchy, and control. They do not account for hybrid work, AI, or the speed of modern complexity. By acknowledging this, organizations free themselves to adopt approaches that match the world they now operate in.

The Forces Reshaping Culture

The chapters identify several forces that are not temporary disruptions but structural shifts:

- Hybrid and remote work have weakened spontaneous connection and belonging.
- Purpose and well-being expectations have risen sharply, especially among younger generations.
- AI and automation are redefining what human contribution looks like.
- Generational shifts are pushing organizations toward transparency, personalization, and authenticity.
- Globalization and diversity make one-size-fits-all cultures unrealistic and exclusionary.
- Leadership trust is under pressure, with authenticity demanded but missteps punished.
- Social media has made culture visible, accelerated, and emotionally charged.

These forces are not signs that culture is dying, they are signs that culture is evolving. When organizations face this honestly, they can begin to design cultures that are fit for the future rather than anchored in the past.

Seeing Culture as a Living System

A central insight across the chapters is that culture behaves more like an ecosystem than a machine. It responds to energy, relationships, and context. It grows in some places and withers in others. It is shaped by informal networks as much as formal structures. And like any ecosystem, it can be restored when the right conditions are created.

This is where the metaphor of rewilding becomes powerful. Rewilding is not about imposing control; it is about removing what suppresses growth, reintroducing what has been lost, and enabling natural processes to regenerate. Reculturing draws on the same principles. It asks leaders to do the following:

- Step back and see the whole system. Culture won't stop being there even if we choose not to see it.
- Remove outdated structures and approaches that no longer serve.
- Reintroduce human practices that create connection and meaning.
- Create conditions where culture can evolve organically and sustainably.

This shift, from control to cultivation, is at the heart of rapid reculturing.

A New Mandate for Culture

The chapters in the part make a clear case: Culture still matters; it is no longer a soft concept or a side project. It is the human infrastructure that determines whether organizations can adapt, innovate, and thrive in a world defined by complexity. Reculturing is not about nostalgia or returning to what once was. It is about building what comes next.

When organizations reculture with intention, they unlock the following:

- Faster, more human decision-making
- Stronger trust and psychological safety
- Greater adaptability and collective intelligence
- Cultures where people feel seen, supported, and connected
- Environments where innovation and collaboration flourish

The fastest organizations in the next decade will be the most human. The most resilient will be those that reculture with clarity, courage, and compassion.

Facing Forward with Honesty and Hope

The chapters close with a hopeful message: By looking honestly at the cultural challenges of this era, we gain the ability to address them. Culture is not yet lost, but it does need to be reimagined. And just as organizations are rethinking strategy, technology, and leadership, they must now rethink culture with the same rigor and urgency.

Reculturing is the human systems response to a human systemic challenge. It offers a way to rebuild connection, restore meaning, and create workplaces where people and performance can thrive side by side. This is not a return to the past. It is an evolution toward a future where culture becomes a source of energy, alignment, and resilience.

1 | Facing the Truth About Where We Are

"Culture is like the wind. It is invisible; yet its effect can be seen and felt."

—Bryan Walker and Sarah Soule (2017)

There is significant challenge within organizations that try to align people to company value sets or behaviors that don't feel true or representative of the whole. Our long-vaunted tools to shape culture, such as our history, values, and top leadership, are no longer enough to cope with the surge of change we are seeing happen to organizations. Culture is being buffeted so hard that we cannot keep up.

For example, take the rise of employee resource groups (ERGs). Most large organizations have a women's network. These help shine a light on the female experience of work. But in the last decade this trend has exploded, and, in some organizations, there can be as many as 15 or so networks that people can join and be part of, each with their own unique agenda and perspective on how the organization should change to meet its needs.

These groups of volunteer champions are often created through engagement commitments from people surveys identifying support required for gaps in the organization. Often these champions have then been relied on for cultural initiatives where internal specialists and expert resources have less investment, so we have developed an overreliance on unqualified change agents. They are given control and influence, yet often unskilled and unsupported at helping their organizations actively deliver what they want without creating challenges elsewhere. The extent to which their power and influence then tips into toxic activism in the workplace, where company expectations fall into a space that conflicts with any individual, is now commonplace.

A large organization in Amsterdam recently recognized that a new ERG had been set up for white men who felt marginalized in the organization, perfectly acceptable according to the organization's policies for ERGs. However, when word got back to leaders that there were conversations within the group supporting racism, white supremacy, and misogyny the private equity firm owners took the action to shut down all ERGs resolving the immediate issue, but leaving many people confused and other groups less supported. The presence and pull of ERGs show that the mainstay culture of the organization is not translating into the workplace nor working for everyone. With the diminishing support for diversity, equity, and inclusion (DEI) initiatives spreading across the globe, will we see less ERG groups searching for community and common values and people simply looking for this human connection elsewhere? It is unlikely that culture can be left in the hands of such groups without better development, investment, and support.

How Does Culture Live Online?

We have seen an explosion of remote and hybrid working environments, a trend we were already seeing but was dramatically sped up thanks to the coronavirus pandemic. Organizations work in a much more distributed way than in the past, and digital workspaces are more common. This shift has occurred alongside the fact that in our everyday lives the average adult now spends 2 hours and 24 minutes on social media every day (Statista, 2025). We move from Microsoft teams to Slack to WhatsApp to Instagram, to LinkedIn, to email multiple times, every day. The virtual spaces in which community and culture now live in organizations would be unrecognizable to a corporate leader of the 1980s or even 1990s. We don't yet know how closely connected organizational culture is to, or driven by, online trends. Does the size of online audience support and reinforce cultural norms? How do we see this happening with the reduction of monitoring on platforms and increasing free speech? Will global media influence reduce significantly with people preferring the thoughts/insights of their online community and where will we find truth? Alongside this, from our experience, most firms don't know how to shape their culture in this setting.

Organizations are experimenting with how to show up in online spaces without the tried and tested guardrails of the past. One example was the tragic 2020 George Floyd incident, which was the catalyst for a major surge of support for the Black Lives Matter movement that catapulted academic ideas around antiracism into the mainstream. According to Pew Research Report "Black Lives Matter stands as a model of a new generation of social movements intrinsically linked to social media" (Bestvater, 2023). The hashtag #blacklivesmatter was used by so many organizations, we thought we were seeing a cultural turning point moment, and in the first two months following the murder of Floyd, more than $5 billion in corporate funding was pledged to organizations for racial equality (Sayed, 2022). Organizations scrambled to put out social media-driven responses and commitments, which by 2025 have been hugely rowed back from (Murray, 2025). The chaos we find ourselves in establishing what organizations stand for—our purpose—risks us continuously getting it wrong, polarizing our narrative from some group somewhere. This demonstrates that perhaps we are now devoid of a mainstay culture in its traditional form.

Cultural fit is no longer something that serves an increasingly diverse workforce or able to serve a diverse customer base. Maybe increasingly we need to accept that the diversity created in our workforce means that all perspectives are appreciated and valued, and that limits the commonality and homogeneity of what used to define culture within organizations.

We used to say don't talk about religion or politics at dinner parties, but that list grows ever longer in the poly-crisis world we live in—don't talk about gender equality, climate change, abortion rights, immigration, on and on. Both the range and the sensitivity of topics seem to be growing, and it's increasingly felt in the workplace.

So How Can We Influence and Evolve Culture with Eggshells Under Foot?

It's vital we step back and make peace with the fact that things have changed. We must see things for how they are now, rather than as we would like them to be.

Nostalgic notions of feeling part of something bigger than ourselves, feeling purposeful through connectedness and interdependence, kept the culture alive yet now we find ourselves more dispersed with many people moving roles post pandemic and shredding what we clung to in terms of organizational culture across all industries. The global pandemic shift to dispersed ways of working has created greater isolation along with the increasingly digital workplace environment.

There is a risk we just give up and ask ourselves questions like these: Have we lost culture altogether? Are we looking for leaders to re-create the cultural norms in this new world of work in a way in which they are incapable? People may be back in the office through return-to-office mandates but how much culture has already been lost during recent times? Is it rebuildable? Or do we need to radically rethink what culture means now for the modern world and how it is created and brought about?

We must face the issues and start to look anew at how we move forward.

What Is Causing Old Corporate Culture to Diminish?

These new and difficult questions for leaders make culture a highly strategic area of business to grapple with. In this new world, the skills and mindsets required for success have changed dramatically. And yet, most of the global workforce and many leadership teams are unprepared for the demands ahead. Perhaps corporate culture feels to some like it is diminishing, but it is simply evolving. Stepping back, organizations can see that both how we define and experience culture has shifted over the past few years and its largely because of a few key factors.

Hybrid and Remote Work

The shift to remote and hybrid work has made culture less about office spaces, and how things are done in the visible sense, and more about the quality of connection and intentional leadership (Clark, 2025). The sudden shift, driven by the rules of the coronavirus pandemic, to remote and hybrid work was a shock to most organizations and individuals. It created a range of complex emotions such as relief of being close to immediate family to deep anxiety and loneliness as jobs were paused or lost. It both brought people together and pulled people very far apart.

We know of one CEO who joined an organization a week before the UK lockdowns began, meaning they had barely met anyone as they started. Traditional culture markers (like office perks and in-person rituals such as birthday cake celebrations) have faded or become complex with the need to ensure everyone can be included wherever they work from, but new forms of engagement, like virtual team building, asynchronous collaboration, and flexible work models are emerging.

What hasn't been addressed is how effective these are in comparison for meaningful human connection? The key aspects of culture that build trust, belonging, and spontaneous collaboration are not easily replicated so people tend to accept a different feel of culture in remote teams on the basis it fits their personal work/life integration needs. Deep questions remain on whether it is good enough for the organization's needs. Some would argue organizations need culture built on those foundations.

Peter Cappelli and Ranya Nehmeh (2025), writing for the *Harvard Business Review*, state that some of the dampening effects of remote and hybrid working on performance "have taken some time to show up." Issues they found in their research range from not helping new people who are struggling early enough, colleagues giving less to support their coworkers with their work and goals, collaboration across teams being almost impossible, virtual meetings are full of people multitasking and not paying full attention, promotions being linked to achievement of individual work as managers can't tell if colleagues get on with others or not, and, most pernicious of all, deep social isolation being bred and culture being eroded.

And yet this is a trend that is here to stay.

Focus on Purpose and Well-Being

Employees today expect more than just a paycheck; they want meaning and belonging in their work with some choosing this over greater financial reward. According to the Deloitte 2025 Gen Z and Millennial Survey, a staggering 89% of Gen Zs and 92% of millennials say a sense of purpose is key to job satisfaction and well-being (Deloitte, 2025). Many companies are actively prioritizing well-being, mental health, and a sense of purpose. Those that fail to do so risk losing talent to organizations that genuinely invest in their people. But how these are seen as a product of, or core tenet of, culture remains to be researched. Since large datasets in the past 10 years show that well-being is critical to organizational performance, it is more likely to be strategically resourced and invested in. There needs to be more studies examining how a focus on well-being and mental health has affected the collective experience and culture, not just how it has had a greater impact on individual experience at work. This might help us understand newer insights that show an intriguing correlation between higher personal resilience and well-being and higher disengagement with the organization.

People with high personal resilience and well-being may sometimes appear more disengaged from their organization—not because they care less, but because they're better at protecting their own boundaries when the culture isn't aligned with their values.

But what's going on beneath the surface? Resilience enables detachment, when needed.

Highly resilient individuals are often self-aware, emotionally intelligent, and able to maintain perspective. When an organization is experiencing dysfunction, unclear values, poor leadership, lack of psychological safety, they may choose to disengage as a protective strategy.

They don't spiral into burnout trying to "fix" a broken system. Instead, they step back, focus on their controllables, and maintain their well-being. After all these are skills we have been promoting in organizations and developing in workforces consistently for the past 5–10 years.

This can look like disengagement, but maybe it's a healthy act of self-preservation.

Well-being supports autonomy. People with high well-being often have a strong sense of purpose and are more likely to be intrinsically motivated. If the organization doesn't align with that purpose, or feels extractive or inauthentic, they may stop trying to "fit in" and instead focus their energy elsewhere (side projects, family, future plans). They're not disengaged from work; they're disengaged from the organization when it's not adding value to their broader sense of meaning.

They may see through performative cultures. People with strong internal grounding can more easily spot when values are performative, when leadership lacks integrity, or when DEI and well-being are used as branding rather than substance. They don't get swept up in surface-level initiatives and may opt out of things that feel hollow.

Again, this can look like cynicism or withdrawal, but it's actually discernment.

Is this a "problem" or an insight? It's an insight and a warning.

When the most grounded, resilient, values-driven people are the ones quietly stepping back, opting out, or mentally checking out, it says more about the organization than the individual.

Potentially it means pushing hard in these areas without substance behind it might exacerbate these issues:

- A lack of meaningful alignment between personal and organizational purpose
- Cultural fatigue, when people are tired of inauthentic messaging
- A gap between what's said and what's experienced

When well-being and purpose lack depth, the most self-aware employees don't disengage from work, they disengage from cultures that no longer deserve their energy.

Generational and Technological Shifts

Younger generations entering the workforce expect transparency, inclusion, and authenticity. At the same time, artificial intelligence (AI), agentic AI, and automation are at pace redefining roles, requiring companies to reinforce the human aspects of work that cannot be replicated by any computer and developing confidence in those such as creativity, social imagination, and collaboration. If a corporate culture has been built over decades on in-depth personal relationships in person in the office, the disruption of recent dispersed ways of working since the pandemic shift means that new generations who have no experience of the past corporate culture have minimal expectations or understanding of it. The "way we do things 'round here" definition is no longer helpful for new starters who work remotely to understand how the culture may support them and without experience of seeing, hearing, feeling leaders role-model organizational values daily.

Dr. Gillian Tett, academic and journalist, speaks to a new phenomenon that has emerged called *Generation P*. This is a cohort of people defined by "its preference for personalization and optionality" (Bottomley, 2025). This growing shift toward hyper-personalization in workplaces is causing organizations to have to offer a complex array of policies, perks, and days off to be able to satisfy the wide range of needs under its roof. Companies are under pressure to offer things like "paw-ternity" leave (time off for new pets), time off for extended travel, and so on. Likewise, managers must be able to make sense of these plus balance the perceptions of fairness and business delivery causing some to back off the job of management altogether. Indeed, according to a report by recruitment agency Robert Walters 52% of Gen Z professionals don't want to be middle managers and 69% of Gen Z say middle management is too high stress and low reward (Robert Walters, 2024).

In addition, AI, and particularly agentic AI, is transforming the way organizations operate, requiring leaders to rethink how they shape culture in the workplace. If culture is the space between humans, where does AI fit in? As AI looks increasingly human-like, automates tasks, enhances decision-making, and reshapes roles, companies must foster an environment where adaptability, security, collaboration, and ethical considerations take center stage. With an estimated $4.4 trillion in long-term productivity gains, AI is advancing at record speed (Kelly, 2025). A culture that embraces AI needs to prioritize continuous learning, ensuring employees develop skills that complement AI-driven processes rather than compete with them. AI is as significant in the workplace as electricity, the internet, and email; therefore, entry-level roles are changing as AI steps in to do what someone new in the workplace would have done for more experienced and senior members of staff. AI is also writing our emails, newsletters, and other content, so our expressions are changing, and with it comes harder to determine rules of the game. This shift is not just about integrating AI but about redefining the cultural blueprint to thrive in an AI-augmented world.

For Gen Z their relationship with technology and AI is different. Gen Z trust AI bots more than human doctors (Glick, 2023) and spend their time conversing with AI about their lives when they are not interacting on social media. Compared with 40% of other generations, 66% of Gen Z use digital tools such as wellness apps and fitness trackers to monitor their health. Yet this extreme connectedness coexists with an epidemic of loneliness; 2025 Ipsos research revealed that 36% of Gen Zers feel lonely every week despite having many friends (Jones, 2025). This dynamic is in our workforce and shaping what happens there.

Trust and Leadership Accountability

With the pace and complexity of business today, command-and-control leadership is fading fast in high-performing organizations because it is too slow. Waiting for the CEO attention or a board meeting coming round in a few weeks can be the difference between winning and losing. We are seeing it being replaced by more human-centered leadership. Trust is the foundation on which this transformation is built. Rachel Botsman, a leading academic on the topic of trust, defines it as "confident relationship with the unknown" (Botsman, 2024).

Companies that embrace open communication and trust tend to move faster and sustain stronger cultures by retaining talent for long tenures, which allows for more time for people to build stronger bonds, while those resistant to change may struggle with engagement and retention. The disruption of recent years and continuous change and uncertainty have meant people are searching for leaders they trust and offer a way forward in a complex world. Research shows people have greater trust in organizational leaders than in politicians or the media, increasing the responsibility that business leaders have to help others make sense of what is going on in the world.

The job of leadership is therefore getting redefined. McKinsey (Maor, 2024) have recently changed their perspectives on leadership too as the "imperial CEO is no more." They cite the need for inner work to be the mainstay of leadership and CEO development—this inner work focuses on resilience, empathy, humility, versatility, and authenticity, which leads to human leadership. This shift in leadership style will also affect the culture as top leaders still hold sway in the culture arena.

Globalization and Cultural Diversity

With teams spread across different countries and cultures, a one-size-fits-all corporate culture is no longer practical or indeed ethical/moral. We can't expect everyone to share values and beliefs in the same way now that we have greater diversity. Companies are learning to build inclusive cultures that celebrate diverse perspectives rather than impose rigid corporate identities. Leaders can no longer assume an alignment between individual and corporate values.

According to Ipsos (Ipsos Global Trends, 2024), large income and wealth disparities are widely recognized as detrimental to society, yet in many countries they have widened over the past decade. The intensity of this feeling has resulted in heightened societal stress and a splintering of traditional structures, with new ideologies and political allegiances emerging.

The World Has Changed Forever

All these forces tell us we are just not experiencing a period of change; we are living through the collapse of an old era. The assumptions and structures that underpinned 20th-century organizations are eroding under the weight of unprecedented global forces. It is time to face the reality: The world we designed our organizations for no longer exists.

The gap between our current capability and future need in organizations is growing:

- From task execution to sensemaking
- From siloed expertise to interdisciplinary collaboration
- From compliance to creativity
- From static learning to continuous adaptability

Despite these future needs emerging steadily over the past years and plenty of resources and budget made available to focus on culture in organizations, we haven't seen large organizations able to keep up with the pace and scale of interventions required. There is a disquiet growing, with CEOs and executive teams now considerably more educated on cultural change than 20 years ago, demanding to know how leaders will get their culture intentionally "match fit" for the future. So with demand and resource available, what is getting in our way?

2 | Why Organizations Are Failing to Shape Culture

We know culture can help us to thrive even in tumultuous eras, yet one of the hardest aspects of shaping culture is its intangibility. It seems we are in a cultural fog. It's okay to not have a deep sense of your company's culture except perhaps a quiet knowing that not all is well. Culture is notoriously hard to define because it's invisible until it's experienced. It lives in the spaces between people, not just in values printed on a wall. It's complex, fluid, and deeply human.

Yet, despite its elusiveness, culture is the undercurrent that shapes everything: how people behave under pressure, what gets rewarded or tolerated, who gets promoted, and how decisions are made. The problem is, most organizations still treat culture as a static artifact and something to be declared, not designed.

The Features of Culture

There are features of culture that we have failed to address that we must now consider as we face the atrophy we are experiencing and confront old ways of working.

Culture Is Lived, Not Just Stated

You can write values like *integrity* or *collaboration* on posters, in hiring booklets, and on the intranet, but the real culture shows up in the everyday. It's revealed in how teams respond to setbacks, how leaders handle dissent, and how recognition is distributed.

We know that disconnects between stated values and lived behaviors create confusion and distrust. Yet we continue to prioritize values in our vision statements, strategic plans, and leadership programs without interrogating whether they're being lived.

Edgar Schein's (2016) foundational model of culture helps us here. He divides culture into three levels:

- Artifacts (visible elements like dress code or office layout)
- Espoused values (what organizations say they believe)
- Underlying assumptions (the unconscious beliefs that truly drive behavior)

It's the third layer, those invisible assumptions, that hold the most power. And they're the hardest to access.

The statement "Culture shapes what people do when no one is watching" popularized by Herb Kelleher, CEO of Southwest Airlines, as he often shared in his leadership learnings, suggests that true culture is revealed through consistent, everyday actions, not just through official policies or statements. Perhaps now, when more people are working remotely in isolation and not side by side, and less visibility and watching is physically possible, that concern about culture has become so critical.

Culture Is Dynamic, Not Static

Culture isn't a fixed asset. It evolves with people, context, and the world around it. A culture that worked pre-pandemic may no longer serve in hybrid or AI-powered environments. Yet many organizations behave as if their culture hasn't changed.

Leaders often define culture once and expect it to stay relevant forever. It's rarely treated as a strategic priority in board meetings or critical conversations. Instead, it becomes another item on the list and something someone else will raise when it's urgent and when there is a new CEO.

Trying to define culture like a static mission statement is like trying to hold water in your hands. And yet, this is how many leaders operate repeating rituals that once worked, too burnt out to imagine redefining culture amid a landscape of competing priorities.

Otto Scharmer's groundbreaking work on *Presencing* (Scharmer and Kaufer, 2007) offers a powerful lens here. He describes culture as something we must sense into not just analyze.

> "The success of an intervention depends on the interior condition of the intervener."

Culture change begins not with action, but with attention. With the ability to listen to what is emerging, not just what is already known.

Culture Lives in Mindsets, Not Just Behaviors

Behaviors are visible, but they stem from collective beliefs, assumptions, and mindsets. These are harder to spot, especially in hybrid environments where people's mental models shift daily.

Take conflict avoidance, for example. It's not just a behavior; it's often rooted in a mindset that "disagreement is dangerous." To shift culture, we need to surface and reshape these invisible patterns. But doing so in a dispersed, digital-first world is incredibly difficult.

Culture change requires more than behavioral frameworks; it demands mindset work. And that's not something you can outsource or automate. Leaders must pause, reflect, and connect with deeper sources of knowing before they can lead meaningful change.

Power and Politics Shape Culture More Than We'd Like to Admit

Culture is often defined by the loudest voices, usually senior leaders, based on their own experiences and biases. This creates a gap between aspirational culture (what we want to be) and actual culture (what we are).

New employee listening techniques are essential to start from a basis of truth. Without them, organizations risk building strategies on a false sense of cultural health.

There's also fear. Fear of naming toxic dynamics. Fear of admitting when culture is inequitable or exclusionary. Fear of confronting political influences, especially when external forces shape internal norms.

We saw this vividly in the backlash against diversity, equity, and inclusion initiatives led by President Donald Trump. The speed at which business leaders retreated revealed how external dynamics can override internal intentions. Culture isn't shaped in a vacuum; it's shaped in context.

Culture Is Fragmented and Subcultures Are Rising

In global or hybrid organizations, culture can feel fragmented. One team's "norm" is another team's "problem." Subcultures form based on location, leadership style, function, or identity group.

A universal definition of culture can flatten important nuances and leave people out. So, if culture is the sum of many lived realities, do we even need to define it? Or should we focus on evolving it?

Subcultures aren't a threat, they're a signal. They show us where energy lives, where resistance forms, and where new cultural possibilities are emerging.

Culture Is Emotional and Personal

Culture touches on identity, belonging, purpose, and safety. Yet when leaders define it, they often focus on performance and strategy, overlooking the emotional core.

Culture isn't just about how we work. It's about how we *feel* while we work.

When we read definitions of culture, do we see ourselves in them? Or do we sense that something vital is missing? Even if we can't fully define the emotional dimension, we must at least acknowledge and respect it.

Culture is not just cognitive, it's emotional and existential. It asks us to be vulnerable, to unlearn, and to cocreate from a place of shared humanity.

Culture Is Decentralizing

We know culture is no longer confined just to office walls. It's shaped by leadership behaviors, digital interactions, and shared experiences across platforms and time zones.

The challenge is ensuring it remains strong, connected, and human.

In organizations marked by constant change, restructuring, and turnover, these connection points are harder to maintain. People are finding deeper connection outside of work through communities, causes, and personal networks that meet emotional needs.

This reduces the desire, or even the dependency, on corporate culture to fill those gaps.

Culture Isn't Just Set By Leaders at the Top

Culture used to be dictated from the top, with often long-tenured leaders setting values and employees expected to follow. Now, culture is more fluid and cocreated, shaped by daily interactions, peer influence, and even external societal trends. How then can organizations still maintain a control or influence on the culture of the workforce when it's much more determined by external factors that might not be beneficial for the vision and strategy? What does this mean for roles such as the board, chief executive and C-suite, who are used to holding much sway and power in their organization?

Company values and behaviors still play a role in defining culture. But how they're expressed and reinforced is changing.

Values Must Be Lived, Not Just Stated

Having values on a website or wall doesn't shape culture and likely never did. Employees expect leaders to be clear about direction, make aligned decisions, and model behaviors.

When there's a gap between what's said and what's done, culture cracks.

But with leadership now distributed across more people and teams, values alignment becomes diluted. Can we still rely on it in the same way we have as a cultural anchor?

Behaviors Can't Be Dictated

Behavioral frameworks often launch with fanfare but miss the nuance of real team dynamics. The official behaviors become performative and can give people more reason to find homes in subcultures. In remote and hybrid environments, culture is less about *where* people work and more about *how* they work together in digital spaces. Companies with a large online presence often find the real conversations, and culture, are held in a series of off-limits online spaces far away from the eyes of the center.

This makes the everyday behaviors of teams—how they communicate, make decisions, recognize contributions, and handle challenges—better indicators of culture than any cookie-cutter framework. Yet with more people working in isolation, these behaviors are harder to see, define, and shape.

So, we must ask: Are rigid frameworks like this still a sensible way to shape culture? How do organizations built on control handle more fluidity?

This isn't yet clear, maybe values and behaviors are more important, and they will likely play a role in defining cultural outcomes. As their role shifts from being inputs to culture in the form of a set of rigid statements of culture to a living framework they help us to define the shared culture and tell us more about the philosophy in which an organization uses to drive forward and act as measures/indicators of a culture—less inputs and more outputs.

For example, a value of trust becomes less about defining trust and trust-like behaviors but more building a culture where people are trusted and feel trusted, which is measurable.

This positioning needs to be constantly reinforced through leadership, communication, and action that demonstrates integrity. Integrity is fundamental for people to feel connected to organization strategy, so while values and behaviors are still important perhaps their function has shifted.

Organizations that revisit and evolve their values and behaviors in response to employee needs and external shifts tend to build stronger engagement. But even then, they may be losing their grip on actual cultural influence.

Culture Must Be Adaptive

Traditional corporate culture was often static, anchored in fixed values and norms. Today, culture must be adaptable to meet the challenges of the day.

Most organizations are trying to respond to complexity with fragmentation. They treat engagement, well-being, diversity, and digital transformation as separate initiatives. They assign accountability to different departments.

They run programs instead of rethinking patterns. Or they are handing over huge parts of the firm to AI and robots, hoping to shortcut themselves out of dealing with the issues.

This approach worked when the environment was predictable and slow to change. It fails when systems are interdependent, adaptive, and volatile.

To reverse cultural atrophy, organizations must move beyond surface-level messaging and treat culture as embedded infrastructure woven into systems, incentives, and everyday behaviors. Leaders must act as cultural architects, modeling values through decisions and tone, while embracing the reality of microcultures rather than enforcing uniformity. Culture should be curated through coherent frameworks that allow for local expression, psychological flexibility, and adaptive norms. This means shifting from performative branding to systemic alignment, where culture is not what we say but it's how we work, decide, and belong.

And another engagement survey won't work!

Engagement as a Bandage

While moving rapidly into an uncertain world of change organizations are still very slow in adapting to the people changes taking place. We've collapsed talk of culture in organization to values and behaviors, employee engagement, and diversity and inclusion initiatives. This is slowing us down. For example, employee engagement is hugely popular in all organizations—both of us have led the charge in setting up employee engagement initiatives over the past two decades.

Employee engagement, in its original guise, is still a valuable idea for businesses. At its core, it shows that when organizations unlock people's abilities and match jobs to their passions and strengths, aligned with the business's direction, employees give more than what's required by their job description or contract. In other words, they offer discretionary effort. This in turn increases pace, innovation and risk management. In their 2009 ground-breaking report to the UK government "Engaging for Success: Enhancing Performance Through Employee Engagement" David MacLeod and Nita Clarke (2009) pointed to some of its major enablers focused on leadership, management, employee voice, and integrity. This is all good thinking for an organization, but as we fast-forward we now see the extreme way some have taken this concept, deconstructed it, commoditized it, and in the process lost what it was trying to tell us in the first place.

Some organizations seem more focused on responding quickly to any perceived unhappiness by giving away policies and benefits (another day off here for this, a new review for that) rather than fix the very basics of what makes a great workplace. And like all methods where we just try and quickly rush to fix the surface problem, most companies are learning that they are not going to move the needle on organizational performance the way it may have done or used to. And these initiatives cost a lot—both in money, added complexity and time. And they become an expected norm to attract people with so-called benefits to working somewhere.

What has happened is that employee engagement has become too narrow and reactive. We have forgotten its core. Engagement when it was first introduced to organizations was led by organizational psychologists and organizational design and development specialists, but this work has slowly given way to automated platforms. Most organization engagement strategies forget the fundamental basis of what makes people connect personally and deeply to their work: purpose, mastery, and autonomy (Pink, 2009). Most instead are obsessed with a focus on short-term sentiment: "Do people feel happy?" "Are they satisfied today?" or "Would they recommend their employer to others?" We started to believe that this is all that matters.

In this commoditization we just take things at face value. If the averages look okay, leaders move on. Many organizations, we have seen, have reduced engagement to score chasing, yet the deeper human experiences, like meaning, connection, and growth, can't be that easily captured with a 1–5 scale. It's become a metric to manage rather than a culture to nurture. When we just chase engagement scores, we often miss the bigger picture of culture and well-being.

We have forgotten to ask why people are happy and satisfied just assuming it means all is well for our systems and processes. But in complex, fast-moving environments, performance requires grounding abilities like commitment, resilience, adaptability, purpose, and deep connection, not just positivity.

Engagement doesn't always reflect whether people are, or indeed the organization itself is, growing, innovating, or sustainably contributing. It is entirely possible to be "engaged" as per an organization measurement scale and still be failing. And we have to be careful that our attempts to create engagement do not simply breed entitlement.

This means that feeling "engaged" doesn't always mean people are thriving or delivering impact, yet the rhetoric for leaders remains in mind: engagement = discretionary effort = productivity = profit. We believe that the engagement measurement industry has to get itself back to core of understanding what will actually help its employees drive high performance.

This is vital because low engagement conversely is often a signal of deeper cultural issues: lack of purpose, toxic leadership, exclusion, or misaligned systems. Trying to solve this with perks, communications campaigns, or wellness webinars instead of addressing the systemic causes won't work. You can't "engage" people out of burnout, inequality, or lack of trust.

Engagement, as we know it currently, is not designed for the complexity of today's workplaces. Engagement frameworks were built for stable, linear systems not today's complex, fast-changing world. In uncertain environments, we need people who can self-lead, cocreate, and evolve, not just feel content in their role. Engagement alone doesn't address collective adaptability, psychological safety, or shared accountability. We need to evolve from "How engaged are individuals?" to "How well do we adapt, collaborate, and thrive together?"

Engagement approaches too often treat symptoms, not root causes. They don't always reflect these deeper needs or help leaders meet them. People don't just want to be engaged. They want to feel human, valued, and part of something that matters and yet the organizational needs are perhaps being minimized in this increasingly empowered human working world. Where is the balance? Do people discuss the balance required to remain focused on the right outcomes for everyone without creating an entitlement shift that negatively affects organizational objectives?

We must stop treating culture as a static artifact and start treating it as a living system. We know you cannot address a planetary crisis in one department. You cannot embed AI through a tech rollout alone. You cannot build inclusion through quarterly workshops. You cannot foster resilience without redesigning how people connect, lead, and learn.

So, with culture, we must shift from top-down declarations to bottom-up cocreation.

We must listen more deeply to emotion, to subcultures, to external forces.

We must design for adaptability, not just alignment.

And most of all, we must recognize that culture isn't what we say, it's what we *do*, *feel*, and *become* together.

> "The emerging future comes into being through our capacity to connect with it" (Scharmer and Kaufer, 2007).

Culture is no longer a side conversation in our business strategies. It is *the* conversation. And it's time we gave it the focus it deserves in our organizations. Alongside this requires us to update what we know about how we evolve culture and undertake cultural change programs.

Change Models Getting in the Way?

Despite the trillions resting on the successful evolution of our organizations, especially in the poly-crisis world of the Digital Era, it is stark how little the theory of change management has changed over the last few decades. Most organizations and change management professionals use the Kurt Lewin model from the 1940s believing they can simply freeze and unfreeze organizations between the current state and the desired future state (Lewin, 1947). Building on that came the management theorists of the 1980s and 1990s to show how to do this, such as the famous Kotter eight-step model (Kotter, 2012).

The ubiquity of these models is that most change efforts fail on the ground and most organizations underestimate what it will take to evolve. They operate as if the organization is static, machine-like, and will respond as expected in direction from above. They also tend to focus only on what the formal system can do; they fail to realize organizations have informal and social systems that are also operating, and it is these systems that can often create change at the greatest speed and scale. With artificial intelligence now a huge additional factor, we have an opportunity to reevaluate how change can happen within an organization and update our organizational practices to use purpose, mindsets, energy, and human connection to shortcut change efforts.

Time and again the Kübler-Ross change curve is applied to organizational settings for change as a simple shortcut framework to encompass how people respond to change, *but* it was designed from the outset as a change response to significant life or death changes for humans being informed they had terminal illness (Kübler-Ross, 2014). The extremes of this research are completely out of context to apply to organizational changes, however traumatic the potential of redundancy at the tricky end of the scale. It is not the same message as one by which a human confronts their own mortality.

Grounded in Evidence: The Foundations of Reculturing

Reculturing isn't a buzzword. It's a convergence of three rigorous, evolving scientific and evidence-based fields:

- Organizational and positive psychology—grounding us in what works, what shifts behavior, builds trust, and enables performance in real workplaces
- Neuroscience—offering insight into motivation, safety, energy, and the conditions required for humans to learn and connect
- Systems theory—helping us see organizations as interconnected, adaptive ecosystems that thrive on flow and feedback, not control

Together, these disciplines allow us to move beyond culture as a concept and into culture as a living, evolving system—one we can design, lead, and scale with intention.

Alongside these fields we also draw evidence from these fields:

- Sociology—how group interactions, social norms, and institutional structures, inform strategies for collective culture shifts
- Anthropology—explores cultural evolution, traditions, and symbolic meaning, which helps organizations navigate deep-rooted customs and belief systems
- Behavioral economics—investigates how incentives, policies, and environmental factors influence behavior, guiding the design of systems that reinforce new cultural norms

Table 2.1   Discoveries Affecting Culture

Discovery	Impact	Year
Neuroplasticity advances	This provides further evidence that the brain can rewire itself, meaning lifelong learning and evolution is possible.	2015
AI & brain simulation	AI-driven models now help simulate brain activity improving understanding of cognition.	2018
Gut-brain connection	Research confirms the gut microbiome's influence on mental health, linking diet and conditions, plus giving scientific evidence to old wisdom such as "trust your gut."	2017
Memory formation mechanisms	These mechanisms provide new insights into how memories are stored and retrieved, giving weight to why storytelling is a vital part of building culture.	2019
Brain-computer interfaces (BCI)	BCI allows direct communication between the brain and external devices aiding communication methods.	2020
Sleep and brain health	Studies show sleep plays a role in removing toxins from the brain.	2021

Behind the concepts of reculturing are the lessons learnt, the growing body of study and practice, and the scientific evidence gained in the most recent times. Our old models of change and running large organizations are built on brilliant work done in the mid-20th century, and yet we know so much more since then. Table 2.1 describes just some of the more recent discoveries from neuroscience since 2015.

This level of evidence and new discovery helps us to have confidence to take bolder steps in our culture practice. We don't need to rely only on expertise that was researched decades ago. This is why updating our practices and embracing our cultures anew is a significant and exciting task to embark on.

Rather than relying on cookie-cutter models, it's about understanding how people engage with change. It draws from psychology, activism, marketing, and communication strategies.

Malcolm Gladwell's *The Tipping Point* explains why some ideas take off while others fade (Gladwell, 2002). Context matters, as do influential voices that are trusted in a community or admired by others.

In large organizations, we've learned this firsthand. Mistakes happen when companies push culture shifts too aggressively too early, without properly planting the seed. Some firms have faced backlash because they rushed into change instead of laying the groundwork for genuine, lasting transformation.

Transformation at pace and scale, therefore, can't be about tearing down what exists; it's about harnessing the strengths that already live within your organization and moving them in service of the future. Real change requires a thoughtful introduction, not just a big announcement.

We must do better and help leaders tap into what feels right to them. We must stop overloading with theory and models that require interpretation and cognitive load and empower them to know how significant an upcoming change might be and support/coach them to focus on outcomes for their teams to work together at pace.

Let us use a story to explain more. In a small town nestled between rolling hills, there was a librarian named Evelyn. She never gave speeches or led rallies, but she believed deeply in the power of her own actions.

In her community, she noticed that young girls in the community were skipping school not for lack of ambition, but because they lacked access to necessary resources. Instead of launching a campaign or making public appeals, Evelyn started subtly reshaping the library. She stocked books on leadership, quietly offered free tutoring sessions, and began leaving small, handwritten notes of encouragement inside novels checked out by young readers. She introduced a "Women Who Changed the World" section, but she never insisted anyone visit it she simply let curiosity do its work.

Interestingly, change began. Girls started lingering longer in the library. They whispered about what they were learning, about the possibilities beyond their town. One by one, they found their own voices not because they were told to, but because Evelyn had quietly shown them that knowledge was power.

Her impact didn't make headlines, but it did transform lives. It's a fantastic example of seeding change in culture. Sometimes, the most powerful awareness doesn't come from the loudest voices; it grows in quiet spaces where minds open and possibilities unfold.

The idea of how to manage change comes largely from the industrial era where command and control is a dominant belief system in how organizations should be run; that is, if someone tells you to do it, you will do it. Yet this belief recognizes nothing from modern behavioral science or indeed the realities of organizational life. Just launching a new culture program is akin to a huge firework display going off in the office catching everyone unawares and probably frightening the life out of them.

Traditional Change Management Versus Reculturing for Pace and Scale

Traditional Change Management	Reculturing Approach
Starts with diagnostics—surveys, assessments, and gap analyses to define current versus future state	**Starts with awareness**—courageous observation, noticing, and sensing what's ready to evolve
Top-down sponsorship—relies heavily on CEO messaging, launches, and formal endorsement	**Ground-up momentum**—begins with a few brave voices shaping dialogue and positioning ideas organically
Structured change plans—milestones, timelines, and interventions mapped in advance	**Adaptive flow**—culture evolving in real time through attention, energy, and presence—not rigid plans
Change agents and training—formal roles and programs to drive adoption	**Cultural evolvers**—leaders modeling change through behavior, dialogue, and relational influence

Traditional Change Management	Reculturing Approach
Manage resistance—anticipating and mitigating pushback through communications and coaching	**Spot resistance early**—using positioning and low-threat seeding to surface and learn from resistance
Celebrate wins and reinforce—tracking key performance indicators, embed behaviors, and reward compliance	**Build shared meaning**—using dialogue to cocreate language, stories, and hooks that sustain change

How then might a new lens and approach on culture help us to not only empower our people to flourish and thrive but also underpin performance and organizational success in this new era of work?

3 | What Reculturing Could Do for Us

"The curious paradox is that when I accept myself just as I am, then I can change."

—Carl Rogers, humanist psychologist

Workplaces, with more than 3.4 billion people, have large potential to give meaning and exert a positive influence over our societies and economies globally. Everything we have typically used to shape culture needs to be dusted off and reassessed to see if it is still fit for purpose. Forces like artificial intelligence (AI), the planetary crisis, power dynamics, diversity, and social media are reshaping what it means to lead, work, and thrive in today's world. The global workforce is rapidly scrabbling to upskill for the future without knowing what jobs will even be needed in an AI-powered future. None of these factors can be tackled by people in separate departments; they are our problem jointly and collectively and pressurizing the need to reculture in all organizations. We must accept now what we have, what we are facing, and understand we need to get to grips with it.

Reculturing not only signals that we are facing into the storm but it also shows we are willing to reframe the work:

- From culture as soft → to culture as infrastructure
- From human resources ownership → to executive stewardship
- From compliance → to conviction
- From optional add-on → to survival strategy
- From internal focus → to societal impact
- From reacting to crises → to building resilience

The Five Forces That Are Reshaping Culture

Organizations are facing existential urgency:

- Disruption through AI and digital worker acceleration
- Climate pressure and regulatory shifts
- Disengagement, burnout, and trust erosion
- A volatile talent market and skills obsolescence
- Fake news and misinformation and the parallel universe of social media

Culture is the arena in which we work together. Our cultures help us be ready for the major forces shaping our working world. Forces such as AI or climate change in our workplaces are not going to go away. If our organizations are fragile, crumbling, and falling apart, we won't do the very best work we can. A 2023 study published in *BMC Nursing* found that toxic leadership predicted 87% of the variance in organizational performance among nurses (Farghaly Abdelaliem and Abou Zeid, 2023). Cultures that create toxicity as the norm won't thrive. As culture is the invisible thread that holds everything together, it influences how leaders lead, how teams work, and how customers perceive the brand. Culture, unlike strategy, uniquely captures the essence of an organization.

Without it, strategy fails. With it, possibility expands. And there are five urgent forces at play in our workplaces where we need culture to support us to speed up, not slow down.

AI: From Efficiency to Human Differentiators

AI enables organizations to automate tasks at scale and reshape job roles, decision-making, and skill requirements. Agents in the workforce now mimic human workers in how they go about completing tasks. Except they don't tire, they don't take breaks, they don't make jokes (unless programmed to), and they don't take holidays. The scale of the robot and agentic workforce alongside their human colleagues is no longer the stuff of science fiction and will become a huge reality for the next generation of organizations.

The human edge will now lie in critical thinking, empathy, creativity, social imagination, judgment, and ethics, not output. We will see more phrases such as *human-led*, *agent-enabled*, *AI-first*, and *co-intelligence* describing our organizations.

Humans are expected to have space once again to look at more macro issues with time to think, likely to become a key feature of high-performing teams.

This requires a cultural shift from valuing busyness, efficiency, and control to valuing human ingenuity, connection, adaptability, and deep learning. Yet in this uncertain world we are doing both, but to what effect? Should this be balanced, or do we need to lean into our human side more so to maintain its essence?

There is a steady shift happening already from fear of AI to coevolving with technology through a human-centered lens. A maturity curve will have us all plotted in our AI adoption journey, and we will all steadily move along, some with more of a push than others; however, will it be fast enough? And who will we leave behind?

It demands that our corporate culture elevates what makes us human, not try to compete with machines. How much do we see this elevation happening with great effect? The huge push for skills-based organizations to create libraries and taxonomies of skills required for the future has largely focused on technical and digital skills and missed the vital human skills that are also depleting as a result of dispersed ways of working. Continuously we hear that the "soft skills" like emotional intelligence (EQ) are prized, yet EQ encompasses a whole range of human skills simply being bucketed under one umbrella and assumed they can be easily picked up in one short online course or bite-size workshop. There is nothing about human skills or EQ that is bite size. Increases in overall EQ correlate with life experience over time, not just in one job, but over entire decades long careers and into retirement. There are ways to accelerate learning, but the time it takes to really apply this into real-life scenarios at work and beyond is nothing that can be shortcut.

We need to reculture to embrace the longevity and breadth of human skill development required to be confident in our differentiators and use AI to its best in organizations.

The Planet: The Forgotten Stakeholder

Why does the planet matter? Climate change, resource depletion, and sustainability are no longer optional issues we get to choose to engage with or not—they are existential, and the scientific facts and data show clear dependency on us to make changes now to reverse the damage already done. Slogans such as "no one makes money from a dead planet" are dramatic but true. The planet is literally our home, not some esoteric thing that lives in our imagination—it's the air we breathe, the water we drink, the soil for the food we eat, and the shelter we need from the sun. Rising sea levels will mean more frequent flooding, loss of land, damage to infrastructure, and displacement of vulnerable communities, with the greatest impacts felt first by coastal and low-lying areas.

Employees, customers, and investors are demanding that businesses embed environmental responsibility into their DNA as a result and yet still it's seen as something for the experts in another department to focus on. Too few organizations recognize the cultural imperative of intertwining sustainability into all we do. John Elkington, known as the *godfather of sustainability* in discussing his latest book *Tickling Sharks* (Elkington, 2024) at Anthropy 2025 in Cornwall, England, wrote a personal message in Kerri's book that said, "All human resources! People. Culture. All key."

For this to really have an impact the cultural shift needed is to move from short-term gains to long-term stewardship. To perhaps refocus on tenure being important in organizations to drive a longer-term shift away from the short-term high-performance burnout we see driving turnover and dwindling culture as a result.

We must switch from "corporate social responsibility add-ons" to sustainability being a core business driver and heard in conversations everywhere within an organization, not just in policies, processes, and documents shared.

Culture must evolve to prioritize regeneration, responsibility, and climate-conscious innovation or else we will suffer as a result, an outcome rarely defined or shared in any great clarity beyond significant weather events.

Do we risk increasing climate anxiety by being transparent about looming outcomes or continue to softly and steadily increase the focus? A level of urgency requires more.

Power: From Hierarchy to Shared Leadership

It is so hard to move away from hierarchy that is entrenched, yet traditional power structures are being challenged by employee activism, transparency, and distributed work. Where self-managing teams and holocratic models struggled to prove effective 20 years ago, perhaps now the world is more ready to embrace it? There are companies at the forefront in industries such as technology and software development where collaborative and agile methodologies are built on self-managing teams. Spotify is famous for its squad model with autonomous teams aligned on products. With increased use of digital platforms that span geographies and increase opportunity to work collaboratively, perhaps this will is already a transition happening steadily that will significantly affect the use of corporate culture to support organization-wide strategy in the way it used to?

People want to work in organizations where they matter. That power is inclusive, accountable, and shared, not concentrated.

This is already taking place where shifts from command and control to trust and empowerment are being recognized in industry and benchmarked with standards and awards for their impact on performance.

Despite servant leadership (Greenleaf, 1998), a continuously popular leadership approach that stemmed from research in the 1970s, there is still a need now for shifts in culture from authority as status to leadership as service and impact. Inclusive organizations are seeing new ways of leading that are deconstructing traditional views and demonstrating role models come in a diverse variety of approaches that are still successful.

Therefore, a culture must flatten, decentralize, and give voice to the many, not just the few, and there are many more ways of this empowerment happening, particularly through employee listening programs, new methods of surveying, and tapping into data across the organization supporting voice in places never offered platforms before. Always-on listening platforms, digital ethnography, employee personas, empathy mapping, and AI mapping sentiment analysis with crowdsourcing dialogue for people vote up those sentiments that most resonate and are taking us to another level in empowering voice for everyone and shifting the leadership power.

Diversity: From Representation to Belonging

Diversity alone doesn't create inclusion; belonging comes from behaviors, language, and systems.

As societies diversify, organizations must reflect and respond to intersectional human experience. Recent events that challenge diversity, equity, and inclusion (DEI) approaches are evolving this work as we write, and this is a fundamental trigger for many people with responsibility for "culture" in their organizations who are desperately searching for ways to enhance the interconnection that was the core heartbeat and essence of the organizational experience.

Shifting a culture away from token inclusion programs that may have caused silent discomfort and marginalized experience for others as a result means reeducating and engaging in the positive opportunity to move to true equity.

Developing psychological safety for people to feel able to be themselves at work comes from the entire organization: managers and leaders encouraging and empowering teams and individuals, systems that celebrate learning through mistakes, processes and structures that remove traditional barriers to development for everyone.

This requires a substantial shift away from surface-level initiatives to deeper cultural fluency and accountability so that we don't absolve influence on volunteers without the understanding or skills to recognize the significant impact their work may have on the whole living organization. Cultural enablers must be those with high EQ and other human skills and with a big-picture perspective of their work. Perhaps this is where the employee resource group and champion group approach needs to stop? Communities of interest and learning are important but have organizations gone too far in using these groups as a cheap resource to tick the box on surface-level initiatives and allowed the empowerment of these groups to polarize sentiment and dominate culture to the point others quietly disengage?

Culture must make everyone feel seen, heard, and valued, not just invited to the table, and this needs to be fully understood from a psychological perspective. Perhaps organizational psychology has been also sprinkled on the top of initiatives without substance for too long. It is rare for organizations to find the budget in significant DEI interventions for the full evaluation and analysis required to determine if it's been successful beyond the short-term face validity measures.

Social Media: From Image to Authenticity

Transparency is the new norm, organizational culture is on display 24/7. In 2006 Robert Goffee and Gareth Jones published their leadership book on authenticity, *Why Should Anyone Be Led by You?* It exploded into the business book market as an international best-seller in the United States and across Europe because it resonated with a distinct need for leaders to step into their own space and embrace what people needed by being honest and transparent leaders. Brene Brown similarly brought vulnerability into management consciousness through her hugely popular Ted Talk, "The Power of Vulnerability" in 2010. Yet with the growth of social media over the past two decades the huge platforms have recognized creators offering a wonderful but fake life. People full of envy as human beings comparing their lives to the influencers selling the dream is leading to a surge of depression as a result. Jean Twenge et al. (2018) note that "adolescent depression and suicidal behaviors have increased considerably." In the United States, depression diagnoses among youth increased from 8.7% in 2005 to 11.3% in 2014 (Mojtabai et al., 2016). Additionally, suicide is the second leading cause of death among youth between the ages of 10 and 34 (Centers for Disease Control and Prevention, National Center for Injury Prevention and Control, 2018), with a 47.5% increase since 2000 (Miron et al., 2019). One suggested cause for this rise in adolescent depression and suicide is the advent of social media (McCrae et al., 2017; Twenge et al., 2018). The shift occurring now is somewhat of a backlash; people are demanding the truth and honesty in their lives even in their imperfection and incompleteness. People are finding more solace in knowing they are not alone. Social media trends are entering our daily work landscape on an increasing basis with new generations more readily using it for everyday tasks. Will this further drive the pace and demand for urgent shifts to reculture with an emphasis on authenticity?

Corporate spin and polished public relations are still the safe, comfortable routes for large organizations with huge brand value, who will do anything to protect and perfect. But how much will general audiences, employees, and customers really buy it? Patagonia at the end of 2025 released a searingly honest "Work in Progress" report highlighting a trend toward more honesty. But it's not easy. What is the experience of those who have taken the plunge into vulnerable storytelling? Where do the topics step over-polarized boundaries and put leaders at risk of being canceled? A big four consulting firm had the chair make open remarks to a 500-strong call that offended his colleagues, leading to his role becoming untenable in one misplaced "authentic" opinionated comment. A 30-year career with the firm finished in one open conversation. What example does this then set for leaders to be encouraged to be their authentic selves? Psychological safety for senior leaders is a topic without enough current research.

How can we support leaders to go from silence to open dialogue on tough issues like ethics, justice, and impact when everyone is watching? And who chooses which topics are safe enough to explore? Do we need to use employee sentiment analysis to open the most relevant topics with guided conversation lines, and how far is too far? It is certainly a significant dilemma when reculturing to know how to approach such a shift which still remaining truly dynamic for sentiment to evolve at such a rapid pace.

Summary of Five Forces

Reculturing is now a strategic imperative because these global forces are nonnegotiable.

Organizations that fail to reculture will lose relevance, talent, trust, and long-term viability.

Those that embrace this moment will lead with humanity, innovation, and impact and this realization is occurring across all industries right now. New realities:

- **AI:** AI has moved from automation to augmentation. It is not just replacing repetitive tasks; it is redefining creativity, decision-making, and the value of human contribution. Organizations built on knowledge hoarding and task repetition are now exposed.
- **Planet:** The climate crisis is no longer theoretical or distant. It is immediate, material, and reshaping the expectations of consumers, regulators, and employees alike. Sustainability is no longer a department, it is a mandate.
- **Power:** Influence is being redistributed. Social movements, activist employees, distributed leadership models, and stakeholder capitalism have all challenged the dominance of centralized authority. Power now moves in networks and influencers, not traditional hierarchies.
- **Diversity:** Diversity is no longer a project or a program. It is a nonnegotiable reality of the workforce. Inclusion is complex, evolving, and essential to performance not just fairness.
- **Social media:** Platforms have become public squares, reputational battlegrounds, and cultural accelerants. Organizational boundaries are porous. Culture is no longer what happens inside the building, it's what people share, believe, and amplify at the touch of a button.

The old era of linear plans, top-down control, fixed roles, and monocultural norms is gone. Clinging to it is not just unhelpful; it is harmful. Traditional upskilling programs, engagement surveys, and leadership pipelines are not designed to close this gap. They are built for stability, not agility. For repetition, not reinvention.

This is not a failure of people. It is a failure of culture.

A New Mandate: Reculture

We see inspiration in rewilding. Reculturing shares its core principles: embracing simplicity, restoring balance, and fostering resilience.

Rewilding focuses on restoring ecosystems by enabling nature to regenerate with minimal human intervention. It involves reintroducing species, remembering forgotten truths and wisdom, restoring habitats, and letting natural processes unfold aiming for a healthier, self-sustaining environment.

Reculturing is similar in an organizational context; it's about revitalizing workplace culture to make it more adaptive, innovative, and sustainable. Like rewilding, it often requires removing outdated structures that suppress growth, introducing new ideas, and reintroducing old wisdom that align with modern needs, and creating conditions where positive change can take root organically.

Both processes require a healthy balance of patience and impatience. You don't just change a forest or a workplace overnight, but you can know you are sowing the right seeds to grow.

Our greatest concern is that within any organization with continuous change, restructuring, and turnover, these flimsier connection points are even harder to maintain. People are looking and have found greater connection beyond work that satisfied those needs, reducing desire or even dependency on corporate culture to fill our personal gaps. Culture matters as it will get back the interconnectedness and interdependence that humans thrive on.

And What Does This Mean for Business Overall?

Culture drives alignment so that the impact and outcomes of collaborative action are greater than the sum of parts. Not only impact but momentum, ripples of joint effort, motivate beyond organizations themselves into society and community for positive change. Culture connects the parts of the system. It is not one priority among many; it is the environment in which all priorities either thrive or fail. When we shift the culture, we shift the system.

Leaders the world over are struggling with decision-making, taking at-pace action and moving forward in this unsolvable and unstoppable world of chaos at a macro level. It feels as if being asked to keep walking into the darkness alone, and yet we know we are more likely to be able to do if we are holding hands with others. Taking this notion of togetherness and collaboration, we should be able to find what connects us universally as humans, what truly takes an inclusive approach to bringing us together in service of the organization. If we're connecting a globally diverse workforce, how much should culture differ between organizations? Should culture always align perfectly with strategy, even as strategy evolves? If not, we risk creating a narrow model of cultural fit that excludes people with different beliefs and behaviors—instead of embracing true inclusivity.

Reculturing is the human systems response to a human systemic challenge. It moves us beyond fragmented interventions and into a cohesive, adaptive, human approach to organizational life. One that works in tune with challenges such as AI and the planetary crisis.

Reculturing is not about going backwards or preserving the past. It is about hardwiring in the conditions for humans to thrive in a world that demands more from us than ever before.

The end of the old era is not a threat. It is a beginning . . . but only if we are brave enough to build something new.

To navigate this we are going forward using a simpler, higher level of truthfulness about how our organizations really can work using human methods and practices that enable them to once again thrive. Just as rewilding uses the knowledge of nature to support nature redevelop, we are using knowledge of how humans work together to drive reculturing. We are going to release the full capacity and brilliance of our people as fuel.

We are at a pivotal crossroads. The urgency for cultural rebirthing is no longer up for debate. What matters now is how we respond and how fast.

We are not starting from scratch; we are evolving forward. Many of the ideas we present are ideas that have been overlooked as perhaps we were not ready for them when they first emerged. Movements happen and things take off when both the attractiveness of the idea meets the right people and timing. Amid the uncertainty of this era lies a powerful, evidence-based promise: Organizations can be reimagined to serve people, planet, and progress. Not through surface-level change, but through deep cultural transformation.

This means seeing patterns, not parts. Relationships, not roles. Dynamics, not departments. Reculturing is not a change program. Its depth comes from thinking about culture for thriving in complexity, helping us to iden-tify leverage points where small changes can create large shifts, look for unintended consequences, and add feedback loops and design for emer-gence, not control. This is the promise of reculturing. It offers a way forward that is both hopeful and grounded. It doesn't just respond to change; it equips organizations to thrive through it. It is science-backed, system-informed, and human-led.

What Can Organizations Do When They Find Themselves in This Place of Cultural Drift?

The way forward starts not with a road map, but with a mirror. It requires pausing not to freeze, but to reflect. To ask: Who are we now? What do we stand for? What do our people need to thrive? Culture can't be restored by force; it must be rerooted in shared understanding. Rebuilt through con-nection, not control.

Organizations that successfully navigate the culture quandary choose a different path.

They follow these steps:

1. Reconnect with their purpose and ensure it doesn't just frame the past but catapults an organization forward.
2. Invite their people into the conversation, cocreating a future that reflects shared hopes and mindsets. Lead with empathy, transparency, and consistency, rebuilding trust from the inside out.
3. Pay attention to the quality and flow of the energy of the organiza-tion and seek to remove blockages and toxicity.
4. Prize human connection, and be intentional about bringing people together emphasizing clarity, autonomy, and psychological flexibility.

These areas make up the four reculture drivers. As this isn't about going back to what was. It's about becoming what's next. Because high perfor-mance in the future won't come from pressure alone; it will come from cultures where people feel seen, supported, and inspired.

The culture quandary is real. But it's also an invitation. To reimagine not just how we work, but why. And in doing so, to create workplaces where performance and humanity can finally thrive side by side. Within this urgency lies immense possibility. There are new models of value and meaning being created every day and in new ways and through new channels. We have incredible tech-enabled collaboration springing up at breakneck speed across geographies and disciplines creating worldwide mega trends within a matter of hours. There is huge possibility for richer human connection if we build for it. We can create organizational structures that adapt and evolve with purpose, even at scale, particularly with the assistance of new AI and technology able to condense complexity into simple models.

We need to reculture organizations, to look anew at culture, not just for internal growth, but because the external world has changed fundamentally and we must face reality that the old era is gone.

The future is not a distant scenario. It's being written now through the choices leaders make about culture.

What Will We See Happen?

Collective high performance and interconnectivity will be created at pace and scale.

Reculturing means you set the right environment for success. High performance can no longer be achieved through individual effort alone or the collection of high-performing individuals. If your organization is operating on the basis that 20% of people add 80% of the most value, then we need to act. The complexity of today's work requires a new kind of collective capacity where insight flows, silos dissolve, and collaboration is intuitive. This only comes at pace through culture.

Thriving individuals and teams will be the outcome, not the input.

Traditional approaches have treated individual well-being and engagement as the fuel for great cultures. But the reality is reversed: Great cultures produce thriving individuals.

Reculturing is about shaping that environment intentionally, continuously, and at scale.

The Fastest Organizations Will Be the Most Human

Speed in the next decade won't come from better processes or more tools. It will come from culture:

- Cultures that allow people to move with trust
- Cultures that activate energy rather than drain it
- Cultures that harness technology while elevating humanity
- Cultures that inspire meaning, not just efficiency
- Cultures that teach people to disagree well—turning conflict into progress rather than division
- Cultures that measure success by impact as well as outcomes
- Cultures that invite people to belong to something larger than themselves

In a paradoxical twist that the more technological our world becomes, the more human we must be to lead in it.

Reculturing is not a luxury. It is the unlock. The way we work, relate, and grow must transform to meet this new era.

The Company That Didn't Believe in Culture

Once upon a fiscal year, there was an organization we were working with. It was a sleek, data-driven enterprise led by executives who believed that strategy, structure, and spreadsheets were the only levers that mattered. Culture? "Soft stuff," they said. "Unmeasurable. Unnecessary."

Their motto: "Performance through precision."

They had policies for everything: key performance indicators, objectives and key results, service-level agreements. But no one talked about how people felt. Or why they stayed. Or what made them care.

The Early Signs

At first, things looked fine. Quarterly targets were met. The dashboards glowed green. But beneath the surface:

- Teams stopped sharing ideas.
- High performers quietly left.

- Meetings felt transactional, not transformational.
- New hires struggled to fit, though no one could define what *fit* meant.

When asked about morale, the CEO replied, "We don't measure feelings. We measure output."

The Culture Collapse

Then came the merger.

Two companies, one vision, but wildly different ways of working. One side valued collaboration, storytelling, and psychological safety. The other? Cold efficiency.

Without a shared cultural language, integration failed. Projects stalled. Trust eroded. Leaders clashed. Employees disengaged.

The board demanded answers. The CEO pointed to strategy. But the problem wasn't strategy it was the absence of cultural stewardship.

The Turning Point

The chief human resources officer finally spoke up: "Culture isn't what we say, it's what we tolerate, reward, and repeat. And right now, we're rewarding silence, burnout, and fear."

She led work to look at the current culture and it revealed the following:

- Low emotional vitality
- Fragmented connection
- No shared purpose

It was the wake-up call the company needed.

The Regenerative Shift: Key Learnings

They began again, not with a reorg, but with listening.
They defined values through stories, not slogans.
They rebuilt trust through rituals, not rules.
They treated human energy as strategic capital.

Performance returned, but this time, it was sustainable and people didn't just comply, they belonged.

Reflection for Leaders

Culture exists whether you name it or not. If you ignore it, it can become your silent saboteur. If you nurture it, it can become your greatest multiplier.

Rapid Reculturing Explained

"Becoming isn't about arriving somewhere or achieving a certain aim. It's forward motion, a means of evolving."

—Michelle Obama (2018)

While we struggle to define culture itself now due to the enormous number of factors that have affected organizational culture, *reculturing* has meaning, particularly to those who recognize what has truly been lost. It represents the opportunity to work together in a way that connects us to be something more than our own self, to be part of something bigger . . . again.

This section will help show what rapid reculturing means in practice. By explaining the three zones and four drivers it will give a global community of leaders new science-backed clarity on what reculturing entails. Too much in the culture space is either too complex or too simple. Our cultures should not need huge constant interventions to keep it in check if it is correctly set. We show what it takes to get our organizations back to a simpler core, restoring only what we need to bind our organization together to flourish and succeed. We share the research and evidence behind reculturing and which help us to know what to focus on and what drives a thriving culture.

We answer what rapid reculturing looks like for companies who have all the values/frameworks/leadership behaviors/skills/systems/processes but still have problems or are still lacking in the human culture, the essence, and the spirit that is needed for us to feel we are on a journey together.

We will see that a human need requires a human solution, and we don't shy away from saying that no one process, culture audit, survey, or program will bring culture back in the way it once existed. It needs to be brought about through experience, connection, relationships, dialogue, sense making, social imagination, psychological flexibility for everyone, not just the chosen few at the top.

Reculturing today requires a shift from rigid, top-down approaches to more dynamic, human-centered strategies. Driving a high-performance culture in the future will be less about rigid structures and more about fluid, human-centric ecosystems. While performance has always mattered, the how and why of achieving it are evolving rapidly in response to societal shifts, technological acceleration, and generational expectations. This tells us what this looks like in practice.

4 | Introducing Three Zones and Four Drivers

Forget the complex culture audits and matrices and endless diagnostic exercises. Organizations are typically in one of three zones when it comes to culture—similar to how water can either be liquid, solid or gas. Many people will try to make culture identification and diagnostics very complex, but this gets in the way. Diagnostics are meant to reveal what's happening and focus attention. But once you've seen the cultural patterns, stop testing—start acting. Endless diagnostics don't build culture; intention, conviction, and movement do. And to know if you need to consider reculturing at its simplest, we only need to know if our culture is lost, a cult, or thriving.

Any organization (or suborganization) can be in any of these zones and may move around them over their history, just as water can move from being a gas to a liquid to a solid. These movements will likely be felt, and events that created the movements will quite often be long held in the organizational memory. Founder-led businesses sell to private equity. Once strong companies lurch from restructure to restructure. A new much-loved CEO arrives and takes the company to new heights. Or one personality dominates, sometimes for good, sometimes for bad. What matters less is the history and more about how it is right now. The label we give our organization is a leading indicator of what is likely to happen next to our organization. It's important to accept truthfully where we are. Given the choice of the three zones, most leaders can intuitively say where they are. In Chapter 10, we describe in more detail how you can get more help to identify where your organization is at.

The zone we are in represents collective decisions over time from the board, CEO, and the senior leaders of the organization and others over what we will let be, and the great news is that wherever our culture is, it can change and evolve.

By embracing the zone we are in means we are seeing clearly, and then we can use the drivers we will explain to leapfrog where we are to where we need to be. These simple but highly effective drivers will enable us to change our cultural trajectory. These forces make reculturing not just possible, but vital.

The Three Zones of Culture

For those whose culture is in the lost zone, our often overriding sense is hope that if we do this one more thing the culture will right itself. We often end up feeling like Alice in Wonderland, where if we don't know where we are going, we think any road will do. We struggle to say what our organization really stands for these days. We see wide variations of "normal" behavior and we can no longer so easily predict how the organization will culturally respond to events.

Those who are in the thriving zone work hard at systemic human activity in their organization and have energy, a balance, and a healthy perspective on the past, present, and future. Shocks can happen but the organization quickly bounces back and learns the lessons. The trick here is to hang onto it, building deeper layers of infrastructure and learning.

Then there are the organizations that have a culture purely driven by the personality or personalities of a few key people. We call this type of culture a cult. The culture is built on the thoughts, opinions, and beliefs of the few, not the many. Teams don't act with confidence unless the personality or personalities give their approval. The organization without these people would no doubt end up as lost unless considerable work is done.

Culture Driven by Senior Leaders—Creating Cults?

Contrary to belief, cult zone cultures aren't always founder-led companies; they can be powerful senior leaders who join an organization and assume their positions with full force. As organizations look to act in the chaos, we are particularly worried about organizations that are now being driven more by the "strong" senior leaders who have the position and power to direct their organizations through a time of such chaos that people are desperate to follow someone. Fewer leaders are enjoying this responsibility of leading in uncertainty, meaning that the ones who do are steadily floating to the top and becoming even more influential. We are increasingly wary of leaders who come in with their playbooks or agenda and action these no matter the context. We are seeing new evidence that suggests those who most want to lead are not always the best at it (Alzahawi et al., 2024).

This strong influence without challenge sways those organizations from lost culture to cult status, meaning we end up acting in agreement vehemently with the top leaders, and large numbers of those not aligned choosing to leave and work elsewhere more palatable to their beliefs.

Where Then Does That Leave the Largest Number of Organizations Looking to Reculture and Thrive?

We anticipate there will be some intense traditional culture interventions that people have used in the past in an attempt to change us back into some resemblance of connection and this may receive a rejection from the more vocal and visible empowered people.

What's more worrying is the potential quiet disengagement and simple avoidance of those uninterested and detached, working at just the distance required to continue contributing but who have found their tribe and human connection elsewhere, beyond the workplace.

People bond through challenge and achieving significant accomplishments together, attracted to wanting to create a positive impact on their team, department, organization that could not be achieved alone, but how much has that outlet for accomplishment reduced compared with sporting, charity, or community events beyond work?

The approach to reculturing offers us a new path—a unifying focus back on the core areas where you can pay attention and enable a focus on a culture that will help us to thrive.

Introducing the Four Reculturing Drivers

"We must be willing to get rid of the life we've planned so as to have the life that is waiting for us."

—Joseph Campbell, creator of the hero's narrative

So how do companies effectively redefine and strengthen their culture in the current landscape?

We have found that there are four reculturing drivers that will supercharge our cultures anew at both pace and scale. Our work over the decades has brought us back to these time and time again. They work in the polycrisis world we are in. They don't need the stability of yesteryear because that is not coming back. All four, both individually and together, can give us the focus and boost we need to get our culture in the thriving zone. The drivers are grounded in the latest human-centered research and evidence of what actually works now.

The next four chapters delve into each reculturing driver in depth with insights to apply to your organization.

- Chapter 5: Reculturing Driver 1: Activating Shared Purpose
  Purpose offers us alignment to others, and being part of something bigger than ourselves and properly put to work is a strong internal motivator for all humans.
- Chapter 6: Reculturing Driver 2: Mindsets as a New Approach to Defining Culture
  Mindsets can be a more dynamic shared approach to collaboration than traditional levers and here we explore how.
- Chapter 7: Reculturing Driver 3: Use Energy to Assess Cultural Health
  Energy is introduced and validated as a new cultural measure that goes further than engagement, commitment, or satisfaction indicators.
- Chapter 8: Reculturing Driver 4: Human Connection in Any Setting
  Ensuring human connection in any setting is consciously prioritizing our human essence in a rapidly advancing technological world.

Reculturing is not about endless diagnostics; it is about clarity, conviction, and movement. By recognizing the zone we are in and embracing the four drivers, leaders can cut through the noise of complexity and return to the simple, human core of culture. What matters is the choices we make now to evolve together. In a world of constant disruption, reculturing offers a path to resilience, alignment, and abundance—a way to bind organizations with purpose, shared mindset, energy, and connection so they can thrive. The chapters ahead will show how these drivers can be put into practice, turning culture from a problem to be solved into the engine of progress.

5 | Reculturing Driver 1: Activating Shared Purpose

"The beginning is the most important part of the work."

—Plato

"To go forward, you must first go back."

—Erin Morgenstern (1998)

Purpose is not a slogan or a statement; it's the shared reason for being that gives culture its coherence, energy, and direction. Without it, culture becomes performative. With it, culture becomes transformative. To reculture effectively, we must begin not with behaviors or values but with purpose, the point of why this organization exists, clearly felt and collectively owned.

Anchoring culture in purpose is critical.

Instead of relying on a static list of values, companies should focus on a clear and compelling meaning and purpose. To influence performance, the purpose must be connected to a core mission of how the organization will grow and what being successful in achieving its purpose in the future will mean for people.

Reculturing is about evolving. It isn't about holding onto the past, reacting to the present, or being newsworthy; it's about setting yourself on a path to shape a thriving future. The most resilient and innovative organizations think ahead to move at pace, and they institutionalize visualizing the desired future. They focus, they look around corners, they obsess with where the company is going, they craft strategies that align with a deeper more enduring purpose.

In today's fast-moving business landscape, organizational purpose is more than a mission statement; it is the strongest possible motivational foundation on which companies can rebuild their strategies, cultures, and long-term success. Purpose is the ultimate intention by which we bring the people together to do their work. It is probably the nearest constant we can now hope for in the turbulent age we live in. It is enduring, inherently outward, and forward-looking and defines why a business exists, guiding strategic decisions, inspiring teams, and forging meaningful connections with customers and stakeholders. It is the very foundation of reculturing.

Companies with Purpose

To craft an enduring organizational purpose, we must encapsulate the core mission and guiding principles, serving as a strategic compass for all organizational activities and decisions. It's not just what the organization does, but what it stands for and why it exists in the deepest sense. Purpose, that is, the point of bringing people together, infuses an organization with direction, coherence, and emotional resonance. It's what galvanizes people beyond their roles, aligning individual motivations with collective aspirations. And like a soul, purpose isn't static. It evolves, deepens, and must be nurtured with authenticity and reflection. When leaders speak to purpose with clarity and conviction, they're not just setting strategy; they're inviting others into a shared journey of meaning.

Here are some companies with deep purpose statements:

- **Microsoft**—"To empower every person and every organization on the planet to achieve more."
- **Goldman Sachs**—"To advance sustainable economic growth and financial opportunity across the globe."

- **Patagonia**—"To build the best product, cause no unnecessary harm, and use business to inspire and implement solutions to the environmental crisis."
- **Chanel**—"To be a creation-driven, human-driven, and committed luxury brand that generates long-term value for both business and society."
- **IKEA**—"To create a better everyday life for the many people."
- **Google**—"To organize the world's information and make it universally accessible and useful."
- **Coca-Cola**—"To refresh the world. To make a difference."

For executives, not only does purpose hugely influence culture but it also offers a powerful competitive advantage. A longitudinal study published in *Harvard Business Review* found that purpose-driven firms consistently outperform their competitors in terms of revenue growth, customer loyalty, and employee retention (Keller, 2019). Research from EY and the *Harvard Business School* indicates that companies with a strong sense of purpose tend to achieve higher long-term profitability and resilience against market disruptions (Gartenberg and Serafeim, 2019). Focusing on purpose does not have to be at the expense of making money or profit.

A study by HSBC Innovation Banking found that purpose-driven companies are four times more likely to earn customer trust, purchases, and recommendations (Clarkson, 2024). This happens because purpose provides a foundation for innovation, brand trust, and long-term strategic alignment, factors that directly contribute to profitability. A McKinsey study found that only 7% of Fortune 500 CEOs (McKinsey, 2020) believe their companies should focus solely on profits. Companies with a clear purpose can hire leaders more effectively as they seek to find aligned individuals who will take the company into the next generation and so while everything else may change, one thing remains enduring.

Shared purpose acts on the culture of the organization because it is a highly compelling motivator of actions, identity, and ideas. When purpose is harnessed effectively, it has the power to help transform organizations into industry leaders, shaping not only markets but also the future itself. Purpose does this because it lifts organizations up and out of merely dealing with the present. Clarity of purpose works because it fulfills a deep psychological need for individuals within an organization. Purpose tells you why this organization exists, why it matters, why it is significant, and what your work is actually contributing to. This is valuable because humans care deeply about mattering. Kellerman and Seligman (2023) argue that people thrive when they feel their lives contribute to something greater than themselves, individuals and teams perform better and experience greater fulfillment. Humans naturally seek meaning in their experiences and want to feel significant.

In Viktor E. Frankl's era-defining work *Man's Search for Meaning*, written in 1946, he argued that meaning is not something we passively receive but something we as humans actively find and create. He observed that those who found purpose, even in extreme adversity, were more resilient and psychologically strong. Neuroscientific studies reveal that a sense of purpose stimulates reward processing centers in the brain. People perform at their best when they believe their work has significance beyond just financial compensation or daily tasks. The self-determination theory, developed by psychologists Edward Deci and Richard Ryan, highlights three basic needs for intrinsic motivation: autonomy, competence, and relatedness. Purpose satisfies the third need, relatedness, by providing employees with a sense of belonging and impact. A 2018 study published in the *Journal of Organizational Behavior* found that employees who perceive their work as meaningful demonstrate higher job satisfaction and productivity (Lysova et al., 2018).

A Stanford University study likewise found that employees working in purpose-driven environments experience greater psychological safety, which enhances collaborative problem-solving and proactive behavior (Edmondson, 2018). When leaders make the effort to integrate purpose into daily operations, employees feel empowered to take initiative and innovate beyond routine expectations. Employees with an effective purpose are more productive. Apart from greater satisfaction, employees with a clear purpose move beyond engagement to being inspired. Data published by Mankins and Garton (2015) suggests inspired employees are 50% more productive: a powerful advantage particularly for growing businesses.

The Purpose Advantage

Purpose-driven companies enjoy real advantages in terms of customer value, productivity, transformation and innovation success, and revenue growth. These advantages come at no extra cost beyond the time and thought required to understand and integrate an effective purpose. Acting early provides a huge advantage due to compounding effects. For example, a 50% advantage in productivity per year, all else being equal, would result in 17 times greater output over 10 years. Purpose as an active force in your business helps it to be successful.

Studies show that storytelling helps individuals construct a meta-narrative that gives their lives direction and significance. When people see themselves as part of a larger story, whether in their personal lives or work-places, they feel more motivated to contribute.

Purpose however cannot be static; it's not enough to have one, it needs to be actively deployed. Done well it will inspire, create energy, and align teams, especially in remote and hybrid environments where physical culture markers are absent. Purpose can help build resilience and calms the nerve center. It has the grounding effect that culture needs; like the presence of the sun and seasons, it can be the constant in the swirl.

Cultures Without Purpose

Viktor Frankl also wrote about a concept of the existential vacuum, which describes a state in which individuals feel that life lacks meaning or purpose. He explained that modern society has lost traditional sources of meaning, leaving many people feeling empty and directionless.

Frankl argued that boredom is a key symptom of the existential vacuum, leading individuals to seek distractions through materialism, pleasure, or power rather than pursuing deeper fulfillment. He observed that people often experience distress when they have time to reflect on their lives, such as on weekends when they are not occupied with work, but dread for Monday and the so-called Sunday blues is a real phenomenon.

Organizations too can operate in the same existential vacuum. The culture is characterized by an emptiness, its workers dread coming in on a Monday, and things can feel directionless. If your business feels this way, it's a vital sign of the need to reculture. Shifting consumer expectations mean that businesses without a clear purpose are likely to lose relevance.

Intensifying Economic Pressure and Its Impact on Profit Versus Purpose

So if we know this, why do so many organizations mention purpose only in the once-a-year statement in the annual report and accounts? Is it that, for some, anything but a focus on profit is a distraction? Both purpose and profit or surplus are incredibly important parts of running a successful business. A singular focus on profit can lead to a risky place for your culture. Henry Ford famously said, "A business that makes nothing but money is a poor business" (Andersen, 2013). What Henry Ford means is that making money is a good outcome for business but without purpose, at some point, someone is going to say, "so what?" Worse still, a sole focus on making money can lead to a culture of narrow-mindedness. This restricts decision-making to short-term financial gains while overlooking broader factors that contribute to sustainable success. We've seen examples where with a single focus on profit, firms can experience a culture characterized by these issues:

- **Limited innovation:** Companies driven solely by profit often resist change if it doesn't yield immediate returns. This mindset discourages bold investment in research, development, and creativity, making businesses vulnerable to disruption by more forward-thinking competitors.
- **Neglecting stakeholders:** When profit is the only priority, companies may ignore the needs of employees, customers, and communities. This short-sighted approach can damage brand trust, employee morale, and long-term customer loyalty.
- **Risk aversion:** Businesses obsessed with quarterly earnings tend to avoid risk, meaning they may fail to explore new opportunities or adapt to market shifts. This can lead to stagnation, as seen in the decline of once-dominant companies like Nokia and Blockbuster.
- **Ethical blind spots:** A profit-first mentality can lead to unethical practices, such as cutting corners on safety, environmental responsibility, or fair wages. History is full of scandals when companies ignored ethics for financial gain leading to lawsuits, reputational damage, and even collapse.

Since 2020 we have seen increased uncertainty and pressure from the global recovery and response to the pandemic, with inflation surging and increased interest rates. Companies must grow to survive. The volatility in markets has made it harder just to maintain historic levels of return on capital. Despite companies focusing on efficiencies from digital transformation to boost margins, recent reports suggest a 23% decline in business performance (Booth, 2025). The United Kingdom has been hit hard with 198,046 businesses struck off the official register in the final quarter of 2024 alone—the highest number in two decades. In 2024, major retailers in the United States announced over 7,300 store closures, a 57% increase from 2023. This marks the highest annual number of closures since 2020, when pandemic disruptions peaked (USA News Independent, 2025).

With this intensifying of pressure on business, the requirement to navigate the right balance of profit focus with purpose focus is strengthening in its urgency to not just "do something about culture" but to fully understand it and get it right and on track with immediacy.

So, while profit remains vital for future growth, the trap of a culture driven solely by profit can lead to a culture that creates excessive risk in the short and long term. Whereas a culture driven by purpose, fueled by profits, helps companies keep a wide field of vision, this builds enduring success to navigate market disruptions and cultivate stakeholder loyalty. Profit becomes key to serving the purpose. It's valued and not rejected. Nor is it the only thing that matters. Businesses that embrace both purpose and profit don't just survive, they lead.

The Reculture Twist: Why Purpose Needs Prospection

So we found our purpose, now what? Perhaps we've even spent a fortune creating new snappy definitions and building exciting communications campaigns for it, but we know from our conversations with leaders is that many haven't necessarily seen the cultural benefits as readily as they would like. One chief product office in the United States told us, "Their work on purpose felt good but quickly peaked and then fizzled out."

So, what is going on here? In some cases, it is likely that we have created generic marketing-esque purpose statements or misdirected efforts in conveying it. Some therefore don't feel authentic and others are long and caveated.

One retailer's purpose statement is so bland people barely register it as a reason to be.

Purpose needs to be something that everyone with global diverse mindsets can feel motivated by: simple, core, human. It must inspire. Peter Senge reminds us that "shared visions compel courage so naturally that people don't even realize the extent of their courage" (Senge, 2006). Think of the American Dream, the 1960s space missions, the Kyoto climate agreement. Engagement with everyone on the purpose needs to come through in all aspects of the people experience, from attraction to onboarding, ongoing performance conversations, well-being, and leadership and career development. The purpose of your firm has to connect emotionally and convey the philosophy with which you will advance and evolve forward.

But reality is, most organizations have missed a big trick with purpose. They leave it on the shelf and don't use it actively within their organization. It's certainly not leveraged as much as it could be from our experiences. To give purpose, what it needs to reboot reculture is to be paired with another future-focused approach and skill known as prospection. *Prospection* is the act of anticipating future scenarios to inform smarter decisions today. For executives, it's the mental modeling that links strategy, risk, and opportunity, turning foresight into financial and organizational advantage. Purpose gives meaning. Prospection gives momentum. Together they become a powerful cultural force that drives long-term success, resilience, and strategic growth.

Going Future Back

Without prospection, even the most inspiring purpose can become static. Future-focused businesses that integrate the skills of prospection into their strategic decision-making ensure their purpose remains relevant and actionable over time. Instead of guessing, we take our purpose and mentally explore what each path might look like in six months, two years, or even a decade. We vividly picture the risks, the wins, the market shifts, and then we make our moves based on those imagined futures. We don't just look at future risks but future opportunities. Cultures that create a natural home for prospection skills alongside a purpose are likely to move more naturally toward the future.

For example, Amazon's customer-centric philosophy is effective because it integrates purpose with prospection. People at Amazon write the press release and frequently asked questions for all investment decisions so people can see, feel, and experience through imagination what future this decision will create. This highly innovative initiative works because people must project forward the impact of their idea, and it builds the momentum and belief to go and make it happen. This type of cultural norm, using skills of prospection, has enabled the company to expand beyond retail into cloud computing, artificial intelligence (AI), and logistics at record speed.

Prospection is a relatively new idea to psychology and is recognized as a natural and core function of human cognition. Understanding prospection better offers a huge amount to organizations that want to utilize uniquely human strengths to achieve its goals. Martin Seligman's groundbreaking work *Homo Prospectus* (Seligman et al., 2016) has brought the concept to a wider audience.

This psychological insight is challenging traditional psychology's focus on past experiences and present circumstances. It is a major shift, as it argues that the basis of human cognition, our natural mental models, is, in reality, fundamentally future-oriented and based on our deeply held intentions. In his book Seligman and his colleagues propose that people are not primarily driven as much by memory or immediate stimuli as we think, but by their ability to anticipate and evaluate future possibilities. His research explores how prospection operates through deliberate thought, intuition, mind wandering, and social imagination, shaping decision-making, creativity, and emotional well-being. The authors argue that both individual and collective cognitive strength lies in our ability to anticipate, imagine, and evaluate future possibilities to guide decision-making and behavior. Seligman's work aims to establish prospection as a measurable and scientifically rigorous concept, with applications in psychology, neuroscience, and philosophy, and, of course, within organizations. By shifting the focus toward how individuals and groups envision and prepare for the future, his research offers new and exciting insights into motivation, resilience, and mental health and how to shape cultures. These results point to prospection as an important component of flourishing, both in the workplace and in daily life (Eubanks et al., 2023).

Prospection for cultures means working on the establishment of practices which enable the organization to, in more places than it does today, to anticipate and look ahead to future possibilities on a collective basis. Rather than one person setting an intention for the future, multiple people, across the organization, are creating a powerful momentum. Prospection as a skill set is closely related to foresight and planning, helping individuals and organizations prepare for upcoming events or opportunities. This is mental time travel, where people envision future scenarios to make better decisions and deepen their intentionality toward something. Research suggests that individuals who engage in prospective thinking tend to be more goal-oriented and resilient.

A study published in *The Journal of Positive Psychology* (Ratner et al., 2022) found that purpose-driven prospection enhances decision-making and long-term planning. Organizations that integrate prospective thinking skills and practices into their cultures are more likely to adapt to change, innovate, and sustain success.

The Four Modes of Prospection and How to Establish Them

As we explained, prospection is our ability to mentally simulate and anticipate future scenarios. It's not just about prediction, it's about envisioning possibilities, preparing for change, and shaping desired outcomes. Four modes, each of which human beings are cognitively built for and discussed by Seligman et al. (2016), can play a distinct role in how individuals and organizations engage with the future, and if developed within our cultures can lead to an acceleration of the future.

Implicit Mind

What it is: Automatic, intuitive forecasting based on past experiences and learned patterns. It operates beneath conscious awareness, guiding decisions through gut feelings and rules of thumb.

Establishing it culturally:

- Foster rituals and routines that bring people together to share their experiences and sensemaking of the world and your organizations role within it. This reinforces shared purpose, enabling intuitive decision-making to align with strategic intent.

- Encourage experiential learning and tacit knowledge sharing (e.g. mentoring, storytelling) to embed future-oriented instincts. Questions such as what would we do next time? What learning are we taking forward?
- Build psychological safety so teams trust their instincts and act without over-analysis in fast-moving contexts.

Deliberate Thought

What it is: Conscious, analytical forecasting using logic, data, and scenario planning. It's the mode most associated with formal strategy and decision-making.

Establishing it culturally:

- Embed structured foresight practices like horizon scanning, trend analysis, and strategic planning cycles in more places than your strategy department. Consider introducing premortems where teams analyze delivery, like a typical project postmortem, before they start on a project. Encourage teams to use foresight tools and techniques as part of their routines of work.
- Promote critical thinking and evidence-based decision-making through training and leadership modeling. Questions such as what have we not thought about? What is the unthinkable that could derail us?
- Create space for deep work, quiet, focused time for individuals and teams to think rigorously about long-term goals.

Mind Wandering

What it is: Spontaneous, unstructured mental drifting that often leads to novel connections and creative insights. Though seemingly idle, it's a powerful source of innovation.

Establishing it culturally:

- Encourage downtime and reflection, recognizing that creativity often emerges in moments of rest or distraction.

- Design physical and digital environments that support curiosity and serendipity (e.g. creative spaces).
- Celebrate nonlinear thinking and divergent ideas, especially in innovation labs or cross-functional teams.

Collective Imagination

What it is: The collaborative envisioning of future possibilities, shaped by shared narratives, values, and aspirations. It's the foundation of purpose-driven culture and transformational change.

Establishing it culturally:

- Facilitate visioning workshops, storytelling sessions, and strategic dialogues that invite diverse voices to cocreate the future.
- Align on a clear and compelling purpose that transcends short-term goals and inspires long-term commitment.
- Build inclusive leadership that empowers people to contribute to the organization's evolving story.

To embed these modes meaningfully:

- Balance structure and spontaneity: Combine deliberate and more formalized strategy with space for intuition and creativity.
- Model future-oriented thinking: Leaders embody and reward prospection in decision-making and communication.
- Design for emergence: Create systems that allow new ideas, insights, and futures to surface organically.

A significant barrier has been that the opportunity for collective daydreaming is seen as a cost and luxury only rarely afforded to the senior leaders of an organization as taking time out of delivery mode for large populations of workers is a significant financial investment. Finding clever methods to offer scalable imagination creation and capture that is efficient and ongoing through daily ways of working will be critical for organizations to take this path at pace.

How Prospection Strengthens Decision-Making

Purpose-driven prospection, in all its modes, enables leaders to embrace proactive strategy. Companies that consistently analyze future trends, anticipate market shifts, and adapt their business models are better positioned to thrive in uncertainty.

Harvard Business School research found that organizations that incorporate long-term future planning into their leadership approach achieve higher financial performance and employee retention. This is because employees are more engaged when they see their work contributing to a meaningful, long-term mission.

To harness prospection effectively, organizations can do the following:

- Define their purpose clearly and powerfully.
- Use the prospection modes to explore different future possibilities for your organization and adapt accordingly.
- Encourage future-thinking within leadership and teams at all levels, fostering innovation. Ask questions such as what would a future team get from this? What possibilities does this enable?
- Maintain flexibility, enabling purpose-driven strategies to evolve with market changes.

Linked to this is psychologist Jonathan Baron's concept of actively open-minded thinking (AOT) (Baron, 2008) can help a company achieve its purpose by fostering a culture of critical thinking, adaptability, and innovation. AOT encourages individuals to seek out diverse perspectives, challenge their own assumptions, and remain open to new evidence, which is essential for effective decision-making in a dynamic business environment.

Purpose as a Future-Proofing Strategy for Culture

The future is not something to be feared, it's something to be designed. A company's purpose tells the world why it exists. Prospection ensures it continues to matter in the years ahead. Businesses that combine these two elements on an ongoing basis gain clarity, resilience, and strategic agility, enabling them to shape their own destinies rather than merely responding to change.

In an era of rapid disruption, by integrating purpose, prospection, and AOT to be a core unifier of people in our organizations, we have the means to leapfrog where we are today and build a new foundation for our culture. We're defining trends instead of reacting to them.

For example, companies such as Patagonia, Chanel, and Microsoft have demonstrated how purpose-driven strategies, combined with foresight, create long-term success. By embedding sustainability and innovation into their future planning, they have remained ahead of competitors.

Case Study: Patagonia—Purpose-Driven Innovation

Purpose   To build the best product, cause no unnecessary harm, and use business to inspire and implement solutions to the environmental crisis.

Prospection   Anticipating the future of business as a force for planetary regeneration, ethical leadership, and consumer activism. Patagonia has embedded environmental and social responsibility into its DNA not as a marketing angle, but as its operating system. From its founding, the company has prospected the future of consumer values, recognizing early that sustainability would become a defining expectation. Its purpose-driven strategy has led to bold moves: donating 1% of sales to environmental causes, pioneering circular product design, and even transferring ownership of the company to a trust and nonprofit to ensure all profits serve the planet.

Patagonia's prospection is evident in its long-term investments in regenerative agriculture, fair labor practices, and climate activism. It anticipated the rise of conscious consumerism and positioned itself not just as a brand, but as a movement. Its "Don't Buy This Jacket" campaign challenged fast fashion and reframed consumption as a moral choice years ahead of mainstream ESG conversations.

The company's ability to forecast and act on emerging sustainability trends has earned it fierce customer loyalty, high employee engagement, and industry leadership. A *Harvard Business Review* study (Malnight et al., 2017) confirms that companies with strong environmental and social missions outperform peers in retention and brand trust; Patagonia is a living example.

By aligning its purpose with future-focused action, Patagonia proves that profitability and planetary stewardship are not opposing forces, they're mutually reinforcing. Its model shows that when business leads with purpose and prospection, it doesn't just survive change, it shapes it.

Case Study: Chanel—Purpose-Led Transformation

Purpose   To be a creation-driven, human-driven, and committed luxury brand that generates long-term value for both business and society.

Prospection   Anticipating the future of luxury through cultural relevance, environmental stewardship, and human empowerment.

Chanel has redefined its legacy of timeless elegance by embedding creativity, craftsmanship, and responsibility into its operating model. Guided by its purpose, Chanel sees creation not just as artistic output but as a force for cultural influence and social progress. Recognizing that the future of luxury demands more than aesthetic excellence, Chanel launched its Mission 1.5° strategy to decarbonize its operations and value chain, aiming for net-zero emissions by 2040. The brand's purpose now extends beyond style to include restoring nature, investing in circular systems, and promoting dignity—especially the autonomy and self-accomplishment of women.

Through prospection, Chanel senses and responds to emerging shifts in consumer expectations for climate action, ethical luxury, and inclusive identity. It has invested in regenerative practices, low-carbon innovation, and durable product life cycles—ensuring relevance in a world where luxury must be both aspirational and accountable. Chanel's selective distribution model's emphasis on emotional storytelling and commitment to human-centric design reflect a deep understanding of future desire—not just current demand.

By aligning its purpose with future-focused sustainability and cultural resonance, Chanel strengthens brand desirability while contributing to global progress. Its transformation shows that luxury can be both enduring and evolving—rooted in heritage, yet responsive to what's next.

Case Study: Microsoft—Purpose-Led Reinvention

Purpose   To empower every person and every organization on the planet to achieve more.

Prospection   Anticipating the future of work, technology, and human potential through inclusive innovation, ethical AI, and global-scale impact. Microsoft's transformation under its purpose has been one of the most studied in modern business. Once known primarily for software dominance, the company reimagined itself as a platform for empowerment—shifting from product-centric to people-centric strategy. Its purpose now guides everything from cloud infrastructure and AI development to accessibility and sustainability. By embedding prospection into its leadership culture, Microsoft has become a proactive force in shaping the future of work, education, and digital inclusion.

Through prospection, Microsoft anticipated the rise of hybrid work, the ethical challenges of AI, and the need for trust in digital ecosystems. It invested early in responsible AI frameworks, carbon-negative commitments, and tools that enable collaboration across borders and abilities. Its acquisition strategy—from LinkedIn to GitHub—reflects a long-term view of interconnected productivity and community-led innovation.

Microsoft's purpose is not just aspirational—it's operational. The company's prospection mindset shows up in its commitment to universal design, skilling initiatives for underserved populations, and its planetary-scale sustainability goals. By aligning purpose with future-focused action, Microsoft has reignited relevance, trust, and growth—proving that tech leadership is not just about speed, but about stewardship.

These examples show us that an active purpose can be a guiding force not just for culture but also the business bottom line. This is what makes it foundational for reculturing organizations. And there is more our purpose can do for us culturally.

The Most Scalable Human Tool for Sharing Purpose: Storytelling

Of course, while we wake up more fully to the role of purpose in our organizations, purpose as the key to culture has been long known to ancient societies, who were among the first to create and harness human culture. And it is in these lessons that we get the wisdom we need to be able to sustain our purpose better. Some organizations have a compelling purpose, but it lacks cultural influence because it is not richly imagined in the day-to-day of the company and only periodically drawn upon.

Aboriginal dreamtime is one of humanity's earliest cultural frameworks, blending mythology, law, and nature. Also known as *the dreaming*, it is a foundational concept in Australian Aboriginal spirituality and culture. It represents the time of creation, when ancestral spirits shaped the land, its features, and all living beings. Dreamtime stories are sacred narratives that encode the origins of the land, the laws of human conduct, and the interconnectedness of all living things. These stories are passed down through generations via oral tradition, song, dance, and art, serving as living guides that shape identity, governance, and ecological stewardship.

Through this it shaped identity, land stewardship, and social norms. Dreamtime illustrates how long humans have used narrative to define values, guide behavior, and embed meaning into everyday life. These stories established the philosophical underpin of the laws, customs, and relationships that continue to guide Aboriginal communities today.

This tells us that one of the greatest learning and guiding tools we have as human beings is storytelling. Ancient civilizations used storytelling to transmit and reinforce their values and beliefs. Myths, legends, and oral traditions helped civilizations like the Greeks and Egyptians pass down knowledge and inspire collective identity. Deep understanding allows for elegant, focused decisions.

In today's complex and fast-moving organizations, storytelling remains one of the most powerful, and underused, tools for shaping culture. Some argue stories are all culture is. Unlike programs or policies, stories scale effortlessly. They travel across teams, geographies, and hierarchies, embedding values, shaping mindsets, and energizing behavior.

Neuroscience confirms this: Research from Stanford professor Chip Heath found that 63% of people remember stories, while only 5% recall statistics because stories activate multiple regions of the brain, including those responsible for emotion, memory, and simulation (Kadence, 2025). This multisensory engagement creates emotional resonance and cognitive imprinting, making stories stick.

Purpose-driven organizations distinguish themselves in competitive markets, and storytelling amplifies this differentiation. When organizations communicate their purpose through storytelling, employees and stakeholders connect deeply with their mission, fostering greater commitment. When people hear a compelling story, they experience empathy and emotional resonance, making them more likely to take action. The company purpose cannot therefore be just a line on a PowerPoint deck, a snappy video, or on a website. It must be alive with image, stories, articulations, rituals, and ceremonies. It must be easy to remember, seen as valuable and desired. During challenges, purpose-driven storytelling reinforces collective identity, helping employees remain focused and motivated. For example, during times of economic uncertainty, companies like Airbnb have used storytelling to remind employees of their core mission, creating a sense of belonging, strengthening internal morale and external brand loyalty.

Yet storytelling in business is often misunderstood. It's not the fairy tales of childhood; it's the strategic act of meaning making. In organizations, storytelling shows up in situations such as these:

- A leader sharing a moment of failure and what they learned
- A team retelling how they overcame a challenge together
- A customer story that embodies the organization's purpose
- A symbolic decision that becomes legend: who was promoted, what was paused, how a value was protected

These stories become the informal curriculum of the organization. They shape what people believe is possible, permissible, and valued. They build trust, coherence, and emotional engagement faster than any slide deck or strategy memo.

For senior leaders, storytelling is not a soft skill, it's a strategic capability. It turns abstract values into lived experience. It aligns teams, accelerates transformation, and creates cultural momentum. And when leaders share stories with clarity and vulnerability, they invite others to do the same, creating a ripple effect of belonging and belief.

In short: If you want to shift culture, don't just launch a program. Tell the right story and let it move through the organization like a wave.

A good place to start with our organization's reculturing story is to start at the beginning—what evolution has our organization taken and why it is where it is. It's important to know who founded the organization and what twists and turns have it taken. For better or worse, those early intentions go on to shape the organization's culture, vision, and values as it grows. We also need to know who owns it as this will help us understand how the culture has been shaped to date. This isn't always as straight forward a question as it seems.

As with humans, the organization origin story is very powerful. Of course, companies change but we are yet to find a company that doesn't carry something of its origin in its culture, and its must have knowledge for anyone seeking to evolve it forward.

Claire Isnard, chief people and organization officer at Chanel, knows all about the power of transmission. At Chanel, stories are core to who they are, and they give life to their identity, values, and how they connect as people. Their approach to onboarding shows how they do this. They have created the Imagine Chanel program, which gives everyone new to Chanel the grounding and understanding of their timeless approach, and they immerse themselves in Gabrielle Chanel's founding vision. They get to appreciate the freedom of creation embodied in the products, discover craftsmanship at the manufacturing sites, and explore the new experiences being created in the boutiques. They deliberately weave facts and figures with the emotion of the brand. In June 2025 it was reported that 28,000 of the 38,000 workforce had experienced this program, and it's a contributor to their ongoing success laying the foundations of the future of the organization. We are constantly surprised when we meet people in our field of human resources, and they don't know who owns their company or the reasons why their company was set up. Of course, not every company is The Body Shop or Patagonia, where their founders had strong, powerful, and compelling purpose and vision for their companies. Most know that it's either private or public listed or owned by private equity, but many don't look deeper. We really recommend doing this. It can usually be found in the annual report and accounts or online. Likewise understanding more about who owns the greatest number of shares in the organization is a relatively easy search and will tell us about their philosophy for investment. Another angle is to look hard at who is on the board or part of advisory committee and again search for them to see what they have done before or if they have approaches or views. For public sector organizations or nongovernmental organizations, find out more about the funding sources and oversight models. Once this is known, look up the public officials in charge of this and see what there is to learn. This knowledge tells us what pressures the organization might be exposed to which influences decision-making and ultimately, culture.

When leaders articulate a clear, compelling story about the organization's purpose, people can feel more connected and committed to achieving its goals.

How AI Can Help

To reculture at pace and scale, organizations must do more than react in line with their values, they must *reimagine* constantly. Purpose sets the direction, prospection keeps it current and builds the momentum, and storytelling keeps the journey alive. When leaders and people align on a shared reason for being and anticipate what's next, culture flows and becomes a living system that is adaptive, coherent, and deeply human. This isn't just transformation; it's choreography. And it begins not with tools or tactics but with a bold return to what matters most.

Purpose and prospection are inherently human endeavors, rooted in imagination, empathy, and ethical reflection, but AI can provide important scaffolding like data, models, simulations, which enable leaders to make more informed choices. The partnership between human intuition and machine intelligence creates a feedback loop: Leaders articulate purpose, AI tests its resonance and feasibility, and employees adapt their behaviors in response. Over time, this loop can strengthen cultural cohesion and resilience.

AI is a tool that can greatly assist organizations in this space. AI can help organizations refine purpose by analyzing vast amounts of stakeholder data such as employee sentiment, customer expectations, and societal trends, and then distill this into patterns that reveal what truly matters. For example, natural language processing tools can scan millions of conversations across social media, internal surveys, and industry reports to uncover themes about sustainability, equity, or innovation. These insights enable leaders to align organizational purpose with the evolving values of their ecosystem, ensuring relevance and authenticity.

For prospection, AI enhances this skill by simulating complex environments and projecting outcomes with unprecedented speed and accuracy. Machine learning models can forecast consumer behavior, regulatory shifts, or technological adoption curves, enabling organizations to test different strategic pathways. More important, AI democratizes prospection: It enables employees at all levels to access predictive insights, fostering a culture where everyone participates in shaping the future rather than passively reacting to it.

Unlike any other technology before it, generative (gen) AI can even help us converse with the future. For example, Ipsos has developed powerful gen AI technology called *Personabots* for its clients to be able to speak to key product and citizen segments and ask them questions based on long-term data sources—it can ask them what they would think of this policy or this innovation and get an instant future-oriented response.

Storytelling has always been central to shaping organizational culture, but AI can transform how stories are discovered, crafted, and shared in ways that directly reinforce purpose. By analyzing employee feedback, customer interactions, and external trends, AI can surface authentic narratives that demonstrate how an organization is experienced in practice. It can then personalize these stories for different audiences, ensuring that the same purpose-driven message resonates across geographies, functions, and roles. Beyond reflecting the past, AI also enables leaders to weave prospection into storytelling by simulating future scenarios and turning them into compelling narratives that inspire action today. In this way, AI democratizes storytelling, empowering employees at all levels to contribute to the cultural narrative, while also measuring which stories truly engage and align with the organization's purpose. The result is a dynamic feedback loop where human imagination and machine intelligence combine to embed foresight and meaning into culture, ensuring that purpose is not just declared but continuously reinforced through stories that matter.

The question now is: Are you ready to lead from the future?

Leaders' Purpose Alignment Checklist

Do you have these qualities at the ready?

- **Clear and authentic purpose:** Our purpose is simple, compelling, and resonates with our history and future direction.
- **Naturally shared:** Employees can articulate the purpose easily and do so willingly in everyday conversations. Alumni from the firm are welcome back to share their stories and maintain a link with the past, present, and future.
- **Talent magnet:** The purpose is a key factor in attracting and retaining people; it surfaces in recruitment and performance discussions.
- **Stakeholder interest:** Progress toward our purpose is regularly discussed and reimagined with investors, customers, regulators, and employees.
- **Strategic integration:** Purpose and the modes of prospection inform scenario planning and long-term strategy development.
- **Leadership commitment:** Senior leaders enable space for analysis and imagination and have personal strategies aligned with the purpose and adapt them to changing environments.
- **Purpose-driven investment:** We allocate resources to initiatives that help us sustain our purpose and ensure high-quality storytelling.
- **Cultural visibility:** Purpose is a frequent and visible part of organizational dialogue.
- **Storytelling and impact:** We share real, inspiring stories that show our purpose in action and how we overcome challenges to achieve it.
- **AI-enabled foresight and storytelling:** We use AI to surface authentic narratives, anticipate future scenarios, and measure cultural resonance. AI insights help us align our purpose with emerging trends, democratize prospection across the organization, and ensure our stories are both data-informed and emotionally compelling.

6 | Reculturing Driver 2: Mindsets as a New Approach to Defining Culture

"Only changes in mindsets can extend the frontiers of the possible."

—Winston Churchill

In his book *Leading in a Non-Linear World: Building Well-being, Strategic and Innovation Mindsets for the Future*, Jean Gomes (2022) presents a new science-based approach to understanding and developing mindset, particularly for leaders navigating today's complex and uncertain environments. This insight opens the potential of mindset to move organizations forward.

Gomes says that mindset is an interplay of feeling, thinking, and seeing. He redefines mindset as the dynamic interaction with our emotions, thoughts, and perceptions. This holistic view emphasizes that, unlike values, mindset is not static but can be cultivated to enhance well-being and per-formance both individually and collectively.

He shares four leadership mindsets:

- **Well-being mindset:** Prioritizing mental and physical health as foundational to effective leadership
- **Strategic mindset:** Developing an understanding of the bigger picture, anticipating trends, and making informed decisions
- **Innovation mindset:** Embracing change, fostering creativity, and adapting to new realities
- **Open mindset:** Cultivating curiosity, flexibility, and openness to diverse perspectives

Two key reflections stood out as key insights into working with mindsets that felt fundamental to reculturing:

- **Mindset as a trainable system:** Contrary to the belief that mindset is innate, Gomes argues that it is a trainable system. By developing self-awareness and understanding the interplay of our internal processes, individuals can enhance their ability to adapt and thrive in changing environments. This gives more impact to working with mindsets as human choice that is universal and not exclusive to those born with particular mindsets.
- **Building self-awareness:** Gomes introduces a framework for exploring the leader's sense of self, emphasizing the importance of self-awareness in cultivating effective mindsets. This involves reflecting on various layers of consciousness and understanding how our internal experiences influence our actions. Thankfully so much leadership development work over past decades has started with "leading self" modules with self-awareness as a foundation to understanding others and our management of self and relationships.

Prioritizing shared mindsets as a driver of reculturing is an important new step because previous work on mindsets in organizations is often limited solely by fixed or growth mindsets for learning. Carol S. Dweck introduced her research on growth mindset in her book *Mindset* in 2006, which had instant impact and adoption into organizations supporting learning interventions for growth. Yet the concept of choosing to share mindsets on any topic is less applied.

What we like most about the opportunity in using shared mindsets to influence culture is the fluidity and dynamic nature that we can choose our mindset and switch it whenever we like. Basically, a mindset is the system of thinking that we use to guide our actions and opinions, and it can shift and flow with our changing context. Tapping into a mindset is likely to create faster shifts than trying to move people's value centers, which are more embedded from years of childhood experiences and hence harder to change.

Comparing Mindsets and Values

Sometimes leaders think that because they have a set of organizational values, they are influential in the culture. But this is dangerous. We are aware of one organization that asked its people what values were being used in the company. Only 7% of people thought their company values were used. This shows how little influence organizational values have on a daily basis in some companies. We worry this is contributing to the blind spots of what really influences culture, which is slowing us down and allowing the crisis in culture to be a very real and present threat for many organizations. So what is the main difference between the two?

Mindset:

- Definition: A mindset shapes how people perceive and respond to the world. It is a way of thinking about the world or your experience of it.
- Focus: It primarily affects your approach to challenges, learning, and personal growth.
- Impact: Mindsets influence your resilience, adaptability, and overall outlook on life.

Values:

- Definition: Values are core principles or standards that guide your behavior and decision-making over time. It's about what you fundamentally believe to be true or believe is important.

- Focus: Values reflect what is always important to you, such as honesty, integrity, and respect. Values can be personal (e.g. family, health) or organizational (e.g. customer focus, innovation).
- Impact: Values shape your ethical and moral compass, influencing long-term goals and priorities.

Key differences:

- Nature: Mindset is about your mental attitude and approach, while values are about your fundamental beliefs and principles.
- Scope: Mindset affects how you handle situations and challenges, while values guide your overall behavior and decisions.
- Changeability: Mindsets can evolve with new experiences, choice, and conscious effort, while values tend to be more stable and deeply ingrained.

Are We Suggesting Values Have No Influence in Organizations?

No. Most organizations are likely to still want and have values, especially if they have strong beliefs and as they are as ubiquitous as having a strategy. But they can be better seen for what they are—as contributors to the work on purpose and shared fundamental beliefs that are part of the story and fabric of the company or industry. They should always be true, lived, and enduring. They give shape to our purpose, which is valuable. However, we can stop pretending our very best people have the exact same values as the firm, and it stops us from trying to force something on people that cannot in truth be forced. Realistically, most corporate values are generally set due to regulation, industry, product, service, and the stage of the organization's life cycle. For example, most oil companies have safety as a corporate value, and it is vital this continues.

Likewise, financial services firms will usually have integrity as a value. Most pharmaceutical firms have patient safety or patient-first values. We'd worry if they didn't. The values an organization adopts are therefore hygiene factors, system design features, or license to operate rather than a dynamic way to shift and shape a culture to meet the challenges of the day.

We can therefore let go of the role of values to try to align people across diverse belief systems, and we can stop trying to extend their influence in artificial ways. By admitting that values are less useful in evolving the culture at pace, we can create some space to bring in something that will help us move forward.

To be valuable values need to communicate a direction and a choice. We hear time and time again that values should be tested in hiring, and of course every person who joins a company can either take a company forward or backwards culturally. We are not denying it's useful to know if someone doesn't believe in teamwork, respect, or integrity (the top three organizational values globally). But that's going to be a rare occurrence as most organizations' values correlate to the values generally held in the population. In hiring, a person can give a narrow story of their alignment with a value, but somehow miss sharing how they think or how they approach life—are they positive or negative? Do they have a victim mentality or a fixed mindset, which slows you down and sends your culture backwards. In short, mindset matters a lot more than we think if we want to go at speed.

We must consider ditching the confusing and often stand-alone language on values, using that label to define something that can't meet future organizational needs. In the same way so many organizations are switching to a skills-based approach from old difficult-to-define-and-influence terms about competencies and behaviors (which are influenced by myriad factors too hard for managers to change), now is the time to reconsider the shift from a static values approach to a collective and dynamic mindset approach.

What's more, collective norms—like cultural values and codes of conduct—are increasingly being rejected. Take common values such as teamwork, innovation, or respect. With rising individualism, we may be losing the ability or willingness to align with these traditional norms that once shaped corporate culture. Despite a strong focus on inclusion, society appears to be growing more divided.

This division seems driven by factors like social media echo chambers, widening economic inequality, identity-based politics, and declining trust in institutions. People are increasingly exposed to views that only reinforce their own, while fragmented information makes it harder to agree on shared truths. Global crises like COVID-19, climate change, and the rise of artificial intelligence (AI) have deepened these divides, prompting people to cling more tightly to familiar identities and beliefs.

Inside organizations, stronger union participation is amplifying divided voices and pushing for more differentiated work experiences—often ignoring the commercial realities of what's being demanded. Leaders of traditional culture change programs, working with limited resources and outdated processes, are struggling. It's clear that people won't simply conform. Many are refusing to follow reasonable directions from managers or others whose power and status once carried weight. Defiance is growing—not necessarily out of principle, but because people don't want to change.

This shift is happening fast, if not already complete. That's why there's an urgent need to embrace collective mindsets to drive positive change and set reasonable workplace expectations. Groups are rejecting corporate calls for accountability because it feels "uncomfortable," leaving even great leaders unable to lead—and often choosing to walk away.

On top of this, upward bullying is increasing. Leaders are stuck trying to honor individual needs while balancing organizational pressure for collective performance. Collaboration and shared ways of working—once essential—are becoming impossible to create. And this is happening even in values-led firms.

Leaders are feeling isolated, operating in a vacuum, even when organizational values are present. It's as if they no longer have an audience. If the old routes of influence through hierarchy and control are crumbling, maybe the shift to more self-managing teams is finally on the horizon—and collective mindsets are the path forward.

The Key to Reculturing: Make It Real and Lived in Shared Mindsets

We are looking at using shared mindsets more broadly, beyond simply growth/fixed, as a faster way to regain traction on culture because mindsets represent the underlying attitudes our organization has when it approaches its work. Working on shifting our mindset is infinitely more possible, at pace and scale, than shifting our values. Our primary aim becomes ensuring we can align on how to approach what's coming at us, rather than try to get consistency in what's core to people.

There is an appealing simplicity to the early definitions of a mindset—attitude and a filter through which we look at the world. This has been oft overlooked, which has no doubt contributed to its underplayed role in our organizations until recently. Even mindset scientists acknowledge this has been an issue (Buchanan, 2024). But early scientists looking at mindsets alighted on an important distinction. Viktor Frankl himself reminds us that "everything can be taken from a man but one thing: the last of the human freedoms—to choose one's attitude in any given set of circumstances, to choose one's way" (Frankl, 1946/2004).

We are used to dissecting mindset particularly in the sporting arena. We can see, in the microcosm that sports offer, the often very immediate difference mindset makes. In England the national women's football team, the Lionesses, credited mindset and specific mantras with what got them through a tough tournament to win the UEFA Women's Euro 2025 for a second time. Despite his extraordinary physical talent, swimmer Michael Phelps attributes much of his success to mental preparation. He used visualization, relaxation techniques, and a resilient mindset to stay focused under pressure, especially during high-stakes Olympic events. His mindset helped him overcome setbacks, maintain composure, and win a record 23 gold medals. As one sports psychologist put it, "Mindset is the difference between victory and defeat."

Organizations that have done something different to the norm on values appear to be more successful. Amazon, for example, places a strong emphasis on guiding principles, particularly its 16 Leadership Principles, rather than traditional corporate values. These principles, or ways of approaching work, serve as a practical framework for decision-making, behavior, and culture across all levels of the organization. For example, one principle is "Bias for Action: Leaders value calculated risk-taking." These are directional statements for what's required of leaders. Unlike abstract values that can be open to interpretation, Amazon's principles are action-oriented and deeply embedded in daily operations from hiring and performance reviews to product development and strategic planning. This approach reflects Amazon's belief that principles should drive consistent behaviors and outcomes, helping the company maintain its customer-centric ethos, operational excellence, and long-term thinking.

Netflix famously has its Culture Memo that explains the mindset and attitude it has: the primary among them being "We aim only to have high performers at Netflix, people who are great at what they do, and even better at working together." It explains its approach to the organizational culture in the form of a handbook rather than a set of snappy but directionless words.

Reculturing Through Collective Mindsets

Focusing on collective mindsets could be one of the most powerful ways to drive reculturing at pace and scale. Culture is and can be shaped by shared attitudes, and ways of thinking, shifting these at a collective level can create deep, lasting change. Moving away from the monolithic attempt to align shared values and beliefs is a bold new step forward for many. Values are held from a young age, developed through childhood experiences and often then difficult to establish as shared in diverse teams, groups and organizations. A shift to a focus on mindsets that are a personal choice at any given time offers the freedom required for our now greater diverse populations to find commonality among our unique differences.

As we deepen our understanding of mindsets we see potential for collection or shared mindsets to really drive our cultures. The features of collective mindsets are compelling.

Collective Mindsets Create Shared Ownership of Culture

When employees feel that culture is something they shape together (rather than something imposed from the top), they are more engaged in living it and owning and shaping it themselves.

Collective mindsets foster a sense of responsibility people actively uphold and reinforce the culture through their everyday actions. Some of the highest performing companies in the world crucially state up front that they will evolve their mindsets and don't attempt to lock them in forever—something we have seen repeatedly over the years in the use of values.

Collective Mindsets Break Down Siloed Thinking

Many organizations struggle with fragmentation, where different teams or locations have their own subcultures.

A collective mindset encourages people to think beyond their immediate roles and see themselves as part of a larger whole, improving collaboration and alignment.

For example, Etsy has set out its approach to its business through these simple statements, which encourage a shared way of thinking about the organization:

- We commit to our craft.
- We minimize waste.
- We embrace differences.
- We dig deeper.
- We lead with optimism.

Anyone can universally sign up to these as mindsets, regardless of personal values held.

Collective Mindsets Strengthen Psychological Safety

When a team embraces a collective mindset, people feel safe to take risks, share ideas, and innovate.

This is crucial in hybrid and remote environments, where trust and connection can be harder to maintain. It may not be easy to create in the first instance, particularly in teams that are pressurized to deliver and execute their plan and in many cases are under-resourced, but the time that it takes to talk through issues and create a safe space can reduce if managers focus on the skill this needs.

Collective Mindsets Shift Culture from Fixed to Adaptive

A fixed mindset culture resists change ("this is just how we do things round here"). This fixed mindset then requires other firm structures to be in place to be able to perform: This is how we do things round here so you must be in the office together to observe this and do the same. This limits possibilities that adaptive mindsets offer for teams to work together in new and agile ways.

A collective learning mindset fosters adaptability, helping organizations evolve as needed instead of clinging to outdated ways of working.

Example: Microsoft's transformation under Satya Nadella was driven by shifting from a "know-it-all" to a "learn-it-all" culture. A simple flip of a word gives new meaning to help condense complexity into easy-to-apply focus.

Collective Mindsets Align People with Purpose

If everyone sees themselves as contributing to a greater purpose, culture can be shaped by something more than just a set of values.

Collective purpose-driven mindsets help teams stay motivated and resilient, even during challenges. For example, Marriott International even calls out embracing change as something fundamental to its collective mindset:

- We put people first
- We pursue excellence
- We embrace change
- We act with integrity
- We serve our world (Qualtrics, 2025)

To effectively state a mindset to use as a cultural driver we can do the following:

- **Clarify core attitudes or approaches that drive us forward:** Express the underlying principles, attitudes, and approaches that drive collective, forward-looking actions.
- **Use simple, inspiring language:** A mindset statement should be easy to understand and resonate with employees at all levels.
- **Make it actionable:** Ensure the mindset is linked to real-world choices, decisions, behaviors, and practices, not just abstract values.

For example, a company focused on growth mindset might state, "We embrace continuous learning, challenge assumptions, and turn setbacks into opportunities for innovation."

Reculturing by focusing on shared mindsets is one of the most powerful ways to future-proof culture at individual, team, and leadership levels.

For Individuals: Mindsets Unlock Growth, Purpose, and Resilience

Shared mindsets create psychological safety for each person, so people feel safe to speak up, take risks, and be themselves. For example, if you create a shared mindset on continuous learning or respecting well-being or being the best you can be, it can shift and encourage people from thinking "What do I need to do?" to "Who can I become here?"

Shared mindsets can help people navigate uncertainty with more confidence, self-leadership, and meaning.

They also help create self-awareness and clarity, especially as research suggests that more people than we often realize struggle to explicitly define and share their personal values.

For example, the United Kingdom Values Survey (Common Cause Foundation, 2016) highlights that individuals recognize broad societal values but may not always identify their own personal ones. This suggests that while values influence people's lives, they are often unconsciously held rather than consciously defined.

Example mindset shifts for individuals:

- From "I need to prove myself" to "I'm always learning"
- From "Change is a threat" to "Change is a chance to grow"

When people share their personal growth-oriented mindsets, they can move from surviving to truly thriving by explicitly naming and sharing growth ambitions with colleagues. When doing so and asking for support through regular feedback from those we work most closely with, we are more likely to get the alignment needed at the right time, in the moment when we need a reminder of the mindset we can choose. This offers immediate and rapid growth opportunities rather than the traditional annual performance cycle with managers who often don't see our actions day-to-day in the same way they perhaps used to if not always working in the same office/environment. This is where our colleagues and team have become much more important for our growth.

For Teams: Mindsets Build Cohesion, Collaboration, and Trust

Teams aligned on shared mindsets (e.g. curiosity, inclusion, experimentation) can work more fluidly and innovate faster together.

Shared mindsets reduce friction so people waste less energy navigating assumptions, misunderstandings, and unspoken norms.

Teams can adapt together in real time because they have a shared lens on how to approach challenges.

Example mindset shifts for teams:

- From "It's safer to stay in my lane" to "We grow stronger together"
- From "Only the leader decides" to "We cocreate solutions"

Mindset alignment across a team creates high trust, which can translate to high performance. It is an assumption that a collection of high-performing individuals put on the same project will automatically result in a high-performing team; however, the collaboration that creates greater than sum of parts does not simply come from working well side by side on our own projects, but by continually building and cocreating together toward team goals and staying on track. This collaboration requires increased effort but is the piece that makes the difference to the purpose of having a team rather than a collection of individual contributors.

For Leaders: Mindsets Create Clarity, Influence, and Legacy

Shared mindsets give leaders a common cultural language to guide teams without micromanaging. They help leaders role model behaviors and make decisions quicker. Example mindset shifts for leaders:

- From "I need to have the answers" to "I empower others to explore possibilities"
- From "Control ensures performance" to "Trust enables excellence"

Mindset-focused leaders shape the culture and leave a human legacy by bringing higher levels of accountability into the day-to-day tasks at the right level to match the skill of the team. If matched well as a stretch, it is an exciting challenge to step out of our comfort zones and take more responsibility; however, if we are not skilled to the right level for the stretch, this simply increases stress levels. The critical element is whether the leader is close enough to the individuals to know this is likely to be healthy and sustainable growth and development for them or tip them into a riskier situation.

Unlike skills or policies, shared mindsets need to be the following:

- Scalable: They apply at every level, across roles and functions.
- Human: They connect people on a personal choice level, not a transactional one.
- Adaptive: They evolve with the world, helping people stay future-ready.

Shared mindsets matter more than ever in the face of AI, human intentionality, and planetary urgency for three key reasons:

- In an AI-driven world, mindsets and the ways we think are what make us irreplaceably human. We know that AI is mastering tasks, decisions, even creativity, but it can't replace human consciousness, ethics, imagination, or meaning making. Therefore, shared human mindsets like curiosity, compassion, and courage can be differentiators that help guide us in how we use AI. Without those shared mindsets, we have a risk that using AI can amplify bias, harm, and disconnection, but with them we can ensure AI serves humanity as a key outcome.
- In the face of planetary crisis, mindsets drive real systemic change. The climate emergency can't be solved by isolated actions or compliance checklists; it needs a collective shift in how we think, prioritize, and relate to the earth. Where sustainability is being embedded into cultures as a choice we make as individuals, teams, or leaders, it can be harnessed through shared mindsets that become explicit and help people feel they belong. In this way, our shared mindsets can support our decision-making and influence us to make decisions that lead to shaping the future of our planet.
- In a fractured, fast world, we must be human on purpose and not by accident.

In the noise of tech, pace, polarization, and overload, it's easy to lose our sense of connection, and interdependence. We can use shared mindsets to explicitly support how we relate to each other, how we create inclusiveness, and how we lead others. We can then build cultures of care, fairness, and purpose, not just efficiency.

In short: Shared mindsets are the new compass, and they help us use AI ethically and wisely, make sustainability part of how we think, and create cultures where human flourishing isn't accidental.

We can't predict what are the right shared mindsets for organizations, as each will need to create and develop them for their context and timing, but we do know there are lots of options, making this an exciting release from rigidly sticking with the values set we have that have often been present for years and created by others we have no connection to.

When speaking to leaders around the world, we are hearing what are likely to be the most critical mindset shifts needed in organizations for successful reculturing for thriving. Here we share six of these to consider their relevance for your own organization:

- Fixed Mindset → Growth Mindset

    From: "This is how we've always done things."

    To: "We are always learning and evolving."

    This mindset encourages experimentation, continuous learning, and adaptability, and since Carol Dweck's research it has been used globally within organizations to help shift away from just filling gaps in skills to a lifelong learning approach that has significantly improved organizational adaptability for the future. To support this shift in mindset, leaders should model vulnerability by calling out failures openly to encourage others to do the same and embrace new ideas without shutting things down prematurely.

    Example: Microsoft's transformation under Satya Nadella focused on shifting from a "know-it-all" to a "learn-it-all" culture.

- Individual Success → Collective Success

    From: "I focus on my own performance and career growth."

    To: "We win together and lift each other up."

Shifts from internal competition to shared accountability have benefitted organizations and aligned reward and recognition systems to support this mindset, particularly in sales functions to work together on team goals and outcomes that better deliver to clients and customer's needs. This shift encourages collaboration and psychological safety so that a supportive team open to offering feedback to each other is part of our joint success.

Example: Companies like Pixar prioritize brain trust meetings, where teams openly give and receive constructive feedback to improve outcomes together.

- Compliance and Control → Trust and Autonomy

    From: "Employees need oversight to stay productive."

    To: "We trust people to take ownership and deliver results."

This mindset example moves away from micromanagement to empowering employees and is often a core outcome of leadership development practices focused on understanding their emotional intelligence. Self-awareness of style, rationale, and approach helps leaders recognize and shift to a more empowering leadership style with others having understood their own needs and reasoning.

This mindset shift is essential for hybrid and remote work environments and is often cited as the reason many leaders prefer office-based working when they struggle to empower others in dispersed teams.

Example: Netflix's "Freedom and Responsibility" approach allows employees to make decisions without excessive rules as long as they act in the company's best interest.

- Perfectionism → Experimentation and Agility

    From: "We must get it right the first time."

    To: "We learn through small, fast iterations."

This mindset shift encourages a test-and-learn approach instead of fearing failure but has a huge impact on agility. People often care about the outcome of their work to such a high extent that for these highly engaged, ambitious individuals, professional outcomes are often deeply intertwined with their personal identity and career trajectory. This can mean individuals who are high performers as individual contributors become siloed in their excellence but create a perfectionism approach that limits others' ability to learn from them because we learn much more through our failures! Simple dialogue encouraging experimentation and highlighting the stages of experimentation that occurred before the perfect outcome was attained might be really beneficial here when first making this shift.

This is a mindset shift that supports innovation by reducing risk aversion.

Example: Amazon's "Day 1" mindset keeps the company agile, encouraging teams to act as if they're always in startup mode.

- Short-Term Thinking → Long-Term Impact

  From: "How does this affect our quarterly results?"

  To: "How does this create sustainable success?"

  When the world is in chaos and turmoil and economies are changing constantly, this mindset shift is critical to balance immediate business goals with long-term employee well-being and societal impact. This is when we need each other more than ever to give each other the side-by-side support and encouragement to make decisions with the best information and data we have. This way we can continue moving forward on long-term actions without knowing the full details of the context we sit within.

  This shift really encourages purpose-driven decision-making, which leaders increasingly benefit from doing collectively rather than in isolation.

  Example: Patagonia embeds sustainability into every business decision, proving that long-term impact and profitability can go hand in hand.

- Task-Focused → Human-Focused

  From: "We need to maximize efficiency and output."

  To: "We prioritize well-being, connection, and purpose."

  This mindset shift acknowledges the overwhelming data and evidence that healthy employees drive better results. This focus helps retain talent and prevent burnout and yet we still see many organizations struggling to get this balance right on a daily basis rather than running "well-being weeks" once a year. Recognizing that these must be woven into conversations at work, and that managers need to be able to talk about this with their team, has to be part of basic management training.

Example: Companies like Airbnb and Salesforce invest in flexible work options, and purpose-driven leadership to ensure that their people have available systems as well as have everyday conversations that create a supportive work environment.

These mindset shifts aren't just about changing policies—they're about changing behaviors, language, and leadership norms. The companies that embrace them will build stronger, more human, and more future-ready cultures.

Case Study: The Bridge Team—A Story of Shared Mindsets in Action

At a global consultancy, a project team called themselves *the Bridge* because they worked across markets, functions, and time zones. But under pressure, cracks began to show.

Tensions rose. Emails became curt. The meetings were tense. Everyone felt overworked and underheard. Performance dipped. Leadership's instinct was to boost engagement with wellness perks and a new communications campaign, but it didn't touch the root of the issue.

Then a new team lead, Amara, arrived not with more tools, but with a question: "What are the mindsets we're bringing into this space?"

She held a conversation, not a workshop, not a directive. Together, the team surfaced what was really going on:

- "We assume speed matters more than quality."
- "We don't feel safe to ask for help."
- "We think mistakes mean we've failed."

So they rewrote their shared mindsets, not as rules but as agreements:

- We lead with curiosity, not judgment.
- We grow stronger together; vulnerability is strength.
- We slow down to think bigger.

Within weeks, something shifted. Meetings felt lighter. People asked bolder questions. Creativity returned. A junior analyst proposed an idea that won the client's trust and a major contract.

Six months later, the Bridge wasn't just a team name: It was a metaphor for how they showed up: connected, trusted, and human.

And it wasn't engagement that saved them. It was reculturing through shared mindsets, the invisible bridge they built together.

How to Embed Collective Mindsets When Reculturing

Mindsets at the collective level are an agreement of how we will face the challenges that lie ahead. We might say we value integrity and for the next year or so we will look at AI with a curious and open mindset; we won't discount the findings we come across. Doing this repetitively is what creates culture as the space between people becomes familiar.

- **Model it at the leadership level:** Leaders can embody the desired mindsets (e.g. curiosity, collaboration, growth) before expecting teams to adopt them. Leaders are the ones who work with and through others and have stepped out of an individually focused role to guide and steward as representatives of the organization's purpose and strategic needs. It is critical leaders step out front first and engage other influencers to come with them.
- **Make mindsets part of daily routines:** Integrate collective mindset shifts into team check-ins, retrospectives, and decision-making.

    Example: Before launching a project, ask, "How can we approach this with a learning mindset?" or "What's the attitude we need to make this a success?" Simply asking questions of mindset and by using this language we are introducing the element of choice of our approach, which invites people to step up and bring mindset to the forefront of attention. It aligns us if part of daily routines.
- **Recognize and reward mindset-based behaviors:** Celebrate individuals and teams who demonstrate collective thinking, whether through cross-functional collaboration, problem-solving, or knowledge sharing. Shared mindsets invite true collaboration, which is

easier to identify when connected to achievement. Most people appreciate recognition of their contribution, so this is a great incentive for team shared mindset outcomes.

- **Create psychological safety for experimentation:** Encourage people to challenge ideas, offer new perspectives, and take smart risks. We know people are more likely to explore if they have a safe path back and are encouraged to experiment. Simply by explicitly vocalizing this and sharing it in teams creates the environment that means people want to try out new ideas more readily.

  Example: Google's "psychological safety" research found that teams that feel safe to share ideas perform better.

- **Use storytelling to reinforce mindsets:** Stories are powerful culture-shaping tools. We use stories to teach children vocabulary, spelling, morals even, and adults continue to develop in their own lifelong learning through watching movies or sharing experiences as stories that help make sense of the world around them. Sharing success stories of how collective mindsets leads to better outcomes once again brings this to the forefront of attention for others to follow as a route to success.

How Can AI Help

- **AI-powered coaching for individuals and teams:** Coaching has always been the gold standard for mindset change, but it's been limited to a select few. AI blows that wide open. By analyzing communication patterns, decision-making styles, and team dynamics, AI delivers real-time, personalized coaching at scale. Individuals get tailored feedback that helps them act in alignment with the desired mindset. Teams receive insights into collective blind spots and collaboration strengths. What was once reserved for executives becomes democratized, embedding shared mindsets across the entire organization.

- **Simulation and scenario-based training:** Mindsets stick when people practice them under pressure. AI-driven simulations drop employees into realistic scenarios like conflict resolution, innovation challenges, cross-functional collaboration, and let them rehearse what to do with the mindset turned on. This isn't theory; it's muscle memory. By learning through experience, employees internalize the mindset faster and carry it into the real world.

- **AI-powered collaboration and knowledge sharing:** Culture spreads through stories and role models. AI curates the right examples through case studies, success stories, best practices, and delivers them to the right people at the right time. It connects employees with mentors who embody the mindset and highlights those who model the behaviors, creating a ripple effect of reinforcement. Recognition becomes automated, and the shared mindset becomes visible, celebrated, and contagious.

- **Personalized learning and nudging:** Workshops fade; nudges stick. AI delivers adaptive learning tailored to each role and context, then reinforces it with timely prompts. A manager might be nudged to give growth-oriented feedback; a team member might be reminded to invite diverse perspectives. These micro-interventions keep the mindset alive in the flow of work, ensuring it's not a one-off initiative but a daily habit.

Shifting collective mindsets isn't a quick fix, it's a continuous process of reinforcing new ways of thinking and behaving. But when done well, it lays the foundation for a more connected, adaptive, and thriving culture. Mindsets can be easier to create as a collective than values or beliefs. A mindset is often more of a choice, a lens we can adopt and evolve from also, so it becomes more flexible and able to develop as a skill.

In today's rapidly changing world, organizations need specific collective mindset shifts to stay adaptable, human-centered, and resilient.

Leader's Mindset Checklist

Purpose: To help senior leaders assess, align, and activate the mindsets that drive organizational success.

Understand the landscape:

- Have I clarified the difference between a mindset and a value—and how each is currently expressed in our organization?
  - → Mindset = habitual way of thinking or approaching situations
  - → Value = principle or belief that guides decisions and behavior
- Can I identify which collective mindsets would most benefit our organization right now?
  - → Examples: growth mindset, adaptive mindset, service mindset, sustainability mindset

Foster organizational dialogue:

- Do we talk openly and often about attitudes, approaches, and mental models in our organization?
  - → Consider embedding these discussions into team reflections, performance reviews, or strategic planning.
- Have I initiated conversations with colleagues to cocreate and agree on the mindset we need to cultivate?
  - → Start small: pilot with one team or project, then scale.

Communicate with clarity and inclusion:

- Is our articulation of the desired mindset inclusive, clear, and easy to understand across diverse roles and backgrounds?
  - → Use stories, metaphors, and real-life examples to make it relatable.
  - → Avoid jargon—focus on shared meaning.

7 | Reculturing Driver 3: Use Energy to Assess Cultural Health

"Energy and persistence conquer all things."

—Benjamin Franklin

"You should think of your energy as if it's expensive, as if it's like a luxury item. Not everyone can afford it."

—Taylor Swift (2025)

Is your company alive?

One of the most underrated yet crucial factors in creating a thriving workplace culture is energy. Not just physical energy, but the human emotional and mental vitality that fuels motivation, collaboration, and innovation. The sun provides us with all our planet's energy, and human energy, likewise, is a vital resource that fuels high performance in both individuals and organizations. Employees who are energized and thriving feel that their current experiences and behaviors at work are intrinsically motivating and supportive of self-development and personal growth (Kleine et al., 2019). This links to high performance and is why energy is our third reculturing driver.

A workplace with low levels of human energy will be blighted by burnout and feel stagnant, uninspired, and resistant to change. If this moves from being an individual phenomenon to localized climate and ultimately being more widespread and cultural, big problems persist, especially once we add bots to the mix.

To move forward, organizations must shift from viewing energy as a wellness perk to recognizing it as a core enabler of innovation, resilience, and sustainable performance. We can use energy to focus attention back on culture. This requires the systemic integration of energy principles into strategy and operations. As we look at it now, our almost complete obsession with employee engagement as a means to drive culture and high performance has distracted us from some very fundamental areas to pay attention to in our organizations. The way employee engagement has been interpreted and operationalized over the years has meant many organizations have not developed the right cultural interventions to drive growth, vitality, and performance, but instead an odd mix of outcomes. The focus on measuring consumer-like recommendations for the workplace has been, in some cases, severely misdirected, and the consequence of which, such as entitlement, disappointment and underequipped and underskilled workforces, is what we are now living with en masse in many organizations.

Engagement typically measures how committed employees feel toward their work in terms of spending their discretionary effort, but it does not always translate into effective action. As Faster Capital, a venture capital organization notes, interpreting engagement scores without context can lead to misleading conclusions about organizational health (Faster Capital, 2025). A highly engaged employee might feel motivated by their role but struggle with burnout, fatigue, or inefficiency. An organization might have high overall engagement scores but lack innovation and a grounded understanding of its financial position, strengths, and weaknesses. We know of one organization that had off-the-charts employee engagement measurement scores and yet was on the verge of collapse. Employees and leaders here had cocooned themselves from reality by looking at these metrics blindly and thinking all was well. And despite knowing that we can improve things in our organization with engagement, globally only one out of five people is engaged. If this is our main culture read, then it isn't working fast enough. Where we should have been looking was at human energy and thriving.

What Do We Mean by Energy?

Scientifically, energy is defined as "the capacity to work or produce heat." Energy cannot be destroyed or created, only transferred or transformed. The term *energy* finds its origin in the Greek words *energia*, signifying "activity, operation," and *energos*, connoting "active and working." The *Chambers Dictionary* defines energy as the "ability for vigorous activity, liveliness, or vitality"; "strength or forcefulness"; and the "capacity to do work" (Onyemelukwe et al., 2023). Energetic shifts are when energy palpably moves, either in consciousness or behavior. Objects have a vibrational frequency that on some level we can feel and experience. We know when we are somewhere with positive energy and we know when we meet people with positive energy. This is called *resonance*. This knowing changes our physiology and psychology—we relax and become alert without ever really realizing. Some humans and cultures are deeply attuned to these shifts, usually those with skills we describe as empathetic, and some cultures can sense what is moving and changing, often way before others. Where we should have been looking to gain understanding of culture was human energy and thriving.

Energy has always been one of the most fundamental building blocks of human progress and culture. Discoveries such as the fire and the wheel were about humans finding new ways to harness energy for survival and growth. Our economy is built off our ability to find new energy sources and power our activity on this planet. Societies have historically evolved based on their ability to tap into and harness energy. Albert Einstein, one of the greatest scientists who ever walked the planet, was deeply interested in energy. He said, "Everything is energy and that's all there is to it."

The amount, where, and on what human energy is directed, is highly important to the organizational culture. The level of energy required to make work happen is also important. If high energy is required to make low-quality things happen, that is a red flag. Researchers Schippers and Hogenes (2011) state that energy can be both a short-term and a long-term process. Just like for instance satisfaction, people can experience long-term (basic energy level) as well as short-term effects on their energy level. Long-term draining effects can result in a burnout and should probably be viewed as deviations from a persons' basic energy level. Organizations and cultures can have the same. Research shows that organizational energy levels can be volatile, just as with individuals, but it can also be better understood and supported (Vogel et al., 2022).

Where energy is going is also very important. When collective energy is focused on the right things, it fuels alignment, innovation, and meaningful progress. Otto Scharmer's (2016) work on Theory U emphasizes that the quality of results is shaped by the quality of attention: where leaders place their focus determines what emerges. Peter Senge reinforces this in *The Fifth Discipline*, noting that intention, what we truly care about, guides the flow of energy and learning across systems. For senior leaders, this means being deliberate about where attention is directed and what intentions are cultivated. When energy is scattered or misaligned, even the best strategies falter. But when it's consciously stewarded toward purpose, possibility, and people, it becomes a multiplier of impact.

Resonance as a Guide

Resonance, in its broadest sense, refers to the phenomenon in which one system vibrates in harmony with another, amplifying its energy through shared frequency. In physics, it's the reason a tuning fork can cause another nearby fork to vibrate without direct contact. When applied to human energy, resonance describes the subtle yet powerful alignment between individuals, environments, or ideas that evoke a deep sense of connection or vitality. It's why certain people "just click," why music can stir the soul, or why some spaces feel instantly calming or invigorating. At its core, resonance suggests that when our internal frequencies—emotional, mental, or spiritual—are in sync with external stimuli, we experience heightened clarity, creativity, and well-being. This concept is foundational in practices like sound healing, energy work, and even leadership, when attuning to others' emotional states can foster trust, empathy, and collective momentum. Given that the energy of individuals can manifest as a higher-level, collective construct, energy is vital to reculturing.

Going back to core ideas and insight that have always been present in shaping human culture is at the heart of reculturing. Energy and culture have long been deeply intertwined, shaping societies, traditions, and ways of life since ancient times. Organizational culture is the heartbeat of a company—it dictates how employees interact, how decisions are made, and how challenges are faced. The quality of the energy in an organization and where it is directed will dictate the quality of the outcomes. A tired or exhausted organization cannot evolve. Yet an organization with abundant and positive energy can. When individuals feel aligned—physically, emotionally, and purposefully—their energy becomes contagious, driving collective momentum and the potential for great things to occur. The level and direction of energy in the organization and where it is directed is a very telling sign or manifestation of a culture. When you focus on a goal or a mindset to frame the world, you give it energy, and the more energy it has gives it momentum. Momentum creates shifts, and shifts create new or realized possibilities. Energy is the base source of performance and transformation.

Energetic shifts are powerful signals of the culture moving. Look at how much attention Mark Zuckerberg got in early 2025 when he said business needed to have more masculine energy. Deep ancient philosophical concepts such as yin and yang in Chinese philosophy are related to energy, and these energies have duality and are interrelated and interdependent, balancing each other to achieve harmony within the natural environment.

When human energy levels are depleted, we see challenges such as poor workplace behaviors, "flare-ups," presenteeism, absenteeism, active disengagement, and spiking health costs, which have a significant impact on organizational success (Owolabi, 2018). Professor Schippers of Rotterdam School of Management discusses that "de-energizers are people who drain people of energy, they act as the black holes of an organization, draining the energy of their co-workers and leaders" (Schippers and Hogenes, 2011). This research suggests that neurotic individuals may be inclined to waste their energy in dysfunctional ruminating, leading to a lowered energy level, fatigue, and in extreme cases depression. Toxic leadership encounters elicit emotions of helplessness, demoralization, stress, and anxiety among individuals (Onyemelukwe et al., 2023).

The level of burnout, which is the ultimate outcome of seriously depleted energy, is affecting our organizations in record numbers. Ipsos research (Ipsos, 2024) shows that 37% of the workforce feel close or at burnout, which in turn is costing the UK alone £102 billion per year. In 2024 Google searches for "burnout" hit a five-year peak. Managers and senior leaders are the closest to burnout with 48% reporting high levels of low energy (Ipsos, 2024).

All this despite record levels of awareness of mental health, investment in well-being initiatives, and a near two decades of focus on employee engagement and experience. This leads us to wonder, how on earth did we miss this?

Why Organizations Have Overlooked the Concept of Energy

The movement for energy still feels very woo-woo to most organizations, yet the interest in energy as a force in our society and economy is exploding. The wellness trend in societies grows and grows and is expected to be worth estimated to be worth $7.2 trillion in 2025 (Wellness Creative Company, 2025). The wellness industry is growing at 8.5% per year (Global Wellness Institute, 2023).

And if you haven't used the word *vibe* in the last month, you're missing out on a massive cultural shift especially among Gen Z. *Vibe* links to the word *vibration*, which is linked to energy. The phrase "I'm vibin'" or "This has a good vibe" has moved from casual slang into everyday business and marketing lingo. Kyla Scanlon in her 2024 book *In This Economy: How Money and Markets Really Work* (Scanlon, 2024) even coins the term *vibecession* to describe how market sentiment and societal mood can influence the broader economy, regardless of what the real numbers say. Yet many motivational constructs do imply energy, but still hardly ever explicitly mention it. Work on organizational energy does not come up very much in our boardrooms or practices; instead, we have focused on employee engagement and, worse still, putting in sticky plaster initiatives such as yoga lessons.

The language linked to human energy is worth considering. Words linked to energy are highly attractive to organizations who care about high performance. Dynamism, vitality, liveliness, and fitness are important focus areas for the task of reculturing our organizations. Even the word *emotion*, which is a large driver of human behavior, comes from

Latin for *emotere*, meaning energy in motion. Organizations have long understood emotions play a role in culture, decision-making, behaviors, and performance but have struggled typically to find a way to analyze the work here.

If energy is fuel, then thriving is the ultimate marker of a healthy culture. The concept of thriving is very simple. Just two elements make up thriving and had we focused on these in the same way we did for workplace engagement, then we could have been looking at a very different future. Thriving happens when you feel vitality (also linked to human energy) and when you feel you are learning and growing (Kleine et al., 2019).

As artificial intelligence (AI) starts to dominate our workplaces with agentic worker bots joining as teammates, human and organizational energy levels are a key differentiator. Our cultures need to pay close attention to how humans are doing and literally where their heads are at.

Despite mounting evidence that energy, both physical and emotional, is a critical driver of performance, innovation, and resilience, many organizations have failed to integrate it meaningfully into strategy or culture. This oversight stems from several interlocking factors:

- **Legacy focus on time and output:** Traditional management paradigms have prioritized time management and productivity metrics over human vitality. As *Harvard Business Review* (Schwartz, 2007) notes, organizations often "take for granted what fuels their capacity to work—their energy," leading to burnout and disengagement.
- **Fragmented understanding of energy:** Energy is often narrowly interpreted as utility consumption or operational efficiency. Broader conceptions—such as emotional, cognitive, and spiritual energy—are rarely acknowledged in leadership discourse, despite their proven impact on decision-making and collaboration.
- **Invisible return on investment:** Unlike tangible assets, the return on investing in human energy—through rest, purpose, and emotional alignment—is harder to quantify. Yet studies show that when organizations support energy renewal, employees outperform peers on financial and relational metrics.

Pioneering organizations are, however, making progress. Microsoft, led by work of EVP Strategy and Organization's Kathleen Hogan, have evolved from measuring how engaged employees are to how well they thrive (Klinghoffer and McCune, 2022). Microsoft define thriving as "being energized and empowered to do meaningful work" (Hogan, 2022). Within this, they looked at the aspects of thriving and measured meaningful work, empowerment, and energy levels. When Microsoft measured employee thriving in 2022, the data showed "energized" ranked lower than any other aspect of thriving.

Human energy isn't therefore just about individuals "being well" or another word for organizational well-being. It isn't linked to work-life balance, which is about the level of integration between work life and personal life. This is about noticing the role and level of energy in play in your organization. It's as if we have taken for granted the power of energy in our organizations. We have wasted energy on things that don't add value, and tragically we have burned through the energy our best people have to stay at the top of their game.

Fostering Human Energy and Thriving in the Workplace

It's insightful to look at organizations through energy lenses. Productivity is about energy efficiency, making sure that human energy is directed at the most meaningful areas of the organization, and using technology to do things that take high amounts of energy and aren't highly valuable. Agility is about energy moving freely and fast and avoiding getting blocked or stuck in energy-sapping processes and ways of working. Well-being becomes about having energized employees and balanced energy in the organization, not overloading focus, or wasting focus, on one area only to the detriment of other areas.

Researchers (Onyemelukwe et al., 2023) state that "in the age of globalization, the words 'sustainability' and 'thriving' are crucial concepts that determine how energy sources like sun, wind, water, and geothermal produce viability. The same is true of human energy, especially in today's rapidly changing world of work." When energy is well matched to the task— flowing and unblocked—people and organizations move at speed. And pace and speed win in uncertain times. Pace is a crucial factor in organizational success, as it determines how quickly a company can adapt, innovate, and respond to challenges. Organizations that operate with speed and agility are more likely to stay ahead of competitors, seize opportunities, and maintain momentum in fast-changing markets.

The importance of human energy in organizational culture is increasingly backed by interdisciplinary research. A systematic review and meta-analysis published in *Sustainability* (Onyemelukwe et al., 2023) highlights that human energy, characterized by vitality, enthusiasm, and psychological resilience, is a critical resource for navigating today's complex work environments. The review found that organizations that actively manage human energy through strategic cultural practices can mitigate burnout, enhance engagement, and foster thriving and sustainable performance. Unpacking the components of human energy helps us to see the opportunity we have to center our reculturing efforts using energy.

As we have seen, thriving is defined in organizational psychology as a dual psychological state of learning and a feeling of vitality, a dynamic condition where individuals and cultures feel both alive and growing. This concept is deeply intertwined with three core energetic capacities: vitality, enthusiasm, and resilience. We notice the double importance of the concept of vitality, which supports both energy and thriving.

These energetic states are not abstract ideals; they are measurable, actionable, and deeply tied to organizational outcomes.

Vitality: The Foundation of Aliveness

Professor Pierre Casse, a globally respected authority on leadership and multicultural management, has long championed the role of vitality as a strategic asset in organizational life (Casse, 2012). Vitality is more than physical health; it's the sense of being energized, purposeful, and connected. Vitality is an inner resource that can foster an abundance of energy available to the self. Vitality traces back to Ancient Greek and Eastern culture and philosophy in concepts like chi in China, ki in Japan, bayu in Indonesia, and prana in India. The common theme of these ancient concepts of vitality is an "underlying life energy or force flowing through living things" (Lavrusheva, 2020).

Research shows that vitality correlates with improved performance, mental health, and somatic well-being. Dan Cable, a professor of organizational behavior, explains that vitality at work isn't just about motivation, it's biological (Cable, 2018). Historically, vitality was linked to moral and spiritual vigor in ancient philosophy and later evolved into a health science construct encompassing motivation and adaptive capacity. Organizational culture practices that create the conditions for vitality include the following:

- Aligning roles with individual strengths and values
- Creating safe environments that reduce chronic stress
- Encouraging movement, rest, and recovery rhythms in daily work
- Promoting autonomy and clarity to reduce energy-draining ambiguity/cognitive overload

Vitality is the difference between surviving and thriving; it fuels the capacity to show up fully and consistently.

Enthusiasm: The Emotional Spark

The word *enthusiasm* has a rich and evocative etymology rooted in ancient spiritual and philosophical traditions. It originates from the Greek term *enthousiasmos*, which combines *en* ("in") and *theos* ("god"), literally meaning "possessed by a god" or "divinely inspired." Today, enthusiasm is understood as intense enjoyment, interest, or eagerness—but its etymological roots remind us that it once signified a profound connection to something transcendent.

Enthusiasm is the emotional spark that drives motivation, creativity, and social engagement. It's linked to dopamine pathways and is reinforced by purpose, recognition, and autonomy. Enthusiasm is a contagious force that drives creativity, collaboration, and discretionary effort. Unlike motivation, which can be externally triggered, enthusiasm arises from meaning and emotional connection. Here are some ways to foster it:

- Leaders model positivity and purpose-driven behavior.
- Recognition and appreciation are frequent and authentic.

- Teams are empowered to pursue meaningful goals and experiment freely.
- Work is framed as valuable and impactful—not just task-driven.

Enthusiasm lifts performance across the board and builds cultures of momentum.

Resilience: The Adaptive Engine

New research into energy shows us concepts such as organizational plasticity and psychological flexibility, concepts characterized by the seamless integration of flexibility and adaptability into an organization's internal processes and networks, present a promising avenue for effectively implementing human energy strategies within the fabric of an organization's culture (UKG, 2023).

Resilience is the ability to recover, adapt, and grow through challenges. It is key to ensuring that energy that has been depleted can be rebuilt. McKinsey defines resilient organizations as those that "bounce forward," turning disruption into opportunity. Key strategies to embed into our cultures include the following:

- Building agile teams with decision-making autonomy and feedback loops
- Investing in leadership development that prioritizes emotional intelligence and coaching
- Embedding routines for reflection, learning, and psychological recovery
- Creating cultures that normalize vulnerability and celebrate growth through adversity

Resilience ensures that energy is renewable, not depleted, through change.

Vitality, enthusiasm, and resilience are not soft concepts; they are strategic capacities. When embedded into culture, leadership, and systems, they transform organizations from reactive to regenerative. The result: thriving people, thriving performance, and thriving futures.

The Power of Energy Flowing

We are interested in organizations looking anew at energy and thriving because they have the potential to become truly regenerative systems. Grounded in the scientific principle that energy cannot be created or destroyed, only transferred or transformed, this approach reframes the workplace as an energetic ecosystem. When leaders intentionally design environments that replenish rather than deplete energy through meaningful work, psychological safety, and rhythms of recovery, they enable energy to circulate, amplify, and evolve across teams and systems. Enthusiasm becomes contagious, vitality fuels innovation, and resilience transforms adversity into growth. Rather than extracting effort, regenerative organizations invest in energetic stewardship: They honor the flow of energy among people, purpose, and place. This shift from transactional to transformational culture not only sustains performance but it also creates surplus energy that can be reinvested into learning, creativity, and long-term impact.

Here are some of the benefits:

- **Resilience and agility:** Employees with high energy levels can adapt more quickly to change and bounce back from setbacks faster. Energy fuels problem-solving, while engagement may sustain only interest.
- **Sustained performance:** High engagement does not always mean high performance. Energy ensures that employees have mental and physical stamina to deliver outstanding results over time.
- **Creativity and innovation:** Energy is essential for innovation and growth. Engaged employees may support an organization's vision, but energetic and thriving employees actively learn new skills, generate new ideas, and push boundaries.
- **Avoiding burnout:** Engagement without energy leads to burnout. Employees who are highly engaged but lack energy may feel obligated to push through exhaustion, leading to long-term disengagement.
- **Human productivity and creativity:** In psychology, flow refers to a mental state in which individuals work at peak energy levels, enhancing focus and performance. Mihály Csíkszentmihályi, the

renowned psychologist, wrote powerfully about how to create flow, which is the act of finding the right focus to work optimally (Csíkszentmihályi, 2022).

Kim Cameron, professor at the University of Michigan, is a prominent figure in the field of organizational studies, particularly known for his work on positive relational energy. His research emphasizes how virtuous actions within organizations can generate positive energy, significantly affecting both organizational success and individual well-being (Cameron, 2021). One of his key concepts is the heliotropic effect, which is based on the fact that living systems move toward positive energy such as the sun and away from negative energy. He suggests that positively energizing leaders can drive exceptional performance by fostering environments where positive energy thrives.

Organizations have spent billions building up levels of engagement or workplaces that employees will recommend. This is part of the disconnect we have found in our multiple discussions with leaders where the benefits of engagement have not necessarily been translated into culture.

Employee engagement has been a hugely popular way for companies to take a read of their culture and performance. Ever since Gallup's Q12 survey released in 1990's based on research by Buckingham (1999), we've pretty much defaulted to the ideas of engagement to manage our organizational human performance. Looking at energy offers us the chance to look anew.

How to Tune into the Energy Levels Within Your Leaders and Organization

Adam Grant's research in *Give and Take* reveals that people in organizations tend to operate as givers, takers, or matchers, and these orientations profoundly shape workplace energy and culture (Grant, 2014). Givers are those who help others without expecting anything in return. Contrary to the old belief that self-serving takers rise to the top, Grant shows that successful givers often outperform others in the long run, generating trust, collaboration, and innovation. Their energy is expansive and regenerative; they create microloans of knowledge, support, and connection that uplift entire systems.

Takers, by contrast, drain energy. They focus on extracting value, often leaving behind toxicity and disengagement. While they may succeed temporarily, their impact erodes trust and resilience. Matchers, those who give only when they expect reciprocity, maintain balance but rarely catalyze transformation. Looking at your leadership styles within your business gives you a sense of the type of energy in your organization.

It's also possible to use real-time listening and feedback (pulse surveys, listening sessions) to help us quickly know where the energy level is in our organizations, and where it is focused. If we can tap into the energy levels and dominant emotions (energy in motion) of our organization (fear, excitement, anger, boredom, frustration, happiness) then we read into the current character and nuances. The more we hone this ability, the more we can understand what is releasing or blocking our energy, and this helps us be agile and expansive in understanding where organizations are coming from and what is going on with them.

Here are some key questions we can ask:

- What energizes or depletes people?
- Where do people feel most connected or disconnected?
- Which rituals (formal or informal) regenerate energy?

We can adapt culture initiatives based on what employees truly need and avoid assumptions bringing potential bias. This is why we've never quite understood why companies focus on one emotion only—usually happiness. Having one, or striving only for one, dominant emotion in an organization isn't realistic; it can create all sorts of blind spots for us and doesn't mean we give the organizations the right interventions it needs (if it needs one). One of the greatest challenges that significantly changes how culture is viewed internally is to forget to use culture as an organizational control but more as a force for good if fueled well with principles of human sustainability as its core.

A focus on unblocking or releasing energy helps us to empower our workforces to generate what they need from within. Elite teams and individuals from the world of sport must play and shape the game with only the information they can get through a human lens; the biggest indicator of success is the energy of the team or person through the game. Is the team fit, alert, open to possibilities, seeing wide, thinking ahead? Or is it head down, exhausted, frustrated, scared. Higher levels of skills and opportunities increase the chances of winning, but it is only when directed with energy that means it will happen. The heads up for those focused on skills-based organizations in modern human resources is that without energy this won't confer advantage. Humans intuit energy in a way that is really honed and unique, and it could be something we harness much more effectively as we lead organizations and shape performance.

How Organizations Can Boost Energy

Fostering energy requires a shift from traditional engagement strategies to more dynamic, human-centered approaches. Here are key ways organizations can fuel workplace energy:

- **Create energizing workspaces:** The physical environment influences energy levels. Natural light, movement-friendly spaces, and inspiring design can help employees feel energized throughout the day.
- **Foster autonomy and ownership:** Energy thrives when people feel empowered. Giving employees more control over their schedules, decisions, and goals fosters a sense of purpose and drive.
- **Create opportunity:** Enable people to learn, stretch, and do what they are dying to do, understand their strengths, and ensure they are using them.
- **Celebrate momentum, not just milestones:** Instead of solely recognizing achievements, organizations should acknowledge progress and movement, reinforcing the importance of continuous energy and growth.
- **Prioritize mental and physical well-being:** Energy comes from health, rest, and balance. Organizations should focus on promoting recovery, movement, and stress management rather than just encouraging commitment to work.
- **Encourage deep work and flow states:** Organizations should reduce distractions, unnecessary meetings, and micromanagement to allow employees to enter flow states where they work at peak energy levels.

How AI Can Help

AI can also increasingly help us to look at the energy levels in our organizations, for example, by interpreting large datasets including more qualitative analysis, and make sense of new data sources such as wearable devices, which can see the heartrate and perceived stress levels of people in the organization. AI can help us aggregate this awareness and show us where hot spots might be. We know of a manufacturing firm that equipped shift workers with wearables. AI analysis revealed that productivity dropped sharply after consecutive night shifts. By redesigning shift rotations based on energy data, the firm reduced errors by 30% and improved employee well-being scores.

By refocusing listening on topics linked to energy we can listen in a different way to what we have done before to get a read on this most important area. AI can help employees understand when they need to pause, and it can build in energy recovery windows for people to ensure they take recovery seriously. We can encourage people to journal and note their energy levels, and this can help create patterns and prompts.

We have also heard of AI being used to give energy boosts to people in the form of recognition and helping people feel the right level of support at the right time.

Leadership Checklist: Fostering Human Energy in Organizations

- **Cultivate self-awareness first:**
  - Regularly reflect on your own energy and enthusiasm levels, triggers, and recovery practices and how you energize teams through your presence, communication and purpose.
  - Seek feedback from trusted peers or coaches on your leadership impact.
  - Practice mindfulness or journaling to stay attuned to emotional and cognitive patterns.
  - Model vulnerability and openness to create psychological safety.

- **Design for vitality:**
  - Ensure workloads and rhythms allow for rest, renewal, and flow—not just productivity.
  - Encourage movement, natural light, and healthy habits in the workplace.
  - Create space for creative expression, play, and nonlinear thinking.
  - Recognize and reward energy-giving behaviors, not just outcomes.

- **Ignite enthusiasm:**
  - Communicate purpose with clarity and emotional resonance.
  - Share stories that connect daily work to meaningful impact.
  - Celebrate progress, not just perfection—use rituals to mark milestones.
  - Invite curiosity and experimentation; make room for joy in problem-solving.

- **Build resilience:**
  - Normalize recovery and emotional regulation as leadership strengths.
  - Provide tools and training for developing psychological flexibility, stress management, and adaptive coping.
  - Foster community and peer social support networks to buffer against burnout.
  - Encourage reflection after setbacks—what was learned, what can evolve.

- **Enable thriving:**
  - Align roles and goals with individual strengths and intrinsic motivators.
  - Promote autonomy, mastery, and connection as core design principles.
  - Invest in growth pathways—mentoring, learning, and cross-functional exposure—even in lean times.
  - Use pulse checks to monitor energy trends and adapt accordingly.

8 | Reculturing Driver 4: Human Connection in Any Setting

"We can't be human alone."

—Margaret Wheatley (2024)

"Invisible threads are the strongest ties."

—Friedrich Nietzsche

No strategy, structure, or system can thrive without the trust, energy, and meaning that flow between people, shaping how we relate, respond, and show up for one another. Businesses are not just systems of productivity— they are communities built on relationships. Culture cannot exist without humans. And humans can't exist without connection.

We are fundamentally wired for connection because it is essential for survival, emotional well-being, and societal progress. From an evolutionary, neurological, and psychological standpoint, human connection is deeply embedded in our biology and behavior and is very important as we move forward as an evolutionary species on this planet.

Innovative studies have shown that the level of human interaction and communication is strongly related to productivity in an organization. Even in our most sophisticated workplaces we have basic needs and skills, which means we are better together. When human beings feel they belong, they focus on positive outcomes. When human beings don't feel they belong, cracks quickly emerge. In the age of AI and automation, our final reculturing focus area is about prizing human connection.

Companies must double down on human connection to remain competitive and build their culture anew. Google, for example, believes an organization's ability to innovate, central to their business and culture, is tied to social connections, especially across disciplines and the power of team cohesion.

Margaret (Meg) Wheatley, pioneering American writer, teacher, speaker, and management consultant, asserts that relationships, not individuals, are the basic building blocks of life and organizations and are rooted in both scientific insight and organizational experience. Drawing from quantum physics, she highlights that even subatomic particles do not exist in isolation; they only manifest their potential in relationship with others. As she writes, "Everything in the Universe is composed of these 'bundles of potentiality' that only manifest their potential in relationship" (Wheatley, 2006). Wheatley argues that our cultural obsession with individualism and hierarchical structures is fundamentally flawed. Organizations, she says, are not collections of isolated roles or boxes on a chart—they are living networks of interdependent relationships (Wheatley, 2024).

Case Study: The Story of Ember—From Buzz to Silence

At Ember & Co. (not its real name), mornings used to hum with energy. The scent of coffee, spontaneous hallway banter, and impromptu whiteboard sessions stitched the team together like a living tapestry. People didn't just work; they belonged. Ideas sparked over lunch, resilience grew through shared setbacks, and laughter echoed through the open-plan office.

Then came the shift.

Remote work was meant to be liberating, flexible, efficient, but as screens replaced presence, something vital slipped away. The team adapted, of course Slack channels multiplied, Zoom meetings filled calendars, and virtual socials tried to mimic the old rhythm. Yet beneath the surface, the culture frayed.

New hires never felt the pulse of Ember's spirit, veterans grew quiet, and without the subtle cues of body language and shared space, misunderstandings festered. Collaboration became transactional. The once-thriving culture of trust and creativity dulled into a polite, distant professionalism.

People stopped reaching out. Not because they didn't care but because the effort felt heavier. The emotional glue that held Ember together had dried. Resilience waned. Turnover crept in.

It wasn't the remote work itself; it was the loss of ritual, presence, and shared meaning. Ember had digitized its operations but forgot to rehumanize its culture.

Months later, a leadership retreat sparked a reckoning. They began rebuilding, restoring connection: storytelling circles, intentional check-ins, and space for emotional truth.

Ember learned that culture isn't just where you are it's how you feel together.

Ember's story reminds us that human connection is essential for reculturing because culture is most strongly built through relationships and invisible threads among people, teams, and places not just policies or structures. When people feel connected and valued, cultural shifts become more organic and sustainable.

Ariana Huffington speaks to the insight that we thrive when we connect deeply—not just digitally, but emotionally and physically.

We Stand at a Crossroad

At the beginning of this book we said that the biggest decision leaders will make is the choice to reculture and how people, artificial intelligence (AI), and the planet feature. Nowhere is this more apparent than in the choices we make this decade on the quality and type of human connection in our organizations. The quality of human connection has been dangerously overlooked since the pandemic. The unprecedented global health crisis forced companies to adopt widespread remote working practices, and it has been a painful reemergence since those days with huge pressure on organizations to abandon the strength of in-person human connection their culture once relied on. This whole premise of reculturing is because without the same presence, we cannot simply revert to the old values and behaviors mechanisms we once had used as levers, and we have lost the in-person context with which those were applied.

Human connection accelerates reculturing because it helps build the following:

- **Trust and psychological safety:** Meaningful relationships create an environment where employees trust, feel safe to share ideas, challenge norms, and embrace change.
- **Shared identity and purpose:** Strong interpersonal bonds reinforce a collective vision, making people more invested in cultural transformation.
- **Social learning and influence:** Culture spreads through interactions—when individuals model new behaviors, others naturally adopt them.
- **Empathy and adaptability:** Listening, understanding different perspectives, and fostering open dialogue helps prevent resistance and makes change feel inclusive.
- **Collaboration and innovation:** Connected teams work better together, enabling the creative problem-solving that drives cultural evolution.

Reculturing isn't a top-down initiative; it happens through daily interactions, shared experiences, and a sense of belonging.

Is Face-to-Face Connection Important?

Isolation and exclusion in the workplace are dangerous. Medical studies have strongly linked isolation to increased stress, anxiety, and depression. Humans are social creatures, and when employees feel disconnected, they experience higher levels of loneliness, which research shows can be as harmful to health as smoking 15 cigarettes a day (Holt-Lunstad et al., 2010). Over time, this leads to emotional exhaustion and disengagement.

We know organizations need to do more. Gallup research in 2025 (Harter, 2025) showed that 32% of workers described their workplace as isolating and impersonal—this rises to 41% for remote workers and 44% for Gen Z workers. This is a huge, missed opportunity to drive the very basics of performance and culture.

Environments where people feel seen, valued, and heard, isn't a peripheral factor; it is central to organizational success.

Nonverbal Communication Is Reducing

More than anyone recognizes, the fact that nonverbal communication is reducing is a huge and pressing issue. Our social skills are slowly but steadily deteriorating and we seem largely unaware that they, along with our attention spans, are declining on a massive scale. We have been duped into believing social skills will remain in us without frequent use. If you don't use it, you lose it—same with physical strength. Our social skills require frequent practice, but hybrid ways of working offer easy excuses to simply text or email someone instead of just calling them in case they are busy on another call or working from home to remove distraction. Our comfort will become our downfall in this regard.

The subconscious connection that occurs through in-person nonverbal communication methods is not replicable to the same extent in a virtual format.

Our in-person social skills enable us to interpret what someone is saying through the combination of their tone, volume, pace of speech, eye contact, facial expressions, animation of face and hands, leaning in or away from us, whole-body positioning, the amount they even "flick their hair," and consequently this enhances the depth of the message in hundreds of ways that an email cannot possibly convey.

Often our next best alternative is for virtual calls using laptop cameras, showing only head and shoulders. According to a 2025 study published in the *European Journal of Information Systems*, participants in virtual meetings spent up to 30–40% of their visual attention on their own image when the self-view was enabled, especially while listening rather than speaking (Abramova et al., 2025). This weakens the idea that we can still tune into someone's nonverbal communication virtually by being on camera. Maybe we can, but in reality, we don't. We are steadily diminishing our ability to be aware of others and becoming more self-focused. Add to these the social media algorithms that feed us more of what we already attend to, and we are shredding our ability to meaningfully connect with each other at an alarmingly rapid pace.

Modern life is increasingly lived through the lens of self-perception, reflection, and curated identity. Digital environments are amplifying our self-focus. Virtual meetings and social media often place our own image front and center, leading to heightened self-monitoring and internal dialogue. This creates the "mirror effect" of seeing ourselves onscreen, which can reinforce a loop of self-consciousness, especially in professional or performative contexts.

Thinking back to the previous focus on energy and vibrations, this reduction of available nonverbal communication means we are limiting our ability to contagiously spread our energy among others by simply putting ourselves behind screens.

With constant connectivity to everything and everyone we are experiencing more of a fragmented presence. We're always "on," but rarely fully present. Notifications, multitasking, and digital immersion pull us into a mental space that's reactive and self-referential. Even our leisure time is often filtered through self-documentation of reflection through photos, posts, and curated narratives.

There is a rise of self-help and encouragement for inner work in many platforms, suggesting a societal emphasis on introspection, mindfulness, and personal growth. While valuable, it can sometimes tip into over-introspection, when we lose touch with external feedback and relational grounding (Vilhauer, 2025).

The concept of the "mental mirror" being our internal reflection of self has become more dominant in shaping both our identity and well-being. Sam Vaknin's work suggests the self now acts as a biased interface, translating external reality into internal narratives that may distort or isolate (Vaknin, 2025).

This is a complex, multileveled amount of interference to be experiencing as a species that previously relied on in-person human connection for effective interdependent functioning. While we are losing social skills of interpreting and understanding others at a rapid rate, are we even aware of the consequences and the futuristic alternatives that either may exist or need to be developed? The concern is that we are stepping into the unknown without any realization or recognition of what is being lost. Our tendency to revert back to what we know about humans and culture when we hit such realizations may hinder our exploration of what could be advanced human functioning.

Fundamental Basics of Human Connection: In the Office and Virtual

In the office we need to focus on embodied connections. These moments thrive on physical cues, spontaneity, and shared space in unstructured time.

Examples include casual chats over coffee, hallway conversations, and shared lunches that build trust and psychological safety. These micro-interactions often carry more relational weight than formal meetings.

Other specific examples to try do the following:

- **Rituals of belonging:** Weekly team huddles, gratitude circles, or storytelling sessions create rhythm and reinforce shared mindsets.
- **Cross-generational mentorship or buddying new starters:** Pairing younger and older employees for mutual learning fosters empathy and bridges cultural divides.
- **Visible appreciation:** Handwritten notes, shout-outs on team boards, or spontaneous celebrations make people feel seen and valued.

When connecting virtually, however, we must focus on our intentional presence over all else.

Digital connection requires designing for depth in a space that can easily become transactional. To do this, try turning off the self-view in video calls. This reduces self-consciousness and increases attention to others. It's a small shift with a big impact.

Structured informality, move on from simple "how's it going" openings to beginning meetings with a tailored check-in question or a moment of reflection. This humanizes the space up front and invites vulnerability and transparency.

Virtual coworking, such as silent Zoom rooms where people work in parallel, re-create the ambient presence of an office, which is especially helpful for remote teams craving connection.

Shared creation functionality on platforms supports collaborating in real time on documents, whiteboards, or storytelling exercises and builds a sense of coauthorship and shared purpose.

Digital rituals such as weekly "wisdom drop" emails, virtual gratitude walls, or asynchronous storytelling threads can deepen culture across time zones or other types of shift working.

Human connection may be easier with all the nonverbal communication impact we can have in person, but that doesn't mean it isn't possible virtually. We simply need to consciously consider what will have the best influence in differing environments and ensure we fully use the tools and functionality available to support us.

Why Building Social Intelligence Is Fundamental to Humans

America psychologist Daniel Goleman's research on social intelligence is another method we have not yet made enough use of as we seek to reculture our organizations. Daniel Goleman's *Emotional Intelligence* has sold more than five million copies worldwide, making it a landmark publication in psychology, leadership, and organizational development (Goleman, 1996). It remained on the *New York Times* best-seller list for more than a year and helped popularize the concept of emotional intelligence (EQ) as essential to success in work and life.

His latest book, *Social Intelligence: The New Science of Human Relationships* (Goleman, 2007), introduced groundbreaking insights into how our brains are wired for connection, and how relationships shape our biology, behavior, and performance.

Goleman's research highlights that we are wired to connect, and our interactions shape not only our emotions but also our cognitive and physiological responses:

- **Neural Wi-Fi and emotional contagion:** This is the most significant area of the research and is the evidence that shows that when we are together our brains sync and emotions become contagious, meaning leaders and employees can spread cultural shifts through positive interactions. Layering this with purpose, mindset, and energy is a powerful driver of pace.

- **Trust and empathy:** Goleman's research shows that trust building and empathy activate neural pathways that strengthen relationships, making cultural change more natural.
- **Social facility:** As we develop our social awareness, facility is about what we do with that awareness, how we skillfully navigate social interactions to build connection, influence, and collaboration. We can use our authenticity and influence to build resonance and persuasion without resorting to manipulation.
- **Social learning and influence:** Organizations can leverage peer influence to reinforce new cultural norms, as people tend to mirror behaviors they observe.
- **Psychological safety:** Goleman's insights into EQ help leaders create environments where employees feel safe to embrace change.

By strengthening social intelligence, in particular social facility, organizations can speed up human connection, making reculturing more organic and sustainable.

Why Social Facility Matters in Organizations

Social facility is the ability to navigate social interactions with ease and influence, and EQ plays a vital role in shaping leadership presence. It's the ability to read the room, manage interpersonal dynamics, and respond with empathy. Leaders who embody strong social facility foster trust and engagement through authentic communication and emotional attunement. They are able to adapt their style to suit different audiences, cultivating psychological safety and resonance across varied contexts.

In team dynamics, high levels of social facility enhances collaboration, particularly within diverse or cross-functional groups. It equips individuals to navigate tension, promote inclusion, and build shared momentum, enabling teams to operate with greater cohesion and mutual respect.

Culture building is deeply influenced by everyday micro-interactions, how people greet one another, listen, and respond. These seemingly small moments collectively shape the emotional tone of a workplace. Social facility levels can transform awareness into action, embedding genuine connection into the fabric of organizational culture.

When it comes to conflict resolution, individuals with high social facility, whether leaders or team members, are better equipped to de-escalate tensions, reframe misunderstandings, and restore trust. Their ability to read emotional cues and respond with empathy makes them invaluable in maintaining harmony and resilience within the organization.

By building connection based on social intelligence we have a strong foundation on which to deliver on trust and autonomy as people no longer want to be micromanaged; they want ownership over their work, they want micro-coaching on demand to deal with challenges and opportunities in real time.

We can rebuild this fragile fabric of social connection by creating rituals (virtual or in person) that reinforce belonging: weekly check-ins, storytelling sessions, or shared learning experiences.

For example, Airbnb fosters connection through "One Airbnb" global gatherings, ensuring employees feel part of a shared mission on a regular basis.

Google's research into the effectiveness of its teams, Project Aristotle, is of course famous for finding and sharing with the world the importance of psychological safety, which made Amy Edmondson, rightly, a household name (Edmondson, 2018). Project Aristotle has spawned thousands of culture initiatives. But this study had other findings worth noting. At the most fundamental level, instead of individual talent or skills, the quality of interactions mattered most. The quality of relationships between team members can significantly influence a team's performance, engagement, and innovation. The researchers sought to distinguish a "work group" from a "team":

- Work groups are characterized by the least amount of interdependence. They are based on organizational or managerial hierarchy. Work groups may meet periodically to hear and share information.
- Teams are highly interdependent—they plan work, solve problems, make decisions, and review progress in service of a specific project. Team members need one another to get work done. A team can really only be identified by team members themselves—an organization chart won't capture it all.

As organizations think about reculturing the way the organization or big work groups connect will likely need to look different to how teams need to connect. We have typically conflated the needs of the work group to the team and vice versa in how we have designed organizations or set rules about office time. When people come together it's important they connect. At Google, half of all-team meetings are often devoted to questions and answers, where any Googler has the opportunity to ask questions or make suggestions. This set up gets everyone's voice in the room and shows others that they are interested in people's ideas and thinking. Asking who is in the room is a vitally important question to ensure there is instant connection.

One of the biggest barriers to innovation is internal resistance to a new idea. Google partnered with researcher Spencer Harrison to study how ideas from new employees end up sticking (Harrison and Sluss, 2017). The study found that good ideas from new employees usually didn't get very far. But when a new employee partnered with a seasoned employee, their good ideas were more likely to develop into something meaningful, thanks to the extra context, support, and connections of the seasoned employee. This evolution seemed to happen behind the scenes as newcomers' outside knowledge became encapsulated within relationships and then, over time, was culturally translated so that when it was finally presented to a broader audience, the outside knowledge seemed as though it was germane to the new context. To bring more of these overlooked ideas to light, think about how you can help your employees connect with one another.

Peer feedback is another great way to build connections. Googlers receive peer feedback as part of their performance reviews each year and are encouraged to give and solicit feedback year-round with the help of a simple real-time feedback tool. Constructive feedback from others, if given as suggestions rather than mandates, can have a positive impact on creativity, which can lead to innovation. This kind of emotional support and constructive feedback is more likely to occur in environments where people feel safe taking risks with one another.

Founded by Arianna Huffington, Thrive Global integrates concern and emotional resonance into its workplace rituals. Leaders are encouraged to check in with employees personally, foster micro-moments of connection, and use storytelling to build shared meaning, all key elements of social facility.

Respect as the Ultimate Leveler in All Forms of Connection

Building back the levels of human connection does one more thing. It stops us from needing theoretical constructs to truly connect with each other. We have seen an explosion of the use of complex identity-based theories in the workplace. These academic theories have an important place in society and help social scientists, policymakers, and academics to understand complex inter-human dynamics, but the way they have pervaded organizations, often through amateur-led strategies, has been highly damaging for most organizations and moved advances on belonging backwards.

Organizations have now long understood they need to be diverse of thought and background to grow and innovate. They also know that being inclusive aids many important outcomes such as avoiding groupthink and creating safety. They know they need to make sure the system doesn't stop people doing that they would naturally do or are capable of. Organizations cannot discriminate.

Diversity and inclusion remain important for culture and so we need to keep measuring and improving levels of diversity, reducing pay gaps and giving people the support and training they need to build respect and use dedication, compassion, and kindness strategically to build belonging. By building a culture of deep respect, of listening and generating ideas, we can leapfrog our way toward belonging. Human connection of the level and depth we suggest for reculturing will help to achieve this.

Recognizable Example: The Culture of Quiet Exit

At the fictional Halston & Co., a midsize consultancy with a reputation for sharp strategy and fast delivery, respect was never explicitly discussed. The senior team prided themselves on performance, not politeness. Meetings were brisk. Feedback was blunt. Recognition was reserved for those who "earned it," usually the loudest voices in the room.

Junior staff quickly learned the rules: Speak only when spoken to, don't challenge senior decisions, and keep emotions out of the workplace. Support roles, finance, and human resources (HR) operations were treated as background noise. Their contributions were rarely acknowledged, and their ideas were never invited.

At first, the culture seemed efficient. Deadlines were met. The clients were satisfied. But something subtle began to shift.

- The most thoughtful team members stopped contributing in meetings.
- High-potential talent quietly declined promotions or left for more inclusive environments.
- Cross-functional collaboration stalled—people didn't trust each other enough to share openly.
- HR flagged a rise in burnout, disengagement, and internal conflict.

The executive team was puzzled. "We've got a great strategy," they said. "Why aren't people thriving?"

It wasn't the strategy. It was the absence of respect—the invisible erosion of psychological safety, dignity, and belonging. People didn't feel seen. And when people don't feel seen, they stop showing up fully.

Eventually, a client asked why their project team kept changing. "We've noticed a lot of turnover," they said. "Is everything okay?"

That was the wake-up call.

Halston's leaders began listening not to performance metrics, but to people. They held story circles. They asked what respect looked like in practice. They realized that culture wasn't just about what they said it was about, what they tolerated, whom they recognized, and how they made people feel.

Respect wasn't a soft value. It was the foundation of trust, energy, and innovation. And without it, even the best strategy couldn't hold.

How Can AI Help Shape the Way People Connect?

As we reconnect both in person and virtually, we must ensure we do not reject AI. Instead, we need to ensure that we are making smart use of AI. We are optimistic about the use of AI to further human connection, but it will need to be consciously achieved and never seen as a replacement for the depth of face-to-face human connection.

Wheatley (2023) views AI as a powerful force that, if left unchecked, can further dehumanize organizations by prioritizing efficiency over empathy, and data over wisdom. She advocates for leaders to become "warriors for the human spirit," those who resist the seduction of control and instead steward compassion, presence, and relational integrity in increasingly mechanized environments.

Culture thrives through meaningful connections, which need to be intentionally designed in digital work environments. AI can support better human collaboration if it is trusted and used to boost collective intelligence. As automation and AI become more prevalent, there is a risk of diminishing personal connection. When implemented thoughtfully, AI can enhance human interactions rather than replace them. A study by McKinsey found that AI-powered communication tools help reduce misinterpretation in business emails by 35%, supporting clearer and more empathetic messaging (Mayer et al., 2025).

This is a fantastic way of demonstrating how simply stepping into a virtual working world and adopting ways of working that replicate in-person work is not enough. If we are becoming more self-focused and reading messages without the external influence or understanding of others, then the AI suggestions of different interpretations of an email message are critical for us to avoid any potential misunderstanding. In effect, it will help us drive out personal bias and maintain healthy and respectful human connection. AI-driven language processing can effectively analyze employee sentiment at scale, enabling leaders to identify engagement trends and proactively address concerns that may be common across populations.

AI-generated feedback is found to improve leadership decision-making by 20% (Medlama et al., 2025). AI, when used effectively, can enhance human relationships by eliminating barriers, improving communication, and fostering deeper understanding rather than replacing genuine human interaction. AI powers platforms that help people find communities, interests, and relationships that align with their values. Whether it's professional networking or support groups, AI-driven recommendations can foster meaningful connections. When used thoughtfully, AI isn't about replacing human interaction, it's about amplifying it. The key is to ensure AI supports empathy, trust, and genuine connection rather than mere efficiency. Remote work doesn't have to mean disconnected work. With intentional efforts, teams can build strong relationships, foster trust, and create a thriving virtual workplace.

Organizational network analysis (ONA) offers compelling evidence that human connection at work is not only measurable but also a critical driver of performance, innovation, and inclusion. By mapping formal and informal relationships across teams, ONA reveals how trust, advice, and collaboration flow through an organization, often uncovering hidden influencers and structural bottlenecks that traditional hierarchies miss. Research shows that employees embedded in diverse and well-connected networks are more likely to share knowledge, adapt quickly, and generate novel solutions. Moreover, ONA identifies "brokers" who bridge disconnected groups key players in fostering cross-functional innovation and psychological safety. These insights enable senior leaders to design interventions that strengthen relational ties, reduce isolation, and cultivate a culture of belonging, ultimately enhancing agility and strategic execution. In essence, human connection when visualized and nurtured through ONA becomes a tangible asset for organizational resilience and growth.

As AI develops, we have an opportunity to use AI to shape our human interactions, so they are better. Studies are already showing that teams who brainstorm with AI support perform better than those who don't (Rosenberg et al., 2025).

Tools such as Conversational Swarm Intelligence will transform how people can come together. Humans are not the only species that deliberate in groups to reach decisions; schools of fish, flocks of birds, and swarms of bees can reach rapid decisions about life-or-death issues before finding an optimal solution. Biologists refer to this collaborative decision-making process as *swarm intelligence*, which enables many social organisms to make decisions that are significantly smarter than the decisions individual members could make on their own; with AI this is supercharged. The unique mix of human and artificial intelligence has powerful potential to bring organizations together in easier ways.

For example, in 2025 the number one use of generative AI was for therapy and companionship (Zao-Sanders, 2025) and numbers two and three were new: on organizing one's life and finding purpose. Fun and nonsense use is reducing from sixth to seventh, suggesting we are moving through the novelty phase, which is an oft-cited stage of radically new ideas and technology. This embedding of tech in our inner lives is very new and so as we navigate this, we need to ensure that real humans, especially those in our organizations, continue to play a role. For example, in 2024, the global AI in mental health market is valued at approximately \$1.45 billion and by 2034, the market is projected to reach \$11.84 billion. Human roles will shift toward supervising AI systems, interpreting complex emotional and cultural contexts, and deepening therapeutic relationships where trust, intuition, and presence are essential. Therapists will also be needed to design, audit, and refine AI tools to ensure safety, inclusivity, and alignment with clinical standards. In short, humans will be used not just to "do therapy," but to elevate it—bringing soul, ethics, and wisdom to a system increasingly powered by algorithms.

AI and automation are reshaping work, but true innovation does not come from machines alone; it comes from human conversations, collective intelligence, and collaborative problem-solving. Businesses that prioritize human connection will unlock new ideas and outpace competitors in adaptability, especially those that have shared purpose, a collective mindset to achieve the future, and the energy to focus.

Leadership's Vital and Evolving Role: From Manager to Sensemaker and Connector

Leaders and managers are the arms that reach into all areas of organizations. They've answered the call to work with and through others, extending work beyond themselves and multiplying performance. They role-model tasks, lead by example, coach teams to stay aligned on performance and well-being, and ensure everyone has space to contribute and move forward together.

Leaders matter. We must position them as culture energizers, have them offer daily role-modeling and an energetic focus to send strong signals about what the organization values. If leaders don't believe in what's required, it won't stick, especially in dispersed workforces across time zones.

We need to train leaders to be authentic, inclusive role models who connect deeply with organizational purpose and foster human connection, both in their own relationships and across the organization. Leaders are essential to creating thriving outcomes without compromising the welfare of their teams or the organization. To do this well, they need to do the inner work and have the tools and armory to stay fit for the job and attuned to what's really happening around them.

Many first-time managers step into leadership after excelling technically, supported by basic training in recruitment, onboarding, performance management, and development. With hierarchy comes added responsibility and remuneration, an enticing career path that often expands across teams, functions, and departments. While personal leadership exists at every level, formal leadership responsibilities typically grow with seniority. Organizations invest in leadership development that mirrors this progression, from leading self to leading others to leading the organization.

The shift from leading others to leading the organization often coincides with middle managers stepping into strategic roles. They become translators of overarching direction for their teams. Leadership development at this level must focus on the skills that help them succeed. Yet, middle managers—often misunderstood and most stressed—are simply told to "step up," while executive leaders forget the platforms needed to support them. At the same time, they must not overlook these leaders' vital role as sensemakers and connectors of culture.

Overreliance on internal communications, engagement teams, or employee resource groups to fulfill this role can be damaging. These teams often operate on rigid calendars and workflows, dictating what can be released and when, without giving voice to the managers and leaders who are closest to the message. This creates bottlenecks and friction, slowing down information flow and weakening critical alliances needed for reculturing.

To step into their roles effectively, leaders need protection from being overloaded with tasks that don't move the organization forward. They need freedom from outdated systems and trust to determine what they and their teams need to perform. They also need learning and development that's current and evidence-based. In a world where reliable content is instantly accessible, it's inconceivable that leadership training still relies on outdated theories disproven by meta-analysis.

There are countless tools on the market, but not all deliver what they promise. Just as we validate media to guide us to truth, we must ensure leadership learning is grounded in 21st-century research. For example, Daniel Goleman's EQ model has proven its validity. By contrast, Tuckman's forming, storming, norming, performing model—based on a 1960s literature review, not empirical data—is still widely used. Do we cling to it because it rhymes? Teams don't always progress linearly, and storming isn't required for performance. Training leaders to have difficult conversations based on a model that creates conflict is counterproductive. Instead, we can focus on human connection, cohesion, collective mindsets, problem-solving, and imagination, freeing ourselves from outdated approaches.

The challenge of determining what's valid is compounded by the gray area between academics and practitioners across HR, learning and development, organizational development, and occupational psychology, each with its own professional body. Leaders need help navigating this complexity. Now, with AI, they can ask better questions and get clearer support.

Yet we're seeing leaders opt out of these sensemaking and connecting roles in droves. Not due to incompetence, but because of psychological, systemic, and values-based tensions. Research like "Worrying About Leadership" shows that internal fears, reputational risk, anticipated opposition cause capable individuals to disengage, especially women and emerging leaders (Karakulak et al., 2022). Broader studies reveal that leaders face growing expectations to address social and ethical issues without adequate support, leading to burnout and selective withdrawal.

At the heart of this shift is a deeper identity reckoning. Leaders are recalibrating their roles to align with personal values, emotional well-being, and a more human-centered definition of impact. But when leaders disengage, their ability to interpret complexity, frame meaning, and foster connection erodes. Effective leadership buffers uncertainty, helping teams make sense of change through shared narratives. When leaders retreat, emotionally, relationally, or strategically, this function weakens, leaving teams adrift.

Their role as connectors also suffers. Disengagement reduces visibility, informal interactions, and relational energy, all essential for cohesion and shared purpose. When leaders pull back, the connective tissue of the organization frays.

Margaret Wheatley's call for leaders to create "islands of sanity" is not just timely, it's foundational. In a world she describes as unstoppable and unsolvable, where systems deteriorate and fear dominates, leaders must reclaim their role as guardians of humaneness. These islands aren't retreats, they're anchors of coherence, where people reconnect to meaning, values, and each other (Wheatley, 2024).

For leaders recalibrating their roles, this offers a transformative reframe: Leadership isn't about controlling the uncontrollable, but about holding space for sanity. It's about fostering relational depth, psychological safety, and shared purpose, especially when the system feels unmoored. Wheatley invites leaders to shift from heroic problem-solvers to stewards of coherence, modeling grounded presence that helps others make sense of complexity and stay connected.

In short, islands of sanity aren't a luxury; they're a leadership imperative. They're where resilience is born, wisdom is practiced, and the future can still be imagined.

So how do we support leaders as sensemakers and connectors? By clarifying their full role: strategic support to senior leaders and cultural guidance for their teams and equipping them with the most efficient, effective, and valid tools. And by helping them build and sustain their own islands of sanity, within and beyond the organization.

Human connection might be the last reculturing driver, but it is no less important. Fostering and valuing this connection is a priority for how we navigate the world of work as we move forward.

Leadership Checklist: Strengthening Human Connection at Work

- **Focus on critical connections:**
  - Are we helping people build meaningful relationships across teams and levels?
  - Do we support communities of practice—not just networks of tasks?
  - Are we creating space for shared purpose and dialogue, not just performance?

- **Build social intelligence:**
  - Do our leaders read emotional cues and respond with empathy and care?
  - Are we training teams to manage relationships—not just tasks?

- Do we encourage face-to-face feedback, mentoring, and coaching?
- Are we helping teams build strong relationships and handle conflict well?

- **Make connection a priority:**
  - Are we designing workspaces and schedules that support human connection?
  - Do we encourage leaders to ask, "What matters to you outside of work?"
  - Are we creating moments of presence, not just productivity?

- **Use AI to support:**
  - Are we using AI to help schedule, surface insights, and prompt connection—not automate relationships?
  - Do our digital tools enhance emotional awareness and team bonding?
  - Are we educating leaders to use AI ethically, keeping human presence at the center?

- **Embed connection:**
  - Do we have regular in-person rituals, gatherings, and shared experiences?
  - Are we measuring trust, belonging, and relational energy—not just output?
  - Do our stories and values celebrate connection as a key to success?

How to Reculture at Pace and Scale

It's easy to say that culture needs to change. It's far harder to shift it. The four reculturing drivers offer powerful new levers to create shortcuts but pulling them requires more than intention. It demands skill, presence, and new practices that embed change deep within leaders and teams. Cultural transformation and change work have become overcomplicated, exhausting, and too often ineffective. But inspired by the success of rewilding, where ecosystems thrive by removing barriers, not adding more, we see a bold opportunity: to simplify how we approach culture change. Not by launching another program, but by restoring what makes culture come alive.

When we stepped back and considered the most, and the least, successful cultural transformation work we had personally done or been involved in across the biggest firms in the world, we saw some regular patterns emerging. We saw five skills stand out more than any other technique as driving positive change at both pace and scale. We have called these five reculturing skills. Taken together they may look a bit like the change methodologies we have had for multiple decades, but there is also something purer, simpler, easier to grasp in what we saw and want to share. In some ways they are deeply intuitive and deeply human, which is part of their power.

In this part, we will take you through each of the five skills in turn to explain how it works, how it helps to speed up the reculture process, particularly for working at scale in large organizations, explain how AI can help and share stories, and best practice and evidence for why this works. Taken together the skills means culture leaders can take their ideas and make a difference.

9 | Armoring

"There is nothing more difficult to take in hand, more perilous to conduct, or more uncertain in its success than to take the lead in the introduction of a new order of things."

—Niccolo Machiavelli, c.1525

Many see armoring as a negative strategy for leaders. We disagree. We see armoring differently. For us, as leaders who have done this, it's not about hiding or controlling. Armoring is about holding better boundaries so we can show up with clarity and care. Healthy armoring enables vulnerability. It gives us the stability to open up without collapsing. It's like wearing boots in a storm—not to run away, but to stand firm. Armoring ourselves professionally and personally is crucial for leading cultural change in organizations because true transformation is rarely smooth; it requires resilience, adaptability, and strong leadership. With the increasing pace and scale required for change in large organizations, we must be aware why this matters so we consciously pay attention to it up front.

Armoring ourselves to lead change requires the following:

- **Emotional resilience:** Cultural change, even positive, often meets resistance and opposition. Ambiguity aversion is a well-known human bias, which means that people will tend to stick to something they know over something unfamiliar, even if the unfamiliar promises a better outcome. Leaders who are mentally and emotionally prepared for this can navigate challenges without losing momentum.

- **Credibility and influence:** Employees look to leaders for guidance. Those who demonstrate professional expertise and personal integrity inspire trust and commitment through a human approach.
- **Adaptability and learning:** Change demands flexibility and continuous learning. Leaders who invest in self-development can better anticipate and be open to continuous shifts, and lead with confidence.
- **Navigating uncertainty:** Organizational change is unpredictable. Leaders who are strategically armored by rooting in their purpose and strengths can make decisions that are anchored and yet focused on overall outcomes.

Ultimately, leading cultural change isn't just about strategy; it's also about personal strength, professional credibility, and the ability to inspire others.

Leading deep cultural change is rewarding but hard work, uncertain and difficult to achieve, even when the upside of the change is quite intuitive and meaningful.

While it can be seen as a defensive move, armoring as a technique actually enables leaders to maintain clarity, composure, and decision-making capacity in volatile conditions, while buffering against burnout and emotional overload. It's different from "armored leadership," which is a posture of protection that is often unconscious, rigid, and resistant to change. This type of "hunker-down" leadership can come from a place of fear, and it may deliver short-term control but undermine long-term trust and adaptability.

Armoring with an open heart as a technique, however, is a tool of intentional resilience and inner growth. Humans can prepare psychologically for hard things and thrive. Strategic change professionals use armoring as a technique to hold emotional boundaries, preserve clarity, and create space for reflection in high-pressure environments. It's not about staying closed; it's about knowing when to pause, protect, and then reengage with empathy and precision.

Two types of preparation for armoring are necessary: both personal and professional. Developing your approach to change and personally/professionally armoring yourself with what you need means you have an opportunity to flourish, find joy, and thrive as you take on this task. Preparing change leaders, especially for the personal challenge of leading change, is an oft-missed step in industrial era change management models. It is also even more critical for those with less equal influence in the hierarchy of power.

Occupations that head into the deep unknown and deal with threatening and changing circumstances, such as astronauts, active military teams, cave divers, and scuba divers, know that most of the job is about the preparation and ability to remain calm and clearheaded as they face untold challenges. Leading big change in our organizations where, commonly, the base belief is profits at all costs, calls for the same approach. Most change efforts fail, and it's simply because they are hard to do and most change agents were grossly underprepared for the effort.

Emotional Resilience: Embracing Opposition

No matter how personally and professionally convinced we become about this important journey of reculturing for our organization, we must be prepared to embrace opposition. We cannot be naive about this.

Armoring is more than just knowing the detail of the topic. We need to find our personal strength, courage, and bravery to be in the spotlight, questioned and challenged without falling down. We must accept early on that there are things we are likely to be wrong on, and we need to stay open to listening and adapting without stubbornness.

Many organizations experience collective terror and suffering at the thought of change. It's not to be unexpected because it's a human condition. The human brain is wired first and foremost to look for and be fascinated by threat. In large organizations, the politics of influence, power, and status are real and affect the impact of well-intentioned work every day. Neuroscientific research by Dr. Tania Singer shows that uncertainty activates the same brain regions associated with physical pain, meaning that organizational change often feels like a genuine threat to employees' well-being even if it is nothing close to it (People Insight, 2025).

It's important to understand that leaders and change professionals will therefore get some opposition, and we need to not be caught out by it but use it as fuel for emotional resilience. It might come in different forms and so being mindful of this is vital.

Why do people resist change efforts? People often resist change unless they see clear, personal benefits. The "worse until better" model, in which disruptive changes like layoffs, relocations, and technology shifts happen up front, has historically fueled fear and disengagement rather than enthusiasm.

Apathy and skepticism are particularly strong when the benefits seem distant or irrelevant to employees. For example, increasing shareholder value might not resonate with workers when very few hold shares in UK-listed companies. Similarly, cost-cutting measures aimed at improving profit margins can feel disconnected from employees' daily realities.

Layoffs and restructuring also have long-term effects on morale and productivity. Studies show that mass layoffs, even when strategically planned, often lead to lower engagement, reduced trust, and increased turnover. Employees who survive the cuts may feel uncertain about their future, making them less likely to embrace further changes.

Ultimately, leaders face an uphill battle in driving change. Successful transformations require clear communication, employee involvement, and a compelling vision that connects change to personal and collective benefits.

Patience and strategic awareness are essential, regardless of level of authority. Listening to key stakeholders across all areas helps gauge readiness for learning. At times, it may be necessary to adapt or sidestep while attention remains on existing initiatives that could otherwise hinder progress toward a more cohesive and expansive strategy.

Preparing for challenges and preventing burnout is not just practical; it's essential. While it may seem like a negative approach, when done well, it can be empowering and liberating.

We prioritize this skill because, in our research with change leaders, it emerged as the most important lesson they wished they had known from the start.

Those who have led change told us they underestimated how long the process would take, who might unexpectedly resist, and the personal toll it would have on them. Many faced deeply personal attacks, moments where they feared their careers were at risk, and crises when external forces—shareholders, media, and consumers—pushed back, causing CEOs and boards to lose confidence.

By recognizing these realities early, leaders can strengthen their resilience and navigate change with greater confidence.

We've both experienced this firsthand. At one organization in the 2010s we were highly trained in the industrial era thinking on change management and so were pretty confident about leading global change initiatives and one big change in which we were reinventing our well-being support for colleagues. We had done all the right things. We had secured CEO support and built a rock-solid business case that was beautifully and clearly presented. It was so logical that we thought it would be easy to introduce, and we were ready to go with getting board approval to go ahead. Therefore, we were not prepared for how hard and relentless it would be to introduce this change and the personal toll leading this change would take. Sometimes leading change is more like death by a thousand paper cuts with small acts of resistance happening regularly; other times it is like being strangled around the throat, especially when a powerful and influential nay-sayer emerges. We remember one board meeting when we were bringing the change to a key decision point and we were personally ridiculed in front of C-suite members as they tried to derail the change. One leader took great pleasure in obsessing over a typo at the back of the deck as if this was evidence of the lack of thought in the paper. What was behind it all? Was it the fact that we were investing in employees as human beings? Was it us? Was it simply that they were worried about their bonus and the profit margin being asked of them? To this day we are not sure. We got it all through anyway, introducing one of the most successful and profound shifts seen in the organization at the time, but it felt at a cost personally. We hang onto the outcome because no one in that room on that day thanked us for literally saving them millions of pounds.

While some people may find themselves organically emerging as change agents in organizations, those with a whole system and long-term remit in their job description and most certainly every chair, CEO, chief product officer, human resources (HR) department head, chief strategy officer, and chief technology officer must prepare, protect, and strengthen themselves with some sort of armory, to avoid burnout, for the challenge ahead.

Kerri's Approach to Emotional Resilience

I couldn't recommend highly enough to change agents the importance of having an "outside the organization" inner circle and friends who know you for who you are and can be there for you as you navigate the twists and turns of changing an organization. Humans work best when there are others around for them—yes, the lone genius type exists, but it's rare and if you find yourself without trusted people to talk to openly about your experiences as a change agent, then you have something to look out for. I am so fortunate that my best friends from university are still with me 25 years on and have their own professional careers. One friend in particular who lives just outside New York is my go-to for confidential advice and guidance. I also have a growing network of people whom I can bounce things off, rant and rave to, and be there when things get more difficult.

Trusting others can be difficult and so that's why having a community outside the confines of the four walls of our organization matters. Our partner, best friend, and family will help but, in this case, even better are people who understand something about how organizations operate and what our experience is like. Sometimes people take on a coach just to have this, but it's even better if you can find it organically.

Traditional change management methods largely skip over this part and simply prioritize the need for change agents to know their stuff and build business cases and PowerPoint decks. They say, "do your research and understand the positive change this will bring to the balance sheet." Be able to quickly respond to all queries, requests, provocations, hook people in, repeat repeat repeat the benefits, and keep people with you as you take on the mammoth task.

Business change leaders may not be able to prepare in the same way as astronauts or Navy SEALs, as the business world is nonlinear and unpredictable. However, organizations can take a proactive approach by embedding resilience-building strategies into their change cycles. By equipping leaders up front with the right tools and mindset, rather than reacting to challenges as they arise, businesses can create stronger foundations for successful transformation.

Credibility and Influence: The Human Touch

To have credibility from the outset of a change is to be regarded as an expert on our topic and armor ourselves and others with the right information, data, research. This is what we call professional armoring. It's a totally necessary and more typical activity for change agents to undertake. This is where the SWOT (strengths, weaknesses, opportunities, and threats) analysis comes into its own. Here is where we can now really use artificial intelligence (AI) to shortcut the research phase and get verified information into the attention space of everyone we need to reach. We can learn here from prior cultural evolution processes that we must meet people where they are and find ways that support their own learning.

In this phase of armoring, we reflect on our own positioning and compare this with the broadest possible insights available of where others are positioned. The great advancements in AI offer us large-scale big data trends at our fingertips shortcutting an extensive research phase that would more traditionally have been time-consuming attendance at conferences in person, using multiple channels to find research in articles existing in different places rather than rapid online search results from a wider range of sources offering far greater diversity of thought.

This part of armoring can take just two weeks or much longer but the need for pace drives us to fully embrace our digital dexterity to advance this using all available avenues, channels, and opportunities at the same time as critically remaining "human switched on" ourselves and open to what may emerge. But this isn't enough as we know people want to feel, not just credibility in leaders but their integrity. This comes from the more human aspect of influence.

How do we not only demonstrate professional expertise but also personal integrity? Integrity is what creates trust and commitment, core to armoring ourselves in multiple stakeholder groups and communities, empowering us to lead the way.

A good place for change leaders to armor for credibility and influence is to understand what makes us uniquely human as a living species.

Going beyond our ability to relay how our knowledge and acquired skills sets us apart as a leader with qualifications to catalyze big change at scale and pace. Eminent climate scientists Simon Lewis and Mark Maslin (2018) note that humans alone mastered the art of mass communication, language, and embracing knowledge and ideas that are not their own, which has enabled us to dominate the course of our natural history and environment.

What we can take from this is that change can be achieved, and leaders offer guidance in the direction others can follow. Humans have shown time and time again that we will move toward the ideas and practices that give us the best guarantee of evolutionary success. We did learn to read at all levels of society, we did end slavery, we did create democracies, we set up the United Nations, and we did fix the hole in the ozone layer. Reculturing our organizations is a powerful way to save the institution of work in the age of AI.

Our ability to anticipate and evaluate future possibilities of the current challenges we face empowers us to change direction, to show psychological flexibility, a skill that will be increasingly fundamental for the future of work. Demonstrating this ability to anticipate and predict change creates a human influence that is critical for leaders of change and innovation that inspires and builds trust for others to follow. Nurturing this natural ability and mastering it in a change role is fundamental for demonstrating human intelligence to others.

Physical Credibility and Influence

It is underestimated how much human beings respond to people in person or through their physical appearance. Our armory techniques can be as literal as having an awareness of how we present ourselves, how we appear and behave and speak and the impact that has on our relationships with other key stakeholders and influencers. This is a controversial area to discuss as it is riven with biases and so it is often less prioritized in change management approaches and therefore grossly underestimated. Ultimately, we work with people we like, we read books by people we admire, we envy and look to emulate those we see as influential—hence the growing power of influencers that affect our daily consumer and employee choices. While change approaches often mention finding champions and sponsors, we wonder if we are transparent in our reasoning and choice? We choose champions in our organizations to lead change because they are liked for their character, their demeanor, their appearance of authority/status/power/service?

What really depicts this? Our armory is often our appearance, which tells others nonverbal cues about who we are and what we stand for—our purpose. In our research we found that women often don't express their personality in their appearance and choice of clothes until they feel they have reached an explicit level of professional accomplishment often associated with higher-level qualifications. One leaders anonymously shared, "I started wearing bright colors that I love, big earrings and bold glasses; I wasn't trying to fit an organizational perception of professionalism anymore—I wanted others to know my authentic self and I stepped into myself." What does this mean for true physical armory? What makes the difference in our ability to truly express ourselves authentically? And how might that affect how we lead change? Our experience tells us that no one should feel they have to look a certain way to achieve change. Power dressing courses for female leaders in the 1990s/2000s were hugely cringeworthy because the positioning was you need to look like a man to succeed but strip some of the crude messaging away and what they were trying to point out was there is a dress code to power in some organizations, which is worth knowing if you are navigating that. Your choices on appearance are best when they are authentic to you, and you are comfortable with the choices you are making for the purpose you are trying to achieve.

Another important element of armory is having voice. For many, we limit our voice; we suppress our intuition and become easily swayed by others we perceive to be more knowledgeable, more powerful, more capable, or even more negatively those we feel judged by. This may be due to microaggressions that limit the psychological safety we perceive and mean we step back from making bold statements, sharing information on important topics, moving the agenda forward, and asking the awkward questions. Our fear that limits our voice often comes from two things: our fear of conflict and our fear of being judged negatively somehow.

Alex's Experience of Amoring

Assertiveness training has long been debated in leadership development for women, aimed at breaking free from the "good girl syndrome." Personally, I was raised in a time when I was expected to be seen but not heard, and I realized that the fear of speaking up runs

(continued)

(*continued*)

deeper than training—it often requires professional therapy to untangle personal insecurities and distinguish between our own fears and the judgments of others.

I built confidence by immersing myself in psychological research, arming myself with knowledge to contribute meaningfully to discussions. I learned to find my voice by actively listening, replaying key points in meetings, and realizing that my ideas were not just valid—they were needed. My mantra became "Say it out loud." Over time, and with the help of vocal coaching, I trained myself to project my voice, refine my tone, and command attention in leadership settings.

But voice alone isn't enough—appearance is another form of armor. As one of the youngest female leaders reporting to the board, I was hyper-aware of how my image shaped perceptions. Early in my career, I wore conservative black suits, avoiding bold makeup to maintain a professional psychologist identity. Over time, I adapted, noticing how dressing the part influenced how others perceived me. When working globally, I shifted to floral dresses, embracing a more senior leadership style. Later, in the startup world, I dressed down, but as my team grew, I recognized that my image mattered for credibility. As a CEO, I refined my wardrobe again—pearls and scarves mirrored the leaders I admired, opening new opportunities.

Now, my armor reflects my authentic self: a balance of professionalism and personality. Ties and waistcoats give me a smart yet distinctive edge, ensuring I stand out in leadership spaces.

Over the years, speaking at global conferences has reinforced the importance of nonverbal communication. While audiences engage with the psychology behind my work, the most common feedback I receive is about my jacket, shoes, or hair. Initially surprising, I've come to realize that these comments aren't superficial, they signal acceptance, a recognition of my presence beyond just my ideas.

Ultimately, armor, whether voice, appearance, or presence, is about consciously shaping the impact we want to have. It's a tool for leadership, a way to navigate perceptions, and a means to command attention and influence change.

Adaptability and Learning: Psychological Flexibility

Learning and being adaptable has long been in the change rhetoric and embraced in change literature, but what we find is that old methods of understanding change as a static, isolated occurrence then dominate how we support and lead others through change. We must armor ourselves with the most up-to-date research in how to be adaptable through being more psychologically flexible, by rapid acceptance that meets the demanding pace of organizational change happening on multiple dimensions.

Psychological flexibility is a relatively new concept in the field of psychology and is the furthest in the right direction we have seen to date that encompasses the exploring of future possibilities that Seligman et al. (2016) describe. It is a skill we can develop, building from growth mindset, resilience, psychological capital, but the difference is it is more dynamic. Not merely the ability to bounce back from a challenge or the way a person reacts to change, psychological flexibility is the open ability to stretch comfort and curiosity to new levels, to suppose alternative possible future scenarios and adapt our behavior toward those influencing the ultimate outcomes.

If we can support ourselves and change leaders to develop psychological flexibility as a muscle, we are absolutely taking the first step in preparing our organization and leaders to lead the change.

Psychological flexibility is inspired by acceptance and commitment therapy pioneered by Steven Hayes, Kirk Strosahl, and Kelly Wilson (1999) and involves several key components:

- **Being present:** Staying fully engaged and attentive to the current moment, rather than getting caught up in past regrets or future worries
- **Acceptance:** Naming and embracing thoughts and feelings without trying to change or suppress them, even when they are uncomfortable or distressing; developing a more granular sense of what we are feeling so we can express what is going on for us better
- **Values:** Clarifying what is truly important and meaningful in life and using these values to guide actions and decisions and to stay aligned to our priorities

- **Committed action:** Taking effective and purposeful action, even when it involves facing obstacles or discomfort, in alignment with one's values
- **Self-as-context:** Viewing oneself as more than just one's thoughts, emotions, or experiences, and recognizing that one has the ability to observe and understand these aspects without being defined by them
- **Cognitive defusion:** Learning to step back from and observe thoughts rather than becoming entangled in them or seeing them as literal truths

Psychological flexibility is a key factor in mental health and well-being, helping individuals navigate life's challenges with resilience and adaptability, and we see it as a key skill for leaders seeking to lead change. Higher levels of psychological flexibility will help us stay the course of the change ahead.

Developing psychological flexibility means taking a bit of a journey inside your own inner being. This does not need to be on a retreat, on holiday, or by taking extended time out. This can be as simple as taking five minutes a day to consider what you are most pleased about in your day, and why. Or it can be creating a vision board or completing a values exercise. Incorporating mindful practice, such as where you simply concentrate on the here and now, is another great inroad. Another example is taking time to just eat your lunch rather than inhaling it or focusing on another person fully who is speaking to you. Even AI can help—if you tell AI what you value, it can help you to navigate things you are experiencing.

Holding Things Lightly

Over the years we've observed how much organizational cultural change can feel like a social movement sweeping an organization. We can therefore learn from these social movements. Hahrie Han, an expert on social movements, says that "most successful movements are simultaneously bold and pragmatic" (2014). The boldness is well understood, the pragmatism less so. In fact it was a lesson Kerri learnt early from her wonderful boss for many years at Aviva, Marie Sigsworth.

Kerri's Experience of Amoring

Marie led huge cultural change at Aviva, playing both leading and unsung roles at times. She led one of Aviva's most sophisticated culture change program, which combined HR and corporate responsibility globally for many years. Her advice one day to me was to hold my powerful ideas more lightly. She could see the frustration I would have when something was so obvious to me and yet people fought against it, and the relationships I was testing as a result. The phrase comes from Buddhism and it reminds us that as much as I might try to control situations and outcomes, I can't, and that I needed to have less rigidity and more fluidity in how I tackled the situations I faced. It took me a long time to get used to the practice and I realize now that I was probably suffering quite a bit from having a fixed mindset: I'd fixed on a good idea and wanted to see it happen. Of course, persistence does pay off, but how you get to your outcome can be flexed, and it was realizing this was a better approach that I became more successful in what I was trying to do.

Recognizing we cannot control everything is key, as well as knowing that pathways, while well intentioned, can still take a tricky/nonlinear path with steps backwards. Being ready to and open to find links and opportunities when they emerge and letting go of control is a central theme throughout this work.

Navigating Uncertainty: Rooting in Your Purpose, Hope, and Strengths

To really engage through the magnitude of micro changes that are part of macro change, we need to know what matters most to us, our own personal purpose, and how that not only influences our seasonal motivations and our inner strengths but also how it roots us. Armoring means we have to be strong in who we are, to be able to navigate through flux without being swept in alternative directions.

Our personal purpose helps guide us to stay focused on outcomes, it helps us evaluate our progress and create meaning and fulfillment in our hard work, and it helps us anchor through uncertainty.

Simon Sinek powerfully brought this to life for many when he launched work in 2011 on "Start with Why" showing that purpose was at the heart of great leadership. His Ted Talk on the topic gained tens of millions of views (Sinek, 2011). Understanding why you are drawn to this mission is a powerful piece of armory—it will help you when things are going well and when they aren't.

In addition, homing in on what our strengths are means we can vitally and uniquely connect ourselves with whatever challenge we have to face. When using our strengths, we are often most authentic and fluent, able to achieve flow and succeed. Our strengths are the ways we have learned to navigate our world best, based on our well-trodden neural pathways in our brain that have worked for us in a plethora of differing scenarios. People who use their strengths for just 10 hours a week have the following qualities:

- Six times more likely to be engaged at work
- Eight percent more productive
- Fifteen percent less likely to quit
- Three times more likely to have an excellent quality of life (Flade et al., 2015)

Putting our human strengths at the heart of organizations has been both our work within organizations for nearly two decades now and is what drew us together as work colleagues in Aviva in the mid-2000s. For Alex this led to the creation of Bailey & French, an organization Alex founded to humanize the world of work. Kerri has introduced strengths and deepened their practical presence in every organization she has worked in for two decades seeing performance, engagement, and energy improvements every time.

Being not only self-aware of our purpose and strengths but also able to use those in the moments that matter means that we can revisit them consciously to help us guide our thinking, reasoning, and decision-making during a change. It takes time to learn to do this well, hence armoring ourselves before a cultural evolution with this personal knowing will help us keep pace with any change through the challenging directions they can take.

Reflective questioning techniques can help us easily focus on bringing our purpose and strengths to the forefront of our consciousness, and one great example is a focus on active hope (Macy and Johnstone, 2012).

Active hope teaches that leaders can grow our abilities by (1) understanding the realities of the context we are in and our own strengths and weaknesses in relation to them, (2) spending time developing a vision for the future that represents where and how we want our organization to be—this can be as expansive as possible, and (3) committing to taking steps in that direction no matter how tough.

Further support to this is Lindsay Foreman's recent hope research exploring the inner emotional and cognitive landscape of goal pursuit, offering a nuanced lens on hope, not as blind optimism, but as a dynamic interplay of thoughts and emotions that shape outcomes. Her doctoral thesis, "An Exploration of the Thoughts and Emotions Associated with Goal Attainment," uses Q-methodology to surface four distinct perspectives people hold during goal pursuit: positive, realist, dreamer, and conflicted (Foreman, 2023).

What's striking is that hopeful thinking alone didn't guarantee success. In fact, the realists—those who experienced self-doubt, overwhelm, and anxiety—were often more successful in achieving their goals than the dreamers or even the overtly positive participants. This challenges conventional coaching wisdom that prioritizes positive thinking, suggesting instead that a balanced emotional experience, including negative emotions, can fuel meaningful progress.

Key questions change leaders can ask ourselves to stay rooted include the following:

- What will happen over the long term if we do not act?
- What is asked of our people to run this business well? Is it at risk?
- How is AI helping to solve issues for the people in the organization?
- What do I personally offer to this change?
- What do I personally want to get out of this change? What different future am I hoping to have as a result? What's my motivation?

- Who am I doing it for?
- What will employees in say 30 years' time say to me about impact of this change?
- What is the smallest step I can take to move toward this vision to feel good about it?
- What's going to be the first sign we see that tells me I am on the right track?

There is no need to show anyone your answers, and no one is going to mark them, but what it gives you is an understanding about yourself in relation to this change that you can review as you navigate the twists and turns which will inevitably arise. These answers help you to flex and can be your own personal guide as you help evolve your culture. Your motivations don't need to be grand or worthy; they might be linked more to survival right now.

How Does Armoring Work in Practice?

The well-being and energy levels (remember vitality, enthusiasm, and resilience of Chapter 7) of change leaders is a key element of reculturing and is missing from nearly every change process we have seen. Armoring ourselves with an open heart as change leaders is something we do through organizational reculturing, and it's essential, not as a shield against vulnerability but as a framework for intentional resilience, emotional clarity, and leadership. Cultural transformation stirs deep resistance, challenges identities, and disrupts long-held norms, requiring leaders to stay grounded amid complexity. This inner armor enables us to absorb discomfort without losing integrity, to model vulnerability with boundaries, and to respond with wisdom rather than react from fear. It protects the emotional bandwidth needed to hold space for others while safeguarding the inner compass that keeps us aligned with purpose. In essence, it's how we remain whole and principled while guiding others through the messy, sacred work of cultural evolution.

This readies us for our next phase, awareness, where we use this context to move forward with others.

10 | Awareness (Building)

We don't fix culture, we evolve it. A key skill of reculturing, especially when aiming to evolve culture at pace and scale, is not strategy, structure, or slogans. It's awareness. And not the kind delivered by fixed diagnostics or legacy frameworks. For too long, we've been reaching for the wrong tools: programs, policies, and playbooks that miss the mark. Real evolution starts with awareness strategic, emotional, and collective. It's the skill of sensing where culture wants to go next, not forcing it somewhere it won't stick.

The leap from one person's vision to a shared reality is one of the hardest parts of reculturing and one of the most exciting. It's where cultural evolution either catches fire or fizzles out. Our deep experience shows that if we want to move at pace and scale, we need to build the muscle of awareness differently. Not through what we've been taught, but through what works.

Too often, culture work starts with a hunt: find the problem, fix the gap, diagnose the distance from some idealized future state. Old models rush in with rigid diagnostics, outdated dimensions, and a mindset borrowed from medicine: spot the symptoms, treat the cause, restore "normal." But culture isn't a condition. It's a living system. And this fix-it-first approach doesn't just miss the mark; it slows everything down.

The diagnostics we have been using are interventions. They can shape perception, freeze momentum, and delay evolution. If we want real cultural change, we need to flip the narrative. That means starting not with judgment, but with awareness. Not with what's broken, but with what's ready to grow. The seeds of the next phase of our cultures are already there; we just might not be able to see them yet.

Awareness building for cultural evolution takes courage, conviction, and conversation. It requires us to start observing at a deeper level; it asks us to start to effectively shape and position the changes required and to engage in meaningful dialogue. These are not soft skills; they're precision tools for leaders ready to evolve culture from the inside out. We begin by noticing, observing things as they are, without judgment or agenda. We learn to notice the subtle signals, energy shifts, relational dynamics, and emotional undercurrents that shape how people feel and behave. The ground in which our people grow. This is where we gather real data and use it later to build conviction in the reculturing journey, and shape the dialogue and conditions for others to engage through conversation.

To build conviction and evidence, we must move from sensing and scanning to crafting simple, resonant messages, testing new language, and building learning-focused conversations. Positioning what needs to evolve becomes a quiet superpower: a guerrilla technique for seeding ideas under the radar, shaping perception, and creating the hooks the organization needs to change from within. It's low effort, low threat, and high impact. It helps us spot resistance early and respond with agility, not defensiveness.

And with that foundation, through dialogue we start to develop the confidence and conversations required to tackle legacy behaviors, outdated norms, and cultural drift. Change lands best when it feels like a build on where we are with who we have, not a wholesale reinvention. As tempting as it is to talk about transformation, big change, or reinvention, these words can trigger fear and resistance. By starting with awareness, through noticing and positioning, we begin organically, with fewer resources and more momentum. We don't need a full cascade from the top.

The traditional diagnostic-based change management practice, by contrast, states that here you need diagnostics, planning, and top-down, often broadcast-style communication. Instead of building your own conviction and conversations we are creating "burning platforms" and business cases. We use fear as the means to motivate versus growth. We have seen that this is often a cause of cultural initiatives failing early, when stakeholders operate with expectations of methodological approaches that don't allow for the fine fabric of culture. For colleagues, findings often aren't attuned to the cultural landscape within the organization and often can land from outer space. This makes them highly likely to be rejected, slowing the whole process down.

Similarly, we have been told by change management programs and gurus that we need to start loudly—with launches, videos, internal marketing booklets, and big pronouncements—and tone from the top from the CEO. This is important work, but it will come better later.

When leaders have the courage to themselves tune into what they want to evolve, through attention, dialogue, energy, and presence, they build conviction. This in turn activates confidence to have new conversations, readying the organization for others to join in. And this begins the work of culture change in real time, rather than a linear phased/milestone plan of diagnosis/assessment/planned interventions and so on. This matters because what we pay attention to doesn't just reflect culture, it reshapes it.

This is how we move from analysis to evolution. As we leave behind cookie-cutter programs and fixed diagnostics, we strengthen our core resolve of what will evolve.

The Courage to Start with Observation and Noticing

"The way to right wrongs is to turn the light of truth upon them."
—*Ida B. Wells,*
investigative journalist and civil rights pioneer

Culture change doesn't need a grand rollout or a program team. It can start today, with you. Right where you are. No new language. No endless slide decks. No waiting for top-down approval. The fastest way to shift culture is often the simplest: tune in, not up. It takes courage as most people don't think they can change culture or that it belongs in another function. Human resources (HR) perhaps, or sales, or technology.

But cultural evolution can start anywhere. Building awareness isn't passive, it's strategic. We call it noticing. It's the art of quietly gathering intelligence by talking to people, listening deeply, and observing how ideas land. Ask about their worries, their hopes, their take on where the organization's headed. Watch what sparks energy, what shuts it down, and what connects to the current way of working.

Here's the magic: Change accelerates when effort is low and threat is low. The more informally you do this, the more honest, and useful, the responses. Like testing a prompt in ChatGPT, you're probing for insight. Every reaction is data. Even resistance is gold; it shows you where the emotional triggers are and what needs to be reframed.

Noticing is about holding ideas lightly, so people can engage without defensiveness. It's how you seed change under the radar, build cultural attunement, and learn what's really going on before you ever launch a thing.

Ida Wells, a key figure in the American Civil Rights Movement and founder of the NAACP, understood that change begins with noticing what others refuse to see—and then naming it with clarity and courage. Her work documenting lynchings in the 1890s was not just journalism; it was a strategic act of observation that exposed systemic injustice and catalyzed national awareness. Observation is not passive, it's catalytic. When leaders turn their attention toward what's hidden, denied, or normalized, or what could be, they begin the work of transformation. Military training treats observation as a survival skill. Observation is the foundation of situational awareness, emotional intelligence (EQ), and strategic foresight. Leaders who cultivate the skill of noticing energy shifts, unspoken tensions, and emerging stories become the most effective culture shapers.

Therefore, the best first move is not structural, it's attentional. It's the courage to actively notice what is going on and beginning to name it. It won't disrupt operations yet. For some leaders this is a good thing. For others who like to make an immediate splash, this might feel uncomfortable. We have learnt that culture is rarely changed by declaration, by proclamation, by telling others it will be so. What gets us started is by what leaders consistently notice, model, and reinforce. As Edgar Schein, early scientist focused on culture, observed, "The behavior of leaders is the most visible and powerful expression of culture" (Schein, 2016).

Fans of the television show *The Traitors* will recognize this technique. The aim of the show is to uncover the "traitors" among a group of faithful. Every night someone can be banished for being a traitor whether they are or aren't and some of the most successful game players are the ones who notice patterns and make astute observations. They are best able to notice the undercurrents, position theories, and suggestions of whom to vote for. People listen more and more to the theories of those who then prove themselves to be correct in their thinking.

This is the phase most leaders skip, mainly because they pay good money for someone else to do the noticing. This is the phase most likely to be outsourced to external consultants. But it's the step that makes everything else work. Culture doesn't shift because we declare it. It shifts because we pay attention and act on what we find.

Conviction Building

"No one will protect what they don't care about, and no one will care about what they have never experienced."

—David Attenborough,
environmentalist, journalist, and broadcaster

Conviction building is an important component in the overall awareness building skill for reculturing, as it means action will be taken. Conviction represents the deeply held belief that something is true, important, and worth acting on regardless of external approval or certainty. We use the concept of conviction quite deliberately, not just as an opinion; it's an unwavering stance that shapes decisions, fuels courage, and anchors leadership. According to *Oxford Dictionaries*, conviction can mean:

- A firmly held belief or opinion
- The quality of showing certainty in what one believes or says

In leadership and culture work, conviction is what moves ideas from concept to commitment. It's the inner clarity that says, "This matters, and I'm willing to stand for it."

Building conviction and intentionality toward change can take few forms. Our experience tells us that data and evidence become important, enabling people to see what we see and framing the changes in the existing context of the organization matters. By looking at critical organizational data and thinking more deeply about the four reculturing drivers and three zones we introduced in Part II we can build deep conviction of where our culture needs to go next. Culture we know is not the easiest thing to study, which means it's easy to not develop strong conviction one way or another. There are misdirections everywhere. It can be like looking at one of those mirrors exhibits at a circus. Reflections tell their own story. In the military everyone is trained to know what to do when they don't know where they are. We share some of these techniques in an organizational context to build the conviction needed to start your reculturing journey. Knowing if an organization is ready to change its culture depends on many factors, but timing often matters most.

Line Up What You Already Know—Organizational Critical Data

Before starting anything it's important to remind ourselves of what we already know. When culture feels unclear, we can't wait for perfect data, start with what we've got. The facts. Every organization has a set of critical data or vital signs, quite often called key performance indicators or outcomes and key results. These tell us how well an organization is doing and provide great data points for reculturing. This information could include data points, and trends in areas such as profitability, operating margin, revenue, customer complaints or satisfaction, attrition, engagement, absence (related to mental health issues), new hire failure rate, tenure, and time to hire. These are hugely important to understand so that it's possible to see where a pull for something is now. It speeds us up if we can link reculturing to an existing opportunity that is on a form of mission control board/balanced scorecard.

Microsoft's cultural transformation in the mid-2010s is a great example of building conviction by gathering and using company data to drive change. Under CEO Satya Nadella, Microsoft recognized that its growth was being hindered by a rigid, competitive culture. Employee feedback and performance data revealed that innovation was suffering because teams worked in silos rather than collaborating. To shift this, leadership used internal surveys and engagement metrics to make the case for a more open, learning-driven environment.

As previously mentioned, the company introduced a "growth mindset" philosophy, encouraging employees to take risks, learn from failures, and share knowledge across teams. Metrics showed increased collaboration and creativity, fueling product innovation, and revitalizing Microsoft's market position. By grounding cultural change in data, Microsoft transformed into a more agile, customer-focused organization that embraced curiosity and teamwork, proving that meaningful change starts with understanding the realities within.

Employee survey data and customer feedback help organizations gauge readiness for change and pinpoint areas where new initiatives can take root. For example, if new managers struggle with development conversations, a straightforward skills-based approach could replace complex competency frameworks, giving them practical, easy-to-apply methods. This creates an entry point to connect with a broader culture strategy, enabling faster learning and progress toward key goals.

Existing data is a powerful tool for shaping awareness of organizational culture, but its real impact comes when it is woven into meaningful conversations. Rather than simply presenting numbers, we can use data to surface trends, highlight concerns, and create a shared understanding of the need for change.

By incorporating data and performance insights into discussions, it's possible to pinpoint what's working and where cultural shifts are needed. Conversations become more actionable when data illustrates patterns, whether it's declining collaboration, gaps in leadership development, or barriers to innovation.

At this stage the key is to frame data in a way that sparks dialogue rather than defensiveness. Instead of dictating solutions, culture leaders can invite teams to interpret findings, explore possibilities, and cocreate strategies. This fosters ownership and ensures that cultural change isn't imposed but built collectively.

When data fuels dialogue, it transforms from a report into a catalyst driving deep engagement and sustained organizational evolution.

Noticing what needs to evolve aligned to critical organizational data works as it gives us a chance to find where it will have the best possible base to thrive without triggering a threat response, which is akin to being able to get a foot in the door.

Some of the biggest opportunities we have to create lasting cultural change in our organizations is through telling a story with data. Over our careers we have seen, and have been part of, the development of the specialism of people analytics and data. The joy here is finding the nugget of insight in the data that can take us to the next level. Once we look at what drives key outcomes in your organization, such as financial performance, sales, customer satisfaction or what reduces speed to competence, or what leaders and themes create engagement and even predictions of who might leave and when, we have the ability to create a healthy sense of urgency on seeing improvements. It's great to have access to studies, which tell us broad trends but there is nothing like our own company data to work with. This is an area that AI is quickly taking over so this type of data and insight will be more readily available for organizations. Using data like this can really change the energy about the work and fuel positive efforts to demonstrate the evidence behind the story.

Using the Reculturing Drivers to Build Conviction—The Reculturing Compass

Knowing our organizational data is helpful but it doesn't always tell us what that means for the culture. We need to build a better sense of this. The most effective leaders don't force alignment, they generate it. Navigation and mapping offers a powerful metaphor: Building enough of a picture of where you are going to build trust but not a detailed sat nav style set of instructions of do this, because culture cannot be navigated like a road.

In cultural transformation, leaders who are internally aligned create a field of influence that guides others through uncertainty. This means getting used to leading from inner clarity, not external pressure. It's not about pushing change; it's about embodying the change. Actions create resonance, not resistance.

To navigate effectively, humans have developed maps and tools like compasses. Our earliest human ancestors understood the earth had a magnetic field and found materials that naturally aligned with it, enabling people to always know which way they were pointing.

For leaders who want to shape culture, not just manage it, building your own compass helps. Culture isn't static, and neither is leadership. Off-the-shelf models and inherited frameworks can't always capture the nuance of our organization's energy, purpose, or human dynamics. A personalized compass, anchored in our own clarity on purpose, mindset, energy, and human connection helps us navigate complexity with conviction. It becomes a reference point when things get noisy, a guide when the terrain shifts, and a signal to others that we're leading with intention, not imitation. The most effective cultural evolvers don't just follow maps, they create orientation. And that starts with crafting a compass that reflects what we stand for, what we're sensing, and where we're ready to go.

A compass can be built for the four reculturing drivers from Part II, and we can position our organizations within one of the three cultural zones we introduced in Chapter 4. This compass is not a fixed diagnostic or a theoretical construct; it's a strategic sensing tool grounded in lived experience and real-world evidence from organizations actively evolving culture at pace and scale. These zones aren't labels or fixed, they're strategic tools. They help frame our language, sharpen our sensing, and guide our reculturing journey with clarity and conviction.

The lost, thriving, and culture zones emerged from patterns we observed across global networks, leadership teams, and transformation programs where culture was treated not as a static artefact but as a dynamic system. What elevates these concepts is their practical resonance: They reflect what leaders and teams actually feel, face, and navigate. From energy audits to executive interviews, from frontline feedback to strategic misfires, these zones help leaders orient quickly, act wisely, and build cultures that are fit for the future. They help bring clarity. And clarity is what makes change possible.

Zone 1: Lost

This is where culture has drifted. Purpose is fragmented or forgotten. Mindsets are passive, cynical, or disengaged. Energy is low, scattered, or stuck in survival mode. Human connection is thin, transactional, or siloed. We feel it in the data—slipped revenue, rising complaints, costly errors or in the atmosphere: a quiet malaise, a sense of "why are we even here?"

Organizations in the lost zone chase shiny initiatives without scaffolding, no narrative, no road map, no link to strategy or commercial imperative. They look busy but lack coherence. HR leaders describe it as "working with 10 trade unions": fragmented, reactive, and hard to unify.

Lost cultures often adopt good ideas for the wrong reasons, like buying a branded item just because others have it. Subcultures dominate, connections fray, and trust erodes. The organization may appear progressive, but it's directionless, pulled in too many directions to move as one.

But here's the opportunity: When purpose, mindset, energy, and connection are reactivated with intention, the appetite for change is high. The pull is strong. You just need to be ready to ride it.

Zone 2: Thriving

This is where culture breathes. Purpose is clear and evolving. Mindsets are curious, growth-oriented, and psychologically flexible. Energy is regenerative, aligned with meaningful goals. Human connection is inclusive, relational, and built on trust.

Thriving cultures aren't perfect, but they're intentional. They know what they stand for, and they're learning how to evolve. The risk here is complacency: clinging to old ideals, outdated leadership behaviors, or values that no longer resonate. Without strategic renewal, even thriving cultures can slip into lost or cult.

To stay here, leaders must protect what's working, reeducate cultural stewards, and cut ties with legacy methods that no longer serve the future of work.

Zone 3: Cult

This is where culture becomes rigid. Purpose is dogmatic and used for control, not inspiration. Mindsets are closed, tribal, and resistant to dissent. Energy is high but performative, fear-driven, or frenetic. Human connection is conditional but based on conformity, not authenticity.

You'll know you're here when no one dares to challenge the narrative. Everyone says the same thing, but not everyone believes it. These cultures can look successful on the surface, but they're brittle. When the world shifts, they struggle to adapt. Founder-led firms often land here, where the culture mirrors the leader's worldview and stifles evolution.

The danger? Harm gets protected. Dissent gets punished. And the culture that once attracted talent becomes the reason people leave.

To evolve, these organizations need humility, external perspective, and a willingness to loosen the grip. Adaptability isn't optional, it's survival.

Exploring Our Own Reculturing Vision

Combining the Reculturing drivers—purpose, mindsets, energy and human connection—with the culture zones in this chapter provides an opportunity to explore and keep building conviction of where we are going. As we said in Chapter 3, it's vital we build our own version of the truth in terms of where to take our culture next.

To help with this, we've described each zone in Table 10.1 based on the organizations we've worked with and studied, but you can use your own. When you build this you create a set of guardrails for the organization and help you see how to observe more effectively.

Table 10.1 Zone Descriptions

Dimension	Lost Zone	Thriving Zone	Cult Zone
Purpose	Fragmented, unclear, absent	Clear, evolving, values-driven	Dogmatic, rigid, unquestioned
Mindsets	Passive, cynical, disengaged	Curious, flexible, growth-oriented	Tribal, closed, defensive
Energy	Low, scattered, survival mode	Regenerative, focused, sustainable	Frenetic, fear-driven, performative
Connection	Thin, siloed, transactional	Relational, inclusive, authentic	Conditional, conformist, exclusive

Visualize this as a four-point compass. The further each point leans toward balance, the more coherent and resilient your culture becomes. If one or more dimensions skew toward lost or cult, the compass tilts, revealing where recalibration is needed.

Mapping our culture to one of these zones helps build strategic orientation. It helps us sense where we are, where we're stuck, and where we could go next. It's terrain building for transformation.

This is how culture evolves through clarity, attention, and action. And it starts with knowing where we stand.

Self Reflection Questions to Strengthen Conviction

- **Purpose:**
    - To what extent is our purpose lived, not just stated?
    - Do people feel inspired or obligated by our purpose?
    - Is our purpose evolving with our context or stuck in legacy language?

- **Mindsets:**
    - How do we respond to dissent, uncertainty, or failure?
    - Are curiosity and psychological flexibility rewarded?
    - Do people feel safe to challenge norms or ask why?

- **Energy:**
    - What's the emotional tone of our day-to-day work?
    - Is our energy sustainable or are we burning out?
    - Do people feel energized by meaning or driven by fear?

- **Human connection:**
    - Do people feel seen, heard, and valued beyond their role?
    - Is connection built across differences—generational, cultural, hierarchical?
    - Are relationships authentic or performative?

The clarity of our own answers to these questions shape how we can frame our culture and the shifts required. Learning from others is then a critical next step to mass awareness.

Building Awareness Through Conversations

> "Change the conversation and you change the outcome."
> —*Patterson et al. (2002)*

In Indigenous communities, where rituals are built from deep human instincts, we see that when communities sense that something is wrong, whether in the land, the community, or the spirit, they often respond not with immediate correction but with conversation and collective listening, ritual, and relational repair. In Māori culture, for example, when something feels off, elders may initiate *hui*—a gathering for open dialogue, reflection, and consensus.

This is the hardest part of any genuine culture change journey. Most leaders are wired to look like they are taking firm action. Ego matters more than outcomes. We ourselves have got this wrong many times and then have seen good efforts slide or take longer as you start to face into the resistance. The moment for big announcements will come, but it's usually later than most change agents would like, and it's better to do it once the change concept is so prolific that it's inevitable.

Cultural evolution doesn't happen in isolation—it's a collective shift—and our role is to help shape the awareness that makes it possible. Once we've found the inner conviction the next step is testing it out and building the confidence of others to join us. Confidence grows not from complexity, but from carefully positioning the evolution through effective transmission and conversation. That means keeping messages about what we've observed simple, grounded, and human. It means shaping dialogue based on our convictions, not just delivering information, positioning it so we can learn what others take from it. It means letting others express themselves in the change, feel safe to engage, and begin to build their own conviction.

Timing conversations to coincide with the open windows of opportunity among the organizations rhythm of fiscal year reporting, planning and goal setting, reviewing and resetting is crucial. Often these windows present themselves perfectly to leadership populations with conference events to develop unity on strategy, and yet only the precisely curated content with structure of required conversations and response is permitted within the agenda. The peripheral conversations are often unattended to and threads of themes have limited resources post conference to be given life. Yet if we are there and with our ear to the ground we can seed ideas in conversations and test appetite with key influencers, no matter where we are. We see those as the unusual suspects—not the normal expected champions and sponsors, the ones who articulate well, who disagree with some strategies, who are brave—but can work the politics that exist: the influencers.

It can help to take note of the number of conversations our idea is generating, how much people seek us out to discuss, who is following us on LinkedIn, who invites us to talk or to learn more. Let this be our gauge and effort focus, not how many people log into the new intranet or web page. Notice where the core message is taking hold.

Clarity in Positioning

> "The leader is one who, out of the clutter, brings simplicity."
> —*Albert Einstein*

Clear positioning is a subtle but powerful skill—especially in culture awareness work—where ideas are seeded quietly, strategically, and often under the radar. Borrowed from guerrilla marketing, it's about placing concepts in the right conversations, with the right tone, at the right moment not to launch them, but to let them land gently and grow. This technique enables leaders to test resonance, shape perception, and gather informal feedback before anything becomes official. It's a form of cultural prototyping: By positioning ideas early and lightly, you reduce resistance, build familiarity, and create space for others to co-own and refine the concept. Done well, positioning turns soft signals into strong momentum and transforms good ideas into great ones before they ever hit a slide deck.

In many organizations where we have worked it's almost inbuilt into the culture that you need to get very senior buy-in and have a snazzy PowerPoint deck to start doing anything differently or to question the status quo. There is often a slightly toxic dynamic of "convince me." We suspect many of those who work in HR might recognize this and hence why they are so grateful for legislative or corporate reporting changes to provide an external hook. However when we mentor leaders we talk about what is in their control to just do. It's vital in this period of raising awareness of cultural change you don't forget the simple power of your own opinion, words, and questions and that you build a hypothesis of what the culture could look like. Being aware of the data in your organization, being curious, and asking informal questions are a great way to navigate very rigid, set, and hierarchical cultures and are less personally risky that just launching straight in to a fully designed change program.

Getting traction is easier when the message is simple and easy to follow. In fact, when we are positioning our messages, simplicity can be quite positively disruptive. In the Western business world, we are mildly obsessed with complicated language, charts, diagrams, models, and stuff to describe change. We have seen 100-page slide decks on strategy.

Business, HR, and culture change is already highly complex, acronym central, and jargon-filled. Jargon is defined in the *Cambridge Dictionary* as "special words or expressions used by a profession or group that are difficult for others to understand." Once we've distilled what we think we need to do and why, at its essence there comes a point when we don't need more knowledge, more expertise, more people, a whole team to get there. We only need the idea. This is a good sign and one where we are close to breaking through.

Haesun Moon is a communications scientist, and her work is an incredibly powerful and persuasive guide here. Moon teaches how simple words and phrases unlock great potential (Moon, 2022). Take for example the word *suppose*. Moon argues that the word suppose can lift people from their dreaded future to their desired future. An example of this could be simply asking people in the organization, "Suppose we can get our culture back? What could that look like?" Or "Suppose we rekindle our purpose. How can we do that?" Learning how to use simple words and questions to the right effect is worth learning as we seek to build awareness.

By making things simple and positioning things in a way that bring others along we make it safe for people to speak about the ideas they hold, and this is ultimately what gives us further fuel for the change. When we catch people off guard with complexity by throwing lots of unfamiliar language at them, immediately we can make change feel clinical, which creates a threat response. Keeping things simple and not overcomplicated is a real lesson in leading change.

When we both worked in financial services in the 2000s there was a huge amount of innovative work underway. Lots was done brilliantly and still today way ahead of its time, but we did fall into some traps. We remember when we bought off the shelf one US company's entire catalog of competency definitions—there must have been nearly 200 competences listed in a book easily thicker than a brick. There was then a rather convoluted way to get clarity on the competencies you were looking to grow. Needless to say, although we in HR were super excited about all this—a sort of Argos catalog or phonebook of competencies, we are not sure they ever made it past us as no business leader had the time to comprehend it all. It is a good example of well-intentioned activity that largely goes nowhere because we wanted to show the world how complicated all this was and that we were rather proud of ourselves for mastering it all. Of course, this is all understandable—you've spent the money, you want to show your wares off, but it is a change trap. There is no need to fall in.

Simplicity has real power in building awareness. An example outside the organization is Rosa Parks' quiet defiance on December 1, 1955, which became one of the most powerful catalysts for the Civil Rights Movement. When she refused to give up her seat on a segregated bus in Montgomery, Alabama, her simple act of resistance sent a profound message: Injustice would no longer be tolerated.

Her refusal was not accompanied by a speech or protest. It was a quiet, deliberate stand against systemic racism. This simplicity made it even more impactful. Parks' action resonated deeply because it reflected the everyday struggles of Black Americans, making the fight for civil rights personal and urgent.

Her arrest sparked the Montgomery Bus Boycott, a movement that lasted over a year and demonstrated the power of collective action. Parks' courage inspired thousands to challenge segregation. Her legacy reminds us that even the simplest acts can reshape history.

The Multiplier Power of Dialogue

The final step to build awareness is to create dialogue and conversation at scale. The most human method to support new learning and seed new learning is to bring information and knowledge into a rich dialogue in groups to explore, debate, and challenge our own understanding and build new ways of thinking about the issues. Having the opportunity to challenge our own understanding and elevate our intuition and wisdom is the bit that AI cannot do.

This approach can feel harder than ever with new generations being more conflict avoidant. We need tools and templates to help structure challenge with psychological safety for people to feel comfortable to stretch and have a voice. For organizations with ever-more dispersed and remote employees, it is harder to ensure dialogue is a common place activity that fuels our human skills into our best work, so ensuring we maximize the available platforms and using the most dynamic functions of those will help. Dialogue is core to us keeping our human switched on and something that is reducing beyond task focus. Creating space for conversations is fundamental for activating a culture, and within traditional hierarchies it is within the power of managers to grant the permission for people to regularly talk beyond task. If we examined what regular opportunities exist in large organizations now for open conversation, despite having human-first values, we assume that they are often limited to employee resource groups, networks, and focus groups on a particular topic from our survey results but time given to "chat" is more limited than ever.

Dialogue is a powerful tool in cultural transformation because it provides a safe space for individuals to test ideas, refine perspectives, and engage constructively. When change is dictated without discussion, it often meets resistance; when it is explored through open conversation, it gains traction. Senior leaders who foster dialogue create a climate where employees feel heard, engaged, and invested in the evolution of the organization.

Dialogue also fosters understanding, engagement, and collective action. Through open conversations, individuals and organizations can exchange perspectives, challenge assumptions, and build empathy, making complex issues more accessible. Dialogue encourages active listening, enabling people to grasp the nuances of a topic rather than relying on surface-level information. It also creates a sense of shared responsibility, motivating individuals to take meaningful action. Whether in workplaces, communities, or global movements, dialogue helps bridge gaps, dispel misinformation, and inspire change.

Beyond just exchanging viewpoints, structured dialogue helps align teams with strategic objectives, turning abstract concepts into practical actions. Through meaningful discussions, organizations don't just introduce change, they embed it in a way that is sustainable, scalable, and widely embraced.

Advanced technology can bring masses of people together in ways that advance the pace of and improve quality of the conversation as well as importantly connecting across previously perceived barriers and creating global community. What's more, social imagination, where we build on each other's understanding through rich engagement, offers the chance for us to have the aha moments that are intuitive leaps in groups and that is innovation at its finest. Collectively we can be more advanced than on our own individually. With the depth of unique human experience, we bring together in social imagination for this purpose, we position our ability through this interconnectedness and interdependence as a core and crucial differentiator from AI.

So how do we then take this and empower people in a team to form their own opinion without being influenced and swayed by consensus and harmony? To prevent the instinct to force agreement, at this stage it can save time to focus on exploration rather than resolution. Encourage participants to share perspectives without the pressure to align. Instead of seeking immediate conclusions, frame discussions as an opportunity to learn, challenge assumptions, and refine ideas. Acknowledge that productive dialogue thrives on diversity of thought, and meaningful decisions often emerge from respectful disagreement rather than premature unity. We can set the tone by valuing debate over conformity—emphasizing that differing viewpoints don't signal conflict but rather a richer understanding of the issue at hand.

Peter Block's work in *Community: The Structure of Belonging* highlights dissent as a crucial element in meaningful dialogue and cultural change

(Block, 2018). He argues, and we agree, that dissent isn't something to be fixed or silenced; it's an essential conversation that fosters accountability and engagement.

Encouraging dissent means creating space for people to express doubts and reservations without the expectation of immediate resolution. Block emphasizes that when individuals feel free to voice concerns, they become more invested in the process of change.

Alex's Example of Dialogue Tool Design

Early on in my career I noticed the intrigue people have with psychology and the desire to use some kind of tool to understand themselves and others in a shortcut way, without doing the degrees and qualifications. Isn't being human in itself qualification enough? Having tools helps us structure the psychological language to appear more scientific about ourselves in what we do and don't know. This has largely fueled the psychometric market, where people get to envision themselves and others as colors with labels and boxes that help us predict how we and others will behave based on our personalities. Ultimately, they answer who am I and how I am similar and different to others. I decided to take this fascination a step further into the so what? I came across a dialogue mat that someone else had developed to structure a conversation for a group, so they had a physical thing in front of them, visually appealing, and taking a level of gamification to an in-depth conversation. I studied its use and application and further developed this idea with the underpinning of evidence-based research I relied on for my intervention design, EQ. In its most basic format, I developed a new conversation mat tool that is self-facilitating and guides a group of people through a positively structured conversation. What I found when observing its use was that having the whole conversation in front of the group without further surprise slides or questions in a focus group/interview scenario meant that people felt psychological safety so that they could open up and be honest without worrying about the next question tripping them up. If we included

(continued)

(continued)

more than five people, the magic number for groupthink, we always had someone who challenged and spoke up, voicing an alternative, unable to withhold a silence. When people were given a rating scale to assess their own level of self-awareness on a topic, they not only completed it and shared their initials but also felt compelled to explain why they chose their score. Open and positively structured questions felt comfortable for people to use to challenge themselves and others on both new topics and those they were aware of. This connectivity lifted off the mat and into rich and in-depth dialogue that created awareness among the group at pace. Within two hours 10 people could explore a new topic and develop their self and other awareness, their self and relationship management related to it, and come up with quick wins and longer-term actions they could take to positively improve it. I took this methodology and applied it to key conversations for humanizing work: how to motivate performance, to explore the PERMA pillars of flourishing (based on Seligman's [2011] research), to establish complementary strengths and offer strengths feedback in a team, to uncover our levels of psychological flexibility, to explore team flow and human leadership. Each fundamental topic was launched with a mat to open up an organization-wide rapidly scalable conversation. These were tools where through creating greater awareness people were also learning human skills in practice, listening, debating, rehearsing, and thinking out loud. These tools give everyone voice: They help managers hear honest upward feedback, they provide qualitative and quantitative data that can be compared with internal data for concurrent validity, they empower people to take action without waiting for permission, they help leaders understand what matters to humans at work and why engagement at scale does not need to be through a PowerPoint deck. These tools birthed from the need to create awareness in conversation at scale and pace, where there is no right or wrong answer but a platform to create shared understanding and human connection. They kickstart 70% of our learning and culture programs at all levels.

How Does Awareness Work in Practice?

Cultural awareness doesn't mean a fixed diagnostic. What it needs is courage to observe and notice what needs to shift, conviction, and high-quality conversations. We need to raise the importance of observation, noticing, data gathering, positioning, and ensuring dialogue—deceptively simple practices that unlock momentum at this stage. To build awareness at pace and scale, leaders must first have the courage to notice, to observe things as they are, without rushing to fix or reframe. This is how we gather real data, build conviction, and use positioning and dialogue to build awareness en masse and spark confidence in others.

From here, we move fast from sensing and scanning to shaping messages, testing ideas, and building learning-focused conversations. Positioning is key: By planting ideas early and lightly, we create the vocabulary and hooks the organization needs to evolve from within. It's low effort, low threat, and high impact. It helps us spot resistance early and respond with agility, not defensiveness.

Change sticks best when it feels like a build on where we are with who we have, not a wholesale reinvention. Big words like *transformation* can sound exciting, but they often trigger fear. By investing in awareness-building skills like noticing and positioning, we start organically, with fewer resources and more pace. We don't need a full cascade from the top, especially if it's not there yet. What we need is a few brave voices willing to ask different questions and act differently.

The best time to start reculturing is when the need is felt. And right now, many leaders feel it, but hesitate to lead. In a climate of cancellation, call-outs, and heightened sensitivity, even well-intentioned leaders fear stepping forward. But when leadership is silenced, the system can't rebalance. Culture stagnates.

Likewise, it's important not to derail the confidence we are building by overlooking the power of our own actions. It can often help to ask, "Are my actions matching the message?" Because without alignment between words and behaviors, efforts risk being dismissed as corporate rhetoric rather than meaningful transformation. We may articulate a vision for change, but people assess its credibility by observing our daily interactions, decision-making, and tangible shifts in the work environment. We can't for example talk about creating a culture of psychological safety with credibility if everyone in our team is scared to speak up.

It's possible to care passionately about reculturing but also remember another truism about real change—people don't simply look at what senior leaders say; they look at what they actually do. Study after study shows that most human communication is nonverbal. An Ipsos Karian and Box study (Ipsos, 2024) shows that people dramatically improve their belief in their company's strategy when they see senior leader actions, not just communications, and this jumps again when the conversation moves from corporate communications to team-level conversations. Action matters. People are wired to pay attention to powerful people's language and behavior and then copy it. If the organization isn't yet ready to act on what it says, don't say it so loudly. Save this for when there is momentum.

This is because we rely on social proof, the psychological tendency to take cues from others' actions to determine what is acceptable or possible. If an organization claims to be moving toward collaboration but we continue to operate in silos, people will assume the change is superficial. Conversely, when leaders actively model new behaviors, such as transparent communication or inclusive decision-making, the shift feels authentic and gains momentum.

So, as we go about building awareness, let's not forget the power of our own actions and approaches day-to-day to drive change.

And let's be clear: This isn't about listening to every voice in depth. This isn't passive. Leaders are under pressure to deliver, and the pace of change often outstrips the time available for full inclusion. Decisions by committee are slow, and not always informed by those with the deepest expertise. That's why ownership matters. Leaders must lead, decide, and deliver.

In today's dispersed, post-COVID reality, gathering the team isn't always possible. But starting smaller, seeding ideas, and positioning with intent allows energy to flow and change to spread. As awareness grows, so does alignment. The goal is to bring people with us, not all at once, but in waves toward a shared vision of what culture can become.

And here's the truth: Awareness never ends. It's not a phase. It's the pulse that runs through every step of the work. And as awareness spreads it's time to get organized about who is working with us on this change. Let's now take a look at the alliances to build.

11 | Alliances

Alliances are where all the groundwork done so far turns into movement. This skill, more than any others, helps create acceleration at the early stages of cultural evolution within an organization. Building nodes of trust and influence in the organization means the changes will spread more organically and reach further. Leadership alliances on culture establish trust, foster collaboration, and surface shared values, accelerating the alignment of mindsets across teams. When influential stakeholders align early, they become champions of the emerging culture, making it easier for others to adopt new ways of thinking and reducing resistance among employees.

Why Alliances Are Critical to Cultural Evolution

Strong alliances encourage cross-functional collaboration, break down silos, and create open channels of communication, all of which contribute to a more unified and resilient culture. During periods of uncertainty, these alliances offer stability and reassurance, acting as support networks that help leaders and employees feel secure as they navigate change. Organizations that prioritize alliances early tend to experience smoother transitions, deeper engagement, and greater long-term success in embedding cultural shifts.

At its core, this is human social skill at its finest; listening, empathizing, finding common ground, offering and inviting relevant input, encouraging, coaching, praising, and staying curious. Organizations are entanglements of people, ideas, skills, and futures. Within them, influential groups naturally emerge, and for cultural change to take hold, these groups must be embraced and engaged. Building alliances means recognizing and empowering others to contribute meaningfully from their unique vantage points.

This empowerment is how we leverage individuals' positions and relationships within the organization to create narrative and character links to the mission. Their trusted relationships, often built over years, become the foundation for cultural development. By tapping into these networks, we create bridges between strategy and lived experience, making the culture feel real, relevant, and human.

As the organization begins to clarify what will change and what will remain the same, early decisions start to take root. These choices of what to adapt, let go of, or reinforce then act as cultural seeds, subtly shaping how people engage with the change ahead. If this stage doesn't connect with enough of the organization's power centers, wherever they may sit, the transformation risks stalling or failing altogether.

In today's social media age, it's easy to mistake visibility for traction. A LinkedIn post might get hundreds of likes or a workshop might draw a full house, but these signals aren't always signs of deep commitment. This stage is about testing the strength of your alliances. We're building the organization's capacity to shift, so we need to look for cues that our alliances have the energy, influence, and perseverance to drive real change and sustain it over time.

It's also important to remember that organizations rarely have a single power center. Even in highly centralized structures, influence is distributed in complex, dynamic ways. We often cling to neat narratives about the dominance of the CEO such as tone from the top, but the reality is far more human. Power lives in relationships, history, and informal networks. Our role is to find these centers of influence, nurture them, and recognize the power we hold in our own position. As senior leaders, we'll likely be aware of where else power resides, and it's vital to engage those nodes with intention.

Relationships are part of this hidden architecture. Who's worked together for years? Who's in a personal relationship? Who shares a commute or has children in the same school or club? These connections form the fabric of organizational life. Organizational network analysis regularly shows just how extensive, and powerful, these informal networks are. We won't know them all unless we're in a very small organization, but we can assume they exist and shape behavior in subtle, powerful ways.

Collaboration is our ally. We might partner with fellow leaders to explore new approaches to team culture, support our finance team in publishing timely data, or sponsor initiatives aligned with broader strategic goals. We can encourage our own departments to map their work to externally benchmarked standards. There are countless ways to influence, and build coalition, across an organization and move it in a new direction, each one rooted in relationship, relevance, and shared purpose.

Evolving culture toward shared purpose and collective mindsets requires more than vision—it demands alliances that span both individuals and groups. When we seek to generate energy and deepen human connection, we're not just shifting behaviors; we're inviting people into a relational ecosystem where trust, reciprocity, and mutual commitment become the fuel for transformation. Individuals bring lived wisdom, emotional nuance, and catalytic insight, while groups offer structure, amplification, and resilience. Together, they form a dynamic web of influence that can hold complexity, bridge divides, and move culture forward with intention. Without these alliances, efforts risk becoming isolated sparks rather than sustained fire.

Alliances in reculturing differ from traditional change management programs in both philosophy and execution. Where traditional programs often rely on top-down mandates, formal diagnostics, and structured rollouts, alliances in reculturing are built on trust, shared sensing, and adaptive influence.

Table 11.1 shows the key differences between traditional change management approaches and the reculturing alliances skills.

Table 11.1   Key Differences

Traditional Change Management	Reculturing Alliances
Hierarchical: Driven by senior leadership with cascading communication	**Relational:** Built through informal networks, peer influence, and trusted connectors
Structured and linear: Diagnosis → Plan → Communicate → Train → Reinforce	**Organic and iterative:** Notice → Position → Dialogue → Adjust → Amplify
Focus on compliance and adoption	**Focus on resonance and cocreation**
Change agents appointed formally	**Cultural evolvers emerge naturally**
Resistance managed through training and messaging	**Resistance surfaced early through low-threat positioning and informal feedback**

In alliances, especially during reculturing, change is invited and co-owned, not imposed. As Joseph Norris's work on collaborative change management highlights (Norris, 2025), traditional models often fail in multi-stakeholder environments because they overlook the complexity of informal influence, emotional dynamics, and cultural nuance. Reculturing alliances succeed by activating trusted relationships, seeding ideas, and building momentum through shared meaning, not just shared tasks.

This approach is especially powerful in today's digital age organizations, where formal structures are stretched and informal networks carry real cultural weight. When alliances are built intentionally—with clarity, presence, and strategic positioning—they become the accelerators of cultural evolution.

Alliances and Resilience

Alliances are essential for building team resilience and surfacing barriers that might otherwise remain hidden. When individuals feel safe and supported, they're more likely to name the obstacles they encounter, inviting diverse perspectives and collective problem-solving. This shared alignment strengthens the core of the team and empowers individuals to carry their own messaging into other parts of the organization. As they test and learn how others respond to their voice, they become agents of cultural evolution.

Sensemaking often happens aloud. People test their thinking in real time, bringing ideas into multiple conversations throughout their day. This process builds courage and momentum and often sparks positive emotional responses from others usually beginning with agreement or admiration. However, without tangible materials or content to support the message, these moments can remain surface level. Admiration alone doesn't drive change. This is where the pull for structured interventions begins. By laying foundations of accessible knowledge across multiple channels, we create the conditions for action to follow inspiration.

As change gains visibility, those outside the base camp, especially individuals who feel threatened or excluded, may begin to assert themselves. Their reactions can take priority within the organization, sometimes manifesting as resistance or even sabotage. These responses often come in the form of sweeping generalizations that distort the core message. For example: "Have you heard what Alex is trying to do? Her budget's been cut, so now she wants us to do her team's work when we're already stretched." In large organizations, where time and effort are precious commodities, such narratives can quickly undermine early engagement and shape how leaders perceive requests for support.

This resistance can also lead to the severing of information flows or exclusion from key stakeholder conversations. When individuals are cut off from strategic dialogue, they lose the opportunity to contribute meaningfully to aligned work, weakening the impact of the change effort. Active stakeholder management becomes critical at this stage. It's often a politically charged space, where power, status, and self-interest can drive destructive behaviors. Navigating this terrain requires emotional intelligence (EQ)—our ability to understand ourselves and others—and strategic foresight, along with a steady commitment to the broader purpose.

It's very rare for a culture to change on one program alone and so part of the skill is not to push forward prematurely, ensuring first that alliances are stable and strong enough to support the next phase of transformation.

This can feel like a game of chess requiring careful pivots, strategic connections, and the ability to bypass persistent naysayers. People are rarely neutral, so a simple stakeholder mapping exercise can help visualize where energy is best invested. One of the most valuable pieces of advice we received was to ignore the strongest saboteurs. Engaging with them only fuels their resistance. Left without attention, they often unravel on their own, creating consequences that expose their behavior without our intervention.

To protect the integrity of the evolution, teams must remain open, adaptive, and attuned to feedback. Dismissive narratives should be anticipated and addressed proactively in communications to prevent them from gaining traction. Frequent regrouping within the core team helps maintain momentum and ensures the messaging, objectives, and purpose remain aligned. This is the moment to safeguard the cultural arc, preserving clarity and coherence so the change can take root and grow.

Dependencies of Reculture Drivers on Alliances

Shared purpose depends on relational anchoring. It doesn't emerge in isolation—it's coauthored. Alliances therefore provide the relational scaffolding where diverse perspectives can converge, challenge, and refine a collective why. Without trusted alliances, purpose risks becoming abstract or imposed rather than lived and felt.

Collective mindsets depend on psychological safety and co-commitment. Shifting mindsets requires environments where people feel safe to unlearn, reframe, and grow. Alliances, especially cross-functional and intergenerational, create the conditions for mutual learning and accountability. They help normalize complexity and foster adaptive thinking.

Creating energy depends on distributed leadership and resonance. Cultural energy is not just enthusiasm; it's the emotional and motivational charge that moves people. Alliances act as amplifiers: When individuals and groups align, energy becomes contagious, resilient, and regenerative. It's through these relational circuits that momentum is sustained.

Human connection depends on trust networks and emotional resonance. Connection is the heartbeat of culture. Alliances cultivate the trust and empathy needed for authentic dialogue, vulnerability, and belonging. They bridge silos, soften resistance, and make space for the emotional truths that often drive behavior more than strategy does.

In short, alliances are not just supportive; they're catalytic. They turn intention into movement, and movement into transformation.

Building Alliances

If we're new to a role or organization, or perhaps made the leadership transition up the hierarchy into a strategic role and not consciously focused on building alliances previously, it's helpful to plan how to build them.

Building transformative alliances, between individuals and groups, is both a strategic and relational practice. It begins with shared inquiry rather than assumptions. Inviting others into meaningful questions like What are we trying to protect, evolve, or create? opens space for coauthorship and reveals the values that lie beneath roles and titles. This kind of inquiry fosters mutual respect and lays the foundation for authentic collaboration. Simply bringing these into our existing meetings schedule whenever possible is a great first step.

Next, it's essential to map the landscape of influence and trust. This means identifying not just formal leaders, but informal connectors, those who carry cultural wisdom, build bridges across silos, and hold the trust of their peers. These individuals often serve as quiet stewards of change and are vital to forming resilient alliances. This is where we go beyond the obvious key players and look for organizational influencers who are more hidden. Finding these people means using the right hooks. The practice of positioning (described in Chapter 10) comes into its own here as the right messaging will bring out those who can help.

Looking for cues in what leaders and people in our organizations say can help build alliances because humans are geared to come together over shared ideas.

Purpose cues: Listen for statements such as these:

- "I just want us to get back to what really matters."
- "It feels like we've lost sight of why we're doing this."
- "There's something powerful in what we stand for."
- "I wish we had a clearer sense of direction."

These signal a desire for meaning, alignment, or reorientation—ideal moments to seed purpose-led dialogue.

Mindset cues: Listen for statements such as these:

- "People are too afraid to speak up."
- "I think we need to shift how we're thinking about this."
- "I wish we could try something different without needing permission."
- "People are stuck in old ways of thinking."

Energy cues: Listen for statements such as these:

- "Everyone's exhausted."
- "There's a buzz around that new project."
- "I'm not sure people have the bandwidth for this."
- "It feels like we're stuck in survival mode."

These help you sense where energy is rising or draining, useful for positioning change in ways that regenerate rather than deplete.

Human connection cues: Listen for statements such as these:

- "I miss the informal chats we used to have."
- "It's hard to feel connected when we're all remote."
- "There's a real disconnect between teams."
- "I just want to feel like I belong here again."

These signal relational gaps or longings, prime territory for building trust, dialogue, and cultural cohesion.

By tuning into these cues, we can build trust intentionally, and activate alliances that move culture forward without needing permission or a program.

Creating low-stakes, high-trust spaces is another key step. Whether through story circles, reflective prompts, or shared meals, these spaces enable people to show up as humans first. Emotional resonance precedes strategic alignment, and these relational moments build the connective tissue that sustains collaboration. Look for opportunities with your employee resource groups (ERGs) for these moments, where relationships are already bonded.

Kerri's Example of Alliances

One of the most impactful ways I have driven change was how we brought leaders together post global financial crisis at a global insurer. Sponsored by one of the most influential leaders in the business, we set up the culture action team (CAT), and senior leaders interested in supporting the work were requested. This group was deeply immersed in what we had found out about the culture so far and the members were trained in culture-building techniques and asked to build their own alliances. We held CAT summits and created a strong bond among the group members, creating trust and even a sense of identity. These leaders did more to spread the change we were bringing through than the formal power network.

Real alliances also require the courage to name tensions and honor differences. Whether generational, cultural, or functional, these tensions hold valuable insight. Facilitated dialogue and storytelling can turn friction that might exist into fuel, helping groups move from defensiveness to curiosity and shared growth. These can come in all formats, from engagement activities on current projects to town hall Q&A opportunities. Honoring differences is a great demonstration of respecting and valuing uniqueness.

From there, cocreating purposeful experiments enables alliances to take shape through action. Rather than pushing for immediate alignment, invite collaboration through small, meaningful initiatives. These experiments offer a way to test new ways of working together, reflect on outcomes, and adapt with agility.

Recognition plays a vital role in sustaining alliances. Celebrate not just outcomes but also the quality of connection, courage, and contribution. This reinforces the alliance as a living system—one built on trust, reciprocity, and shared purpose. Sometimes this can be where new alliances are formed, with groups previously unnamed or organized, and often injects new energy.

Finally, embed rhythm into the culture. Alliances thrive not through one-off events, but through ongoing touchpoints, rituals, and feedback loops. Establishing a cadence of connection ensures that relationships deepen over time and remain responsive to change. It's amazing how we know the importance of this, yet often forget to build it in from the outset. Aiming for longevity and consecutive consistency helps create a rhythm others naturally fall into as it eases the cognitive load to know someone has already set up a pathway forward for continuation.

The most effective alliances are built on trust, shared purpose, and mutual curiosity—not just shared tasks. They thrive when we engage early, position ideas lightly, and cocreate meaning before formal plans take shape.

Alliances in the C-Suite

No change stems from one person alone. Hence the reason even a CEO with responsibility for vision and strategy will get nowhere near executing the strategic priorities without a unified senior leadership team. It is sometimes the simplest issues that get in the way of a great senior leadership team from operating well in their own function and truly collaborating every day with their peers. Often superstar talent has been brought in with a sharply focused remit, for example, to implement a new tech platform or to create new customer evaluation processes, and the enormity of understanding the complex strategies of all their counterparts plans means we only focus on clear overlap. However the CEO often then is the only one with sight of it all, and becomes very internally focused to maintain execution of a clear strategy. Unless time and space is dedicated to sharing and developing plans together, the natural segmentation can remain and alliances can take on a new meaning. Beyond simply team collaboration at any level, an alliance is something much more: It's a more bonded relationship, a more reliable partner, able to speak for and represent one another on key topics as well as overall strategy on behalf of any of your team's plans. Too often senior leaders stay within their realm of technical expertise. Chief people officers (CPOs) and chief human resources officers (CHROs) are one of those key roles that naturally operates overall and is therefore a great center of alliance building activity. When a CPO is tasked to evolve a culture explicitly, the intricacies of doing so can be misunderstood, with others expecting more process-driven change management techniques. The strength of bond and trusted relationship at this critical point can be a key success factor in establishing workplace influencers at the C-suite.

If the right champions don't exist at C-suite level it might be possible to wait for the right leader to champion it from the top and not squander our efforts on someone who will get a worse reaction if done inauthentically, which will come back to us as champion of the change.

How to Build Alliances with C-Suite Influencers

When we are evolving a culture without the official remit, we have to develop alliances that power any change with a base camp of diverse thinking, expertise, and approaches to be able to light fires across any organization in a variety of ways. This includes upward influence to the C-suite at the right timing, often with early pilot data demonstrating initial testing and trialing.

Building meaningful alliances with C-suite influencers begins with understanding their strategic lens. Before initiating any cultural conversation, it's essential to grasp what drives their decisions—whether it's shareholder value, operational efficiency, innovation, or risk mitigation. By framing our cultural insight as a strategic enabler rather than a soft add-on, we position ourselves as someone who speaks their language and understands their priorities.

Once trust is established, use their language to build rapport, but gently expand the conversation to include human dynamics, cultural levers, and long-term adaptability. This helps shift their perception of us, from a values advocate to a strategic partner who can translate between operational goals and cultural outcomes. It's about meeting them where they are, then inviting them into a broader, more human-centered view of leadership.

Credibility is built through quiet wins. Rather than starting with bold requests, offer support on initiatives they already care about. Help them navigate team dynamics, interpret cultural signals, or amplify engagement. These small but meaningful contributions demonstrate our relevance and build trust over time, showing that we understand their context and can add value without demanding immediate buy-in.

True alliance building requires cocreation, not just consultation. Invite C-suite leaders into reflective dialogue with questions like "What kind of legacy do you want this strategy to leave culturally?" or "How do you want your team to feel during this transformation?" These questions elevate the conversation from tactical execution to visionary leadership, fostering a sense of shared ownership.

To influence effectively, pair data with story. Bring early pilot results, behavioral insights, or engagement metrics to the table, but humanize them with stories that reveal emotional impact. C-suite leaders respond to both rational and emotional cases for change, and stories make the invisible visible, anchoring abstract ideas in lived experience.

For roles like CPO or CHRO, it's especially important to position ourselves as a cultural strategist not just a process owner. Demonstrating understanding of the emotional architecture of the organization can shape the conditions for strategic success. This reframing makes our role indispensable to execution, not peripheral.

Finally, understand and leverage informal networks. Influence doesn't always flow through formal hierarchy. Whom does the C-suite influencer trust? Whom do they turn to in moments of doubt? Sometimes the path to alliance is indirect, through shared allies, long-standing relationships, or social proximity. Timing also matters. Watch for inflection points, strategy rollouts, leadership transitions, or cultural tensions, when openness is higher and influence can land more deeply.

Where to Direct Our C-Suite Alliances?

If we have built trusted relationships with our most senior leaders well, they will quickly look for direction on their responsibilities at pace so where do we direct this influential group in terms of cultural drivers?

While C-suite influencers can shape all four cultural drivers, their most profound and immediate impact tends to be on shared purpose. They are the stewards of organizational vision, strategy, and narrative. When they articulate purpose with clarity, conviction, and emotional resonance, it cascades through the system: aligning priorities, inspiring commitment, and anchoring change in something meaningful. Their endorsement turns abstract ideals into strategic imperatives.

That said, their influence on collective mindsets is also significant, especially through modeling. When senior leaders demonstrate psychological flexibility, curiosity, and openness to learning, it legitimizes those mindsets across the organization. But this influence is often indirect and depends on how consistently they embody those traits.

Generating energy and human connection is more distributed. C-suite leaders can spark energy through bold moves, storytelling, and visible support, but sustaining it requires middle leaders and informal influencers. Similarly, while they can set the tone for connection through relational leadership, empathy, and inclusion, the depth of human connection is built in the everyday interactions across teams.

Alliances in ERGs

As diversity, equity, and inclusion strategies continue to dissolve across Europe and North America, many organizations are shifting ownership and responsibility for inclusion into the broader fabric of company culture. Rather than being led by dedicated teams, this work is increasingly driven by ERGs, often operating with limited budgets and relying heavily on volunteer efforts. This shift places pressure on organizations to bring inclusion and belonging to life through everyday practices—requiring new ways of thinking, operating, and collaborating across functions.

In this context, alliances become essential. For employee experience and people teams, the ability to build strong, trust-based relationships is now more critical than any single initiative. Innovation in this space will depend less on formal programs and more on the quality of connection, influence, and shared purpose across the organization. Relationship building must become a core capability, especially as teams navigate cultural change without the structural support that once existed.

Language also plays a pivotal role. Terminology evolves over time, shaped by education, awareness, and lived experience. However, as meanings shift, certain terms may begin to carry unintended or negative connotations. This makes it vital to listen closely and adapt continuously, ensuring that language remains inclusive, resonant, and positively received. When resistance arises, reframing concepts or introducing ideas under more approachable titles can help maintain engagement and foster understanding.

Cultural evolution in large organizations often unfolds across multiple programs and multiyear strategies, typically spanning three, five, or even seven years. Within this landscape, the energy generated by ERGs can be a powerful internal force. Tapping into that momentum is essential, but it must be done with care. There is a risk, albeit rare, of negative activism that becomes so forceful it isolates the ERG's message and undermines its inclusivity. This risk is amplified when the activist is a strong workplace influencer, making it crucial to balance passion with openness and ensure that the message remains accessible to all.

How to Build Alliances with ERGs?

Building alliances with ERGs begins with presence and listening. It's not enough to observe from the sidelines; leaders must show up with genuine curiosity and humility. Attending ERG events, engaging in dialogue, and listening to the stories and lived experiences of members builds relational equity. This isn't about extracting insights for strategy; it's about being in the relationship, signaling that their voices matter and their perspectives are valued.

True partnership means coauthoring, not co-opting. ERGs should never be treated as implementation arms for top-down initiatives. Instead, invite them into the design process. Ask questions like "What do you see that others don't?" or "What does meaningful change look like from your vantage point?" This shifts the dynamic from transactional engagement to transformative collaboration, where ERGs become cocreators of cultural evolution.

It's also important to align on purpose, not just projects. While initiatives may come and go, shared purpose creates a durable bond. Whether the focus is inclusion, belonging, equity, or resilience, anchoring the alliance in a deeper why ensures that the relationship can adapt and endure through organizational shifts.

Offering strategic visibility is another key step. Help ERGs connect their work to broader organizational goals and translate their insights into language that resonates with senior leaders. Advocate for their inclusion in strategic conversations, positioning them not just as affinity groups but as cultural contributors with valuable influence.

Support doesn't always mean funding; it means intentional resourcing. Even when budgets are tight, leaders can offer time, access, platforms, and sponsorship. Mentoring ERG leads, amplifying their voices, and helping them navigate organizational complexity are powerful forms of support that build trust and momentum.

Sustaining the alliance requires ongoing feedback loops. One-off engagements aren't enough. Regular check-ins, shared reflection spaces, and collaborative planning sessions help maintain alignment and adapt to evolving needs. These rhythms build resilience into the relationship.

Finally, it's essential to amplify the energy ERGs bring while respecting their boundaries. ERGs often carry the emotional labor of culture work. Recognizing their contributions, celebrating their wins, and ensuring they're not overburdened is critical. Support should feel empowering, not extractive, fueling their mission while honoring their humanity.

Where to Direct Our ERG Alliances?

When building alliances with ERGs, the most effective cultural drivers to focus on are human connection and shared purpose as they form the emotional and relational backbone of any meaningful partnership.

Human connection is foundational. ERGs are built on lived experience, identity, and belonging. They thrive when relationships are authentic, trust is mutual, and voices are truly heard. Directing alliances through this driver means showing up with empathy, curiosity, and respect. It's about creating space where ERG members feel valued not just for their advocacy, but for their insight, leadership, and humanity. This connection builds the psychological safety needed for collaboration and influence.

Shared purpose is the strategic glue. ERGs often carry deep clarity about what matters whether it's equity, visibility, or systemic change. When alliances are anchored in a shared why, they gain coherence and momentum. Aligning on purpose enables ERGs and organizational leaders to coauthor change, rather than operate in parallel. It turns advocacy into strategy and ensures that inclusion is not a side initiative, but a core cultural commitment.

While collective mindsets and generating energy are also important, they tend to emerge more naturally once connection and purpose are in place. Mindsets shift when people feel safe and aligned. Energy builds when people believe their efforts matter. So, by leading with connection and purpose, you create the conditions for the other drivers to flourish.

Alliances Through Workplace Influencers

To build a core base camp of true allies, those who are not just supporters but believers and agents of change, we must move beyond traditional champion groups. We're now in the era of micro and macro influencers: individuals people genuinely listen to, emulate, and view as role models. Often, they're the unexpected voices, the unusual suspects, who carry quiet credibility. At this stage of cultural evolution, we don't need cheerleaders. We need people who can embed inclusive language and strategic projects into their everyday work, aligning with the deeper cultural shifts required. These are individuals who know what drives impact and what drains energy, and who connect with others on a fundamentally human level.

The rise of content creators and influencers in consumer platforms has reshaped how influence works and this shift is now moving inside organizations. Internal influencers are redefining traditional internal communications, bringing authenticity, creativity, and reach. The challenge is how to harness this influence to build alliances that support the organization's cultural direction. These individuals need freedom to express honest views through blogs, videos, or commentary, but that freedom comes with risk. One misstep can lead to reputational damage or cancellation. Many influencers may lack deep experience in navigating internal politics or strategy, making it essential to support them in aligning with cultural evolution. This is a new frontier for alliance building, and one that CPOs and CHROs must understand and act on quickly.

Some of these key influencers may have emerged during earlier awareness stages. Now is the time to amplify their voices as extensions of our own. This means replaying and reinforcing their contributions through the lens of cultural change highlighting how their work supports transformation, boosting their visibility, and helping them benefit from the spotlight. Once identified and amplified, they should be connected into the broader base camp community, where their influence can be shared, strengthened, and multiplied.

As part of this process, it's important to reflect on how others are responding to their efforts. Show the impact they're having, and feed in data-driven insights that build their confidence to lead through future challenges. Influencers bring excitement, curiosity, and emotional resonance. They are often masters of human connection in digital spaces able to distill complexity into powerful, relatable statements that hit home and spark reflection.

These individuals build trust at scale by sharing vulnerabilities that make them feel real, familiar, and likable. Their visual style, nonverbal cues, and curated environments create a sense of intimacy and recognition. They speak directly to the camera to foster closeness, and they stay attuned to global trends and omnichannel language to appear informed and relevant, engaging followers in more than they initially came for. Many avoid sharing personal values that could be polarizing, instead leaning on others' opinions or media-driven drama to spark conversation. This delicate balance of authenticity and strategic communication is critical for workplace influencers, especially those operating through digital channels like Teams, Slack, Substack, and beyond.

Gaining their commitment to the change we're leading is essential. These influencers represent the new organizational grapevine, a powerful, informal network we must learn to navigate and, when possible, integrate into our alliance-building strategy. Their reach and resonance make them invaluable partners in shaping the future of culture.

Influencer Verification

Generation Alpha (born after 2010) have grown up with a heightened awareness of digital risks. They've been educated to recognize misleading information and value fact-checking as a core skill. By contrast, many older adults who didn't receive online education or digital literacy training have experienced a surge in scams. Decades ago, interactions with strangers were more likely to be genuine, and elaborate fraud schemes were rare. Today, however, many individuals have had negative experiences with online platforms, leaving them more vulnerable to deception and distrustful of digital engagement.

Generation Alpha, by comparison, is inundated with media designed to capture attention and influence spending. Fortunately, they've been offered early awareness training that helps them navigate this reality with discernment. Gen Z (born between late 1990s–2010), however, may have endured the most intense initiation into mass online discourse often under the guise of "free speech," resulting in widespread issues like addiction, negative self-image, and emotional harm. The long-term effects are still unfolding. Yet, amid political fluctuations, there's growing awareness among parents, educators, and younger generations about what constitutes digital reality and how to protect it supported by legislation such as the Online Harms Act of 2023 in the United Kingdom.

So, what does this mean for workplace influencers driving cultural evolution? It means we must equip them with verified, reliable, and accessible information in all formats. By doing so, we shortcut their research process and allow them to focus on what they do best: translating complex ideas into fluent, engaging dialogue. Their creative genius lies in how they assimilate and communicate information in ways that resonate deeply with others.

Influencer admiration stems from a unique blend of strengths that appeal to our most basic human instincts. EQ is central to this. EQ develops naturally over time, shaped by life experience. Research consistently shows that lived experience is a powerful driver of emotional maturity. When influencers demonstrate this awareness through their behavior, they become more relatable, trustworthy, and effective in shaping culture.

In practice, this looks like sharing authentic thoughts, purpose, and mindsets with skill and intention. Influencers know how to reveal aspects of their true selves that align with their purpose, their why, as Simon Sinek (2011) puts it. This isn't about oversharing; it's about connecting personal authenticity to a broader mission. While the "bring your whole self to work" movement had noble intentions, it sometimes led to emotional overspill in professional environments, placing undue pressure on colleagues untrained to respond. Influencers navigate this with finesse, sharing what's meaningful and relevant without overwhelming others. Their centered self-awareness creates subtle but powerful connections to the cultural story arc, drawing admiration and curiosity from others. This admiration, rooted in healthy comparison, becomes a catalyst for growth, people naturally gravitate toward those who embody confident authenticity and want to learn from them.

Influencers are also deeply attuned to others. Their ability to notice, understand, and articulate universal aspects of human experience makes them highly relatable. When they speak, it feels personal even in a mass communication setting. This is when influence becomes scalable—when a video or message feels like a direct conversation. The moment they begin receiving personal messages from viewers who feel seen and understood is a breakthrough, an opportunity to embed key cultural messages with precision and emotional resonance.

Self-management is another hallmark of influential leadership. It's demonstrated through restraint, courage, and integrity, whether role-modeling new behaviors, facing conflict, or stepping into unfamiliar territory. Influencers often face provocation from trolls or critics. Their ability to respond with grace, rather than react defensively, is a powerful skill. These moments when values are challenged and emotional instincts are triggered, are defining. The way influencers handle public conflict, especially in organizational settings, is closely watched. When they respond not just with composure but with clarity and reinforcement of cultural values, they elevate the conversation and strengthen the message.

Finally, relationship management is the culmination of self-awareness, awareness of others, and self-control and is what enables influencers to build trust at scale. It's the fabric of connection that supports future collaboration. Influencers do this by responding thoughtfully, welcoming engagement, sharing humor, affirming others' experiences, and creating a sense of belonging. Watching how they cultivate this relational depth across digital platforms is essential for cultural evolvers and change agents. It offers a blueprint for how influence can be harnessed to drive meaningful, human-centered change.

Alliance Building with Influencers and Creating the Organizational Cult

> ### Alex's Example of Reaction to Alliance Building
>
> The phrase "drinking the Kool-Aid" was often used to discourage me from speaking about influencing organizational culture, especially decades ago when behavioral change was met with skepticism. The concern was that shaping culture might resemble cult-like indoctrination, forcing people into a singular way of thinking that suppresses individual diversity. But that's a fundamental misunderstanding of cultural evolution. As Malcolm Gladwell explores in *Revenge of the Tipping Point* (2024), true cultural change is not about conformity; it's about creating conditions where diverse perspectives can thrive within shared purpose.

That said, we must acknowledge the darker side of mass influence. The rise of social engineering, particularly through online alliance building, has shown how influencers can dramatically shift public understanding using clickbait headlines, provocative imagery, and high-conflict narratives. This power to shape perception is real and potent. But it doesn't negate the opportunity to harness influencer methodology for good. In fact, workplace influencers can become powerful agents of cultural evolution when their influence is grounded in authenticity, purpose, and human connection.

Recognizing the positive potential of workplace influencers is now an urgent priority. If the world beyond work is already shaping how we spend our attention, time, and money through digital influence, then the workplace must evolve to match that pace. Influencers when aligned with values-driven leadership can become the key alliances that guide organizations into a more adaptive, inclusive, and human-centered future.

Alliances Building with Influencers as Entertainers

To build meaningful alliances with workplace influencers, we must offer platforms that go beyond traditional organizational norms. This means granting them creative freedom to push boundaries that have long been held tightly by brand and public relations (PR) teams. In many companies, the brand is considered a prized asset carefully curated and fiercely protected. We've seen how quickly external celebrity influencers are dropped from brand partnerships when their behavior or character comes into question (Think of Adidas cutting ties with Kanye West or Balenciaga distancing itself from controversial campaigns.) These examples highlight the fragility of brand association and the caution that surrounds it.

So how do people experience teams work alongside PR and brand functions to loosen these restrictions and enable internal influencers to thrive? One example is live streaming organizational conversations. For some departments, this idea is terrifying—imagine employees representing company strategy live, without a script or the safety net of post-production edits. The risk is real: It only takes one poorly chosen sentence to spark backlash. In today's climate, cancellation can be swift and unforgiving.

Yet, if we want influencers to truly engage audiences, we must support them in bringing the entertainment element that people crave. External influencers captivate followers by blending glamour, humor, and relatability. They create fun, human experiences that draw people in. Inside organizations, however, the need to control the narrative often stifles this potential. But people don't want another scripted panel webinar or a staged fireside chat. They want authenticity. Imagine a leader talking into a GoPro while running a marathon, sharing their most exhilarating thoughts about future strategy. That's the kind of content that grabs attention, sparks curiosity, and makes learning feel alive.

To compete with the endless entertainment options available externally, organizations must radically rethink their internal communication channels. We need to offer more freedom, more creativity, and more humanity. Celebrities like Matthew McConaughey, Drew Barrymore, and Oprah Winfrey are already creating life/work learning content that blends insight with entertainment. They understand how to engage audiences because they come from a world built on storytelling and emotional connection. The question is: Can we re-create this internally?

Workplace influencers give us that opportunity. Not only can we identify those naturally suited to this role, but we can also develop others in succession building a pipeline of authentic voices who can shape culture from within. This approach is far more sustainable than paying $60–$100k for a celebrity keynote speaker who may or may not connect with the strategic journey we're on. By investing in our own people, we create influence that is relevant, resonant, and rooted in the lived experience of our organization.

How to Build Alliances with Workplace Influencers

Building alliances with workplace influencers begins with genuine recognition. These individuals aren't just amplifiers, they're sensemakers, storytellers, and emotional connectors. Acknowledging their unique contributions, whether through creativity, insight, or relational influence, lays the foundation for trust. When influencers feel seen and valued, they're far more likely to engage with authenticity and purpose.

Rather than presenting a fully formed change strategy, invite influencers into coauthorship. Their proximity to everyday sentiment and informal networks gives them a pulse on what's resonating and what's being resisted. By involving them early in the design process, you unlock language, tone, and framing that feels real to the wider organization. This shifts the dynamic from top-down messaging to cocreated movement.

Influencers thrive when given freedom, but they also need clarity. Offer them creative space to express ideas in their own voice, whether through video, storytelling, or informal dialogue. Instead of scripts, provide context, verified insights, and strategic framing they can translate into compelling content. This balance of autonomy and alignment ensures their message is both authentic and impactful.

Support their growth, not just their output. Many influencers are still developing their strategic fluency and understanding of organizational complexity. Offer coaching, peer learning, and access to leadership conversations. Help them connect their personal authenticity to the broader cultural arc, turning them from content creators into cultural catalysts.

Amplify their message with intention. Use formal channels such as town halls, newsletters, leadership briefings to spotlight their work, but also build informal momentum by sharing their posts, referencing their insights, and connecting them with other change agents. This creates a web of influence that's relational, distributed, and resilient.

Protect their credibility. Influencers walk a fine line between visibility and vulnerability. Be their ally when they face backlash or misunderstanding. Help them navigate conflict with grace, reinforcing their role as trusted voices rather than entertainers or amplifiers. This kind of support builds long-term trust and psychological safety.

Finally, measure impact through connection, not just metrics. Don't rely solely on clicks or views. Look for signs of cultural traction, are people quoting them? Are their ideas surfacing in meetings? Are they sparking new conversations? These are the indicators that your alliance is not just visible, but transformative.

Where to Direct Our Alliances with Workplace Influencers

Workplace influencers, when activated as strategic allies, have the most profound impact on generating energy and human connection—the emotional and relational lifeblood of cultural evolution.

Generating energy is where influencers truly shine. Their ability to spark curiosity, excitement, and emotional resonance makes them natural amplifiers of cultural momentum. Whether through storytelling, visual content, or authentic dialogue, they create moments that feel alive, moments that move people. They don't just communicate change; they embody it, making abstract strategies feel tangible and inspiring. Their presence can turn passive awareness into active engagement, especially when they connect cultural shifts to personal relevance.

Human connection is their second major domain of influence. Influencers build trust at scale by being relatable, emotionally intelligent, and attuned to the nuances of human experience. They know how to speak to the individual within the collective, making each person feel seen, heard, and valued. This capacity to foster belonging and psychological safety is essential for cultural evolution, especially in hybrid and digital-first environments where connection can easily fray.

While shared purpose and collective mindsets are often shaped by formal leadership and strategic framing, influencers play a vital supporting role. They help translate purpose into everyday language and behavior, and they model adaptive mindsets through their own evolution. But their greatest leverage is in energizing the system and weaving the relational fabric that holds it together.

What Do Alliances Look Like in Practice

Building alliances for cultural evolution is a necessary skill for reculturing at pace and scale. It's more than doing a stakeholder engagement plan because the alliances are ultimately anchored in stewardship, and we create a network of individuals who choose service over self-interest and act as trusted transmitters of culture. These are not just formal power holders, but people across the organization who demonstrate a commitment to shared purpose, relational integrity, and the long-term health of the system. As change agents, we may begin with a clear list of known influencers and established groups, but true stewardship requires reaching beyond the obvious and engaging lesser-known individuals who hold quiet influence and relational depth.

This phase of alliance building must be carefully tended to before accelerating change. While the urgency to move forward is natural, especially among those energized by the vision, skipping this foundational work risks leaving gaps in engagement and trust. Once the base camp of alliances is solid, diverse, inclusive, and aligned, these individuals become conduits for ongoing communication, sensemaking, and cultural reinforcement. They help carry the message into new spaces, test its resonance, and adapt it in real time.

Stewardship also means meeting people where they are. Leveraging existing events and channels while weaving in cultural messaging subtly and strategically ensures alignment without overwhelming. Novelty plays a role, too. Our human curiosity and fear of missing out make us receptive to fresh formats and unexpected routes of influence. When workplace influencers begin sharing key messages with enthusiasm and authenticity, it signals that the alliance is ready to move. Their engagement becomes both a thermometer and a transmitter indicating readiness and spreading energy across the system.

In essence, alliances built on stewardship are not just tactical; they are cultural infrastructure. They embody the relationships that make change sustainable, and they ensure that evolution is not just initiated, but carried forward with integrity.

The strength and range of our alliances, extending from the awareness stage and building on the personal and professional armoring work that's been done, is now our best source of stability as we reach one of the most exciting skills in reculturing—acceleration.

12 | Acceleration

> "The tipping point is that magic moment when an idea, trend, or social behavior crosses a threshold, tips, and spreads like wildfire."
>
> —Malcolm Gladwell (2002)

Successful movements of change are built on participation. When change feels exclusive or reserved for a select few, it inevitably loses momentum. But when many people are invited in, when they feel part of something larger than themselves, it activates the cultural driver of shared purpose. People begin to see themselves reflected in the change, and that sense of belonging fuels energy and momentum. This is what makes cultural evolution sustainable: It's not imposed, it's cocreated.

The acceleration stage is where reculturing efforts truly take flight, and harnessing it is a key skill to master. By this point, the movement has gathered support not just from known allies but also from unexpected voices across the organization. Some of these individuals will emerge as ambassadors and protectors of the change, while others will quietly carry the message into new spaces. This is the moment to shift from control to trust, from managing every spark to lighting a thousand fires. As new leaders and interpretations of the change emerge, we must embrace the evolution and realize that this change no longer belongs just to us. The cultural driver of collective mindsets comes alive here, as people begin to adapt, interpret, and personalize the change in ways that reflect their own context.

Acceleration is also the phase and skill of generating energy. It's both the go and let it go moment—the release of built-up momentum into action. It's chaotic, exhilarating, and often unpredictable. It's like a balloon that's come untethered from the string. Talks, training, workshops, and reflections begin to multiply. We start to hear of people rolling with the ideas and concepts and doing their own thing with it. The language feels like it is everywhere—in presentations, in meetings and on LinkedIn posts. People start piloting new approaches, sharing stories, and experimenting with new ways of working. The buzz is palpable. And while resistance may surface from those not yet ready, the overall energy signals that something real is happening. This is the cultural heartbeat of change.

Perhaps most important, this phase deepens human connection. As stories are exchanged and people take risks together, relational bonds strengthen. The change becomes emotionally resonant not just strategic. People begin to feel seen, heard, and part of a shared journey. And with that, the change process we've worked so carefully to build is no longer just ours. It belongs to the system. It's alive in relationships, the conversations, and the collective imagination of the organization.

The Momentum Effect

Once an idea resonates, it can spread faster than anticipated through social networks, informal conversations, team rituals, and word-of-mouth. This surge is often catalyzed by a perfect storm of timing, relevance, and emotional appeal. People latch onto ideas that reflect their desires, frustrations, or aspirations, and when they do, momentum builds. But this isn't just a communication phenomenon, it's a cultural one. Momentum is the lifeblood of cultural evolution because it activates and amplifies the four drivers that make change stick.

Shared purpose becomes visible when momentum takes hold. The idea becomes a mirror for what people care about, and that emotional alignment fuels commitment. Momentum validates that the purpose is not only shared but felt.

Collective mindsets shift when momentum reaches critical mass. Early adopters begin to model new ways of thinking, and others follow not because they were told to, but because they see it working. The idea spreads not just as a message, but as a mindset. This is where cultural norms begin to bend, and adaptive thinking becomes contagious. Momentum accelerates the repatterning of beliefs and behaviors.

Generating energy is perhaps the most immediate effect of momentum. When people feel part of something exciting, their emotional engagement spikes. They talk about it, experiment with it, and bring their own creativity to it. This energy is self-reinforcing and it creates a buzz that draws others in. But it's also volatile. If not guided, it can burn out or veer off course. That's why momentum must be stewarded, not just celebrated.

Human connection deepens as momentum spreads. The idea becomes a social experience, not just a strategic one. This is where belonging grows and where people feel not just informed, but included. Momentum, when rooted in connection, becomes a cultural glue.

However, rapid momentum also brings risk. Misinterpretations, unrealistic expectations, and resistance from stakeholders who feel blindsided can derail progress. Once an idea is out in the world, it cannot easily be contained. The skill of it comes in as we shift from gaining attention to managing it and ensuring the message remains clear, inclusive, and aligned with the original intent.

To prepare for the acceleration phase, we must build readiness into our alliances and think about the onward structures that will keep it in place. This means equipping influencers and change agents with the tools, language, and emotional intelligence to guide the wave rather than chase it. Helping them to imagine the organization once the idea is in full flight can help anticipate what to expect and how to guide it—then crucially sustain it. We know we're in acceleration when intentional conversations multiply, not just exploring a topic but actually doing something about it. This is when people start referencing the idea without prompting, and when new leaders emerge organically. At that point, our role is to support, adapt, and amplify ensuring the momentum translates into meaningful, sustained impact.

Capitalizing on momentum means protecting the core message while allowing for evolution. It means listening closely, responding quickly, and staying anchored in the cultural drivers that brought us here. Because when momentum is aligned with purpose, mindset, energy, and connection, it doesn't just move people. It transforms them.

Case Study: Recognizing Acceleration: The Thousand Fires at Liora Health (Name Changed)

Liora Health had always been known for its clinical excellence, but behind the scenes, something deeper was stirring. A few months earlier, the CEO and chief human resources officer had quietly launched a reculturing initiative rooted in a bold purpose: "Healing through human connection." It began with leadership circles and reflection guides, but now something had shifted.

Suddenly, the language was everywhere. A nurse posted on LinkedIn about "micro-moments of belonging" in the intensive care unit. A finance analyst redesigned onboarding to include storytelling rituals. A regional director started hosting "energy huddles," where teams shared what gave them life at work. None of this was mandated. It was emerging.

The movement had escaped the confines of the original steering group. A janitor in Manchester began hosting lunchtime "connection cafés." A skeptical compliance officer in Dublin became an unlikely ambassador, translating the mindset shift into audit protocols. People weren't waiting for permission; they were interpreting the purpose in their own way, lighting fires in places no one expected.

Workshops multiplied. Teams began experimenting with regenerative scheduling, peer-led reflection pods, and purpose-infused performance reviews. Resistance still flickered and some leaders clung to control but the energy was unmistakable. This wasn't a rollout. It was a groundswell.

And in the midst of it all, something beautiful happened: People began to feel seen. A junior pharmacist shared her story at a town hall and received a standing ovation. A facilities manager and a surgeon codesigned a "culture pulse" dashboard. The walls between roles, regions, and ranks softened. The change was no longer owned by the few; it belonged to the many.

Liora's culture wasn't just evolving. It was alive. In the relationships. In the experiments. In the shared imagination of what healing could mean together.

Preparing for the Acceleration Phase

Preparing for the acceleration phase of change should begin from the very first moment we start seeding ideas and building awareness. As we've seen in the alliances phase, every person who joins the journey, every individual on the bus, has the potential to tip the initiative into acceleration. Momentum doesn't always come from the most obvious sources; it often emerges when the right combination of timing, relevance, and emotional resonance is reached across the system.

To be ready for this tipping point, it's essential to ask ourselves a few key questions. Are we prepared to respond if someone asks for help or wants to engage more deeply with the change? What resources, conversations, or support can we offer quickly and confidently? Is our narrative clear and compelling, simple enough to be shared with a new audience at a moment's notice? Can we consistently articulate the top three things people need to know about this change?

Equally important is our ability to connect the change to personal meaning, a skill we explored in Chapter 9 on armoring. Can we explain why this matters to us, and why it matters to the organization? And beyond ourselves, could at least three people in our network, internal or external, speak to its importance with clarity and conviction? These questions help us assess whether the foundation is strong enough to support acceleration.

In some organizations, the acceleration phase is artificially constructed. All the materials may be ready, but no one picks them up. When this happens, it's often a sign that earlier phases of change weren't fully realized. The program team may find itself pushing uphill, trying to force movement rather than riding the natural energy of the organization. In these cases, it's wise to pause and revisit the groundwork, to reconnect with the purpose, reengage the alliances, and rebuild the emotional and strategic momentum.

A broken-down car offers a useful analogy. A driver trying to push a stationary vehicle alone faces an uphill battle. But when a few willing volunteers join in lining up behind the car, strongest at the back, they can slowly get it moving. At the right moment, the driver jumps in and starts the engine. Change works the same way. It needs collective effort, timing, and readiness before it can truly accelerate.

As we set up a change program or team, we must give it space to breathe. Let it find its language, build its alliances, and form a solid foundation. Only then can we move with the energy of the organization, rather than against it—and ensure that when acceleration comes, we're ready to harness it.

How Do We Know We Are Accelerating?

Cultural evolution is often not a linear rollout. It's a dynamic, adaptive process shaped by context, participation, and energy. The pace of change varies across organizations, and even within them, due to several strategic and human factors. Large, matrixed organizations may experience uneven speeds due to silos, legacy systems, or varied readiness. Some pockets may leap ahead while others lag. This is normal and should be embraced, not resisted.

As we develop our skills of acceleration, here are some of the signs the organization, or pockets of it, is in an acceleration phase:

- The idea or change program is dominant in conversations across the organization.
- People are doing something differently—conversations are happening in a different way or with a different focus.
- There is a feeling of pull not push on the topic or materials.
- New information is prominent.
- Our alliances are active in moving the change forward.
- Those who disagree with the change emerge and potentially disrupt progress.
- Spontaneous supporters emerge and change groups emerge.
- Stories are told about how someone is moving forward differently internally and on social media.

If this isn't happening then the organization is not accelerating just yet. If the idea is launched and these described changes aren't happening on either a big or a small scale, it is worth going back to revisit earlier parts of the change journey.

As we become aware of this process of change, it's possible to get a feel for whether the organization is accelerating gently or hard. A gentle acceleration would be similar to the examples provided happening, but in influential pockets. If it's accelerating hard, it is a change in the full spotlight of the organization.

> ### Kerri's Example of Acceleration
>
> At Aviva I've experienced that acceleration can move at different speeds—the culture shift toward customer centricity built steadily. We even summed it up using the song "this revolution will not be televised." But the change toward a focus on well-being was dominant and visible—a conference for well-being warriors was packed to the rafters.

Indicators of Acceleration

Let's take a closer look at what is going on in the acceleration stage:

- **The idea or change program is dominant in conversations across the organization.** When a change program becomes dominant in conversations across the organization, appearing on meeting agendas, embedded in strategic plans, and echoed by senior leaders and influencers, it signals that the idea has transcended its origin. It's no longer just a proposal or initiative; it's becoming a shared narrative. People begin to align not out of obligation, but out of desire to be part of something meaningful. The presence of FOMO (fear of missing out) is a powerful indicator that the idea has emotional and strategic resonance. It reflects a collective recognition that this matters, and that being part of it affirms one's relevance and contribution.

  This is the moment when shared purpose shifts from concept to culture. It's visible, contagious, and self-reinforcing. Others want to align not just because it's strategic, but because it feels like the future and they want to help shape it.

- **People are doing something differently—conversations are happening in a different way or with a different focus.** When people begin doing things differently, especially in how they communicate, it signals a shift in how they think, relate, and make decisions. The introduction of upwards feedback, for example, fundamentally reorients power dynamics and challenges long-held assumptions about leadership and voice. It's not just a procedural change; it's a cognitive and emotional recalibration. Leaders must learn to receive feedback as a growth tool, and employees begin to see themselves as contributors to leadership culture, not just recipients of it.

This shift in conversation from hierarchical monologue to inclusive dialogue is a hallmark of evolving collective mindsets. It reflects a growing openness, psychological safety, and shared responsibility. People start asking different questions, consulting more broadly, and engaging with complexity rather than deferring to authority. The organization begins to think together, not just act together.

- **There is a feeling of pull not push on the topic or materials.** This is a huge, sudden change that can almost feel as if no one will ever listen or make time to incorporate the changes, yet quickly the pull for input becomes strong:
  - Can you join my next department meeting to share?
  - Can you share a one-pager on this?
  - Can you put together measures to be incorporated into our performance targets?
  - Can you demonstrate how this works with our online skills system?
  - Show me how this affects our recruitment strategy?
  - Can I get rid of this part of our onboarding?
  - What are the five-year plans for this change?

  And it keeps coming; hence having a pack of evolving information/FAQ's that can be used and shared easily in response to everyone's asks is critical. Having time and space in the diary to attend many new events to be the spokesperson and key communicator helps. Resource is also helpful here! In large organizations it's a matter of asking for resource time from other departments rather than increasing the full-time head count of your own team, which can mean our people management time is stretched. Find people who can prioritize the change alongside their focus; running a codesign strategy meeting can help. Simply looking for all key points to align action and focus, create and collaborate in a similar direction.

> ### Alex's Example of Aligning for Acceleration
>
> When at Aviva working on people leadership strategy we connected with the customer service representatives and diversity, equity, and inclusion teams early on as they had ownership of the global engagement survey and dedicated resources worldwide. These had been functions that operated differently and separately from human resources for the 17,000 employees in the United Kingdom. This was an incredible network that already had significant expertise and experience in the challenges managers and leaders were facing every day and knew what would and wouldn't work on a local level as Norwich Union became part of Aviva with 27 countries and 65,000 people.

- **New information is prominent.** When a new approach begins to take hold and confidence builds across the organization, new stories inevitably surface. These may be celebratory or challenging, but both are signs that the culture is shifting. As people engage more deeply, they often feel safe enough to share experiences they've previously kept hidden. This emergence of new information is a powerful indicator that collective mindsets are evolving, and people are beginning to think differently, speak differently, and relate to change in more open and reflective ways.

  Stories about past challenges offer more than catharsis; they provide insight. They help us understand what didn't work, what caused harm, and what needs to be done differently. When we process this feedback with intention, we strengthen new initiatives and avoid repeating old patterns. This is how collective learning becomes embedded in the culture and not just through formal training, but through shared reflection and dialogue.

  Rather than shutting down difficult conversations, we must create spaces where employees can speak honestly and explore solutions together. Framing these discussions as opportunities for growth fosters psychological safety and collective accountability. It signals that the organization values truth telling and is mature enough to learn from it.

Change isn't just about moving forward; it's about integrating what came before. When we embrace honest dialogue and make room for diverse perspectives, we reinforce the cultural driver of collective mindsets. We shift from reactive to reflective, from defensive to adaptive. And in doing so, we turn past criticisms into catalysts for progress and fueling a culture that learns, evolves, and leads with wisdom.

- **Our alliances are active in moving the change forward and building communities.** When our alliances become active and communities begin to mobilize, the energy of change becomes unmistakable. Suddenly, the individuals we've resourced, coached, and quietly supported step forward en masse. It feels like a groundswell. The program expands beyond what we can track through project plans and workstreams. The movement begins to outgrow our original scope, and with that, it starts to leave our direct realm of responsibility. And that's exactly what should happen.

This is the moment when generating energy becomes the dominant cultural driver. The belief in the change is so strong, so contagious, that it spreads faster than any formal rollout. People are acting on conviction, not instruction. The idea has taken root emotionally and socially, and it's now being carried forward by a network of energized contributors. It's exhilarating and sometimes disorienting. The momentum can be so powerful that we forget the careful measures and metrics we put in place early on. It may even feel unnecessary to revisit them.

But this is where discipline meets dynamism. In the next attention phase, it's critical to maintain focus on the key measures that track and sustain progress and impact. Cultural evolution must be designed to endure beyond early success. This means focusing on building structures that can adapt and evolve. While energy propels the movement, metrics anchor it. They ensure that the enthusiasm translates into outcomes aligned with the organization's goals. Without this balance, we risk drifting off course or losing sight of the deeper purpose behind the change.

So, while we celebrate the surge of energy and the rise of new leaders, we also stay grounded. We continue to monitor, reflect, and recalibrate ensuring that the movement remains not just vibrant, but effective.

- **Those who disagree with the change emerge and potentially disrupt progress.** As change begins to take hold, it's natural for dissenting voices to emerge often from those who excel at analyzing every angle of a proposal. Rosabeth Moss Kantar wisely reminds us that "change is disturbing when done to us, exhilarating when done by us" (Kantar, 2004). The individuals who disagree bring valuable perspective; cultural resistance is often rooted in fear or fatigue. Working with dissenters requires empathy, not enforcement. It is true their scrutiny can also slow momentum if not managed thoughtfully but how can the person's dissent be brought into what is happening? This is where the cultural driver of collective mindsets becomes essential. Shifting how we think about disagreement, from obstruction to contribution, enables us to engage with resistance as part of the learning process, not a threat to it.

  When a new initiative challenges tradition say, reimagining a long-standing company celebration it's easy to default to legacy thinking. But the question isn't simply whether the change is "right" or "wrong." It's whether our current mindset enables us to reevaluate the purpose behind the tradition. Is it still serving the culture we're trying to build? Or is it time to adapt? These moments require fast, inclusive thinking and a willingness to explore workarounds that preserve progress without dismissing history.

  At this stage, disruptors are unlikely to halt the movement entirely, but they can make progress more difficult. We might see all parts of the organization start to enjoy the evolution but one area is behind. That's why cultivating a collective mindset, one that values curiosity, flexibility, and shared ownership, is critical. When teams are encouraged to think together, not just defend their positions, resistance becomes a source of insight rather than derailment. It's not about silencing dissent; it's about integrating it into a broader, more adaptive cultural conversation.

- **Spontaneous supporters emerge and change groups emerge.** As spontaneous supporters and change groups begin to emerge, we witness the quiet but powerful rise of human connection as a cultural driver. This critical mass often consists of individuals who may not be vocal activists or early adopters, but who are deeply influenced by the trust and relational cues within their networks. They tend to move with the emotional rhythm of those around them, relying on shared belief and social validation to engage with new ideas. Their participation signals that the change is no longer confined to formal leadership or structured alliances; it's becoming socially embedded. These individuals amplify momentum not through loud advocacy, but through relational alignment, modeling openness, and reinforcing the sense that "we're in this together." Their emergence is a sign that the cultural shift is resonating at a human level, where belonging, trust, and emotional safety drive engagement more than strategy alone. Nurturing these connections through storytelling, peer-led dialogue, and inclusive rituals ensures that the movement continues to grow organically, sustained by the very relationships that make culture real.

- **Stories are told about how someone is moving forward differently internally and on social media.** Storytelling is one of the most powerful expressions of the cultural driver human connection. From childhood, we use stories to pass on values, spark imagination, and make sense of the world. As adults, we continue this journey through films, books, and shared experience seeking deeper understanding of life and each other. In organizations, storytelling plays the same role: It connects people emotionally to ideas, values, and change.

When culture begins to evolve, it's often the emergence of new stories that signals the shift. These stories carry meaning morals, lessons, and reflections that help others understand not just what is changing, but why it matters. They humanize strategy, making it relatable and memorable. A single story told with authenticity can ripple across teams, sparking conversations, curiosity, and alignment. It's through these narratives that people begin to feel part of something larger than themselves.

As stories spread, they weave a relational fabric across the organization. They build trust, foster empathy, and invite others into the journey. This is how cultural evolution becomes real, not through directives, but through shared human experience. When people hear a story and see themselves in it, they don't just understand the change, they feel it. And that feeling is what sustains momentum.

What Do You Do If There Is a Need to Move Quickly?

In our experience we can plan when we'd like the acceleration phase to be—the organization might have a launch in mind or developed a careful communications campaign, and then sometimes it just happens to us anyway. No one can ever predict entirely what takes hold when and why.

Alex's Example of the Change Taking Its Own Pace

When we were seeding the idea at Aviva that people management had to include positive psychology, things moved fast. It went from a quite academic idea to one that had huge pull across the organization to embark on a strengths-based journey. In this phase new approaches to strengths-based recruitment were trialed and launched. We had hit the acceleration phase before we were ready. We didn't have broad communications materials, we didn't have easy to use tools or key measures ready to do, we didn't have simple one-pagers for managers. This is when things became very interesting. After initiating a pilot in our Norfolk call center, I was meeting with a manager in York to discuss a second pilot in his area, and he suddenly said he had a managers' "cheat sheet" on this already. I panicked wondering what he was talking about. Had someone launched something similar? How could they be doing the same thing we had developed? How far away from our design was it already? Then he said, "I was at a managers conference last week and someone from Norfolk said he had good questions for interviewing, and he shared a cheat sheet with me. It's awesome." I suddenly felt so relieved and also fascinated that the acceleration was already on us. People were creating their own content for the change we were implementing because they found it so useful and wanted to share with others. And apparently it had gone viral as it was so good! A major win. It was a great lesson for me early on to recognize that it helps to get short, simple, and practical tools and resources packaged up quickly so that there is no barrier to the acceleration when the timing and energy is right.

(continued)

(*continued*)

Similarly, I know one organization who was launching a large program to evolve culture who managed to create barriers to access that stifled the acceleration at a critical point.

When you are planning communications to be exactly right, at the right time, in the right way, with the right channels and asking people to view a document/video/link to more information it needs to be immediately available. In this instance a whole new portal was created full of research, recorded podcasts with senior leaders, quizzes, access to innovative learning, discussion threads for different populations (this was all at a point of lockdown in the United Kingdom when everyone craved learning and connection). A teaser campaign had already been launched, and this was the go point, but no one had realized the registration for logins had a 24-hour delay to access. Twenty-four hours may seem insignificant, but over 10,000 people tried to get access and were told to come back at a later point. The moment was lost. Despite further communications only about 3,000 tried again to access once they had logins authorized. That's 7,000 people who tried once and gave up. A huge lesson in getting mass engagement right first time. People don't want to go away and come back. In this world they are used to instant access, one-click buy, immediate chat response, and so on. Acceleration points are the culmination of huge amounts of effort and best-laid plans, so don't waste the critical mass point with any barrier. Think about the end user experience before releasing content even if you need to delay as a result.

Sometimes the acceleration phase comes quicker because of external events and contexts, which mean your idea has sudden prominence and resonance.

Kerri's Example of External Influence of Pace

At a UK regulator we took time to sow the belief that we would be able to hire tech experts from the biggest global platforms to take forward the new online safety regulation. There was deep skepticism that people would leave highly paid, prestigious jobs with bonuses and share schemes and join a regulator. We stuck at it though because these were the only people who had the inner knowledge of how decisions were made and the processes underpinning key areas such as content moderation and programming decisions for algorithms. We prepared and decided early that the major hook was going to be purpose. We couldn't offer bonuses, but we could offer legacy. We couldn't offer ping pong tables, but we could offer the knowledge you were stopping horrible things happening to people. We had job descriptions ready that were created from blending the strengths of similar roles. We had done work to ensure the look and feel of the organization wouldn't put people off, and we are created the narrative of why our jobs were different from the tech sector. This preparation all came in useful because suddenly we landed our first big hire from Meta, and it became a tidal wave. Then we were inundated with interest from very talented technology sector individuals. We were ready and capitalized hugely on that moment.

What Acceleration Looks Like in Practice

Lots of external activity is core to this skill area. Learning to be attuned to what is happening across the organization and leveraging momentum of the change being built is vital. If we are fortunate in the acceleration phase happening before we are ready, it's important to find ways to capitalize quickly. Rapid success requires flexibility and creativity. Be prepared to adjust strategies, respond to feedback, and pivot as needed without losing sight of the bigger picture. This might be putting on a panel discussion to give people content. It might be organizing a speaker. It might be producing a one-pager of the idea in concept. Whatever it is, feed the energy. Don't let it dissipate as once an organization moves in a direction it can be hard to get it back. Be transparent with stakeholders about what needs doing to keep momentum going. Culture evolves when people do things differently and so prioritize helping people channel their efforts into doing things differently, for example, gathering people in a workshop.

Likewise, don't forget the power of asking for help—this alone can bring surprising support and keep acceleration going. If we are working without resources, it's important to have conversations with those who can provide them. In the acceleration phase, movements thrive when leadership is distributed. Asking for help shifts the dynamic from "I must lead this" to "We are building this together." It invites others to step in, contribute, and carry the message into new spaces.

It's not always clear how long the acceleration phase will last—while enthusiasm and momentum are still building, the acceleration phase is still happening and feeding the energy is vital throughout. However, this is now also time to look at the next and final skill of evolving culture—attention—and how to maintain the effort so things don't fall back to where they were.

13 | Attention

"Progress, not perfection, is what we should be asking of
ourselves."

—Julia Cameron, *The Artist's Way*

Cultures are never finished. Our cultures may have reached a waypoint, but
they will keep evolving, and this will unfold through experimentation,
reflection, and adaptation—not flawless execution. When shaping culture,
it's important we reach the stage when it no longer depends on a single
champion but is carried forward by the collective. The skill of attention
kicks in when this is how the culture is, rather than something we are moving toward. It occupies unspoken space between people and is part of the
fabric of how the organization works through people.

Both the skill and phase of attention is highly strategic. Culture change
isn't a one-time event; it's a living system. Attention skills ensure that the
shifts in rituals, language, and mindsets don't fade into background noise. It's
the difference between a launch and a legacy. Traditional change management goes quiet on this—assuming everything that needs to be done is
done. But the quality of the attention we now place on our cultures will
determine how deep the evolution goes.

We need our attention skills when we reach the phase that our shared
purpose is now widely understood and emotionally resonant. People
aren't just following a directive; they're aligning with a vision they believe

in. The change feels relevant, meaningful, and worth investing in. Collective mindsets begin to solidify as new ways of thinking become normalized. Conversations shift, assumptions are challenged, and adaptive thinking spreads across teams and functions.

At the same time, generating energy is palpable. The buzz of experimentation, storytelling, and visible progress creates momentum that fuels further engagement. People are no longer waiting to be told; they're initiating, contributing, and amplifying the movement. And underpinning it all is human connection. Relationships deepen as trust grows, and the emotional fabric of the organization begins to reflect the values of the evolving culture.

When we're at this stage, our role is no longer to control; it's to empower. The moment to step back is a judgment, and it isn't when everything is perfect but when the wider collective has the confidence and capability to carry the vision forward without feeling like this is part of a change effort. The key is to shift from guidance to ownership ensuring the purpose, mindsets, and energy introduced don't disappear when leadership steps aside but instead become part of how the organization operates. The transition from leading change to embedding and sustaining it requires intentional handover, clarity of message, and trust in the system. It's about letting go, knowing that the culture is now alive in the hands, hearts, and minds of many. That's when change becomes not just successful, but self-sustaining. We move from talking to listening. From changing to sustaining.

This means moving to activities that help to reinforce habits and allowing teams to refine and adapt the change in their own way. Ownership drives longevity. For example, it's encouraging the culture to emerge in the everyday, such as in job descriptions, feedback criteria, meeting norms, and so on, as it's these activities that show there is no going back to how things were before.

Ways to Sustain

Over the years, there's a number of ways we've seen organizations sustain what they have built. Some of these methods come a lot later in any change than many expect, which is an exciting part of the reculturing skills because they turn so much on the head of the traditional change models we are accustomed to using.

Mastering Ease Versus Control

When a change that's been orchestrating for some time suddenly starts to accelerate at a pace, it's easy to fall into the trap of trying to control, contain, and direct where it is going. We tend to hold on when we need to let go.

Conversely, it can be easy to assume that now it's taking on a life of its own, we can fully let go and allow other people to take the reins and move on. It's like the phase parents face when their child reaches points of maturity—what do you do when they ask to walk to school with friends? Make their own way home from a party? Travel abroad?

Observing and developing an ease (despite what's going on inside) gives cultures space to stay evolved, stay adapted. Nancy Kline in her seminal book *Time to Think* (2022) reminds us that "ease is deceptively gentle catalyst." And, of course, ease isn't easy.

This point can feel overwhelming when others at a senior influencing or hierarchical level take on sponsorship and use new language and tone. This action can take on its own form within new areas of the organization without your involvement, and it can feel things are running away from us.

When early on we were building a base camp of alliances with key stakeholders, champions, and influencers, now we are now working with allocated resource either dedicated to culture or borrowed from change/ human resources/learning and development/leadership populations/ employee resource groups, and more, with initiatives reaching large numbers of people in the organization. This is the elevation moment when we know the change has knitted into all areas of the strategy and with many people beyond our direct influence.

We have seen some senior leaders use this point to reinforce their need to take on a more senior strategic-level promotion and create larger teams beneath them; however, this stealth team growth isn't required and can hamper a change influencing culture broadly by maintaining leadership control. This desire to control and own the change ultimately limits its reach.

We have seen that control is typically a huge issue for change evolvers. Letting go of how we achieve an outcome is the most important way to empower others to take on more accountability and find innovative ways to bring it to life. Letting go while also staying close to the outcome required means we take on a coaching approach, using positive enquiry to build capability in others around us.

Despite this letting go, part of the skill is that we also paradoxically need to remain steadfast and focused on achieving the overall outcome. Ensuring this golden thread is clear and communicated throughout helps us ask those curious questions of how it's being achieved with a positive regard. Reinforcing this focus by highlighting, praising, and sharing the wins that demonstrate real progress toward the outcome is good practice.

Good questions to develop skill in attention and to ask at this stage include the following:

- If we stepped back from active culture work, would the new norms sustain themselves?
- What scaffolding (rituals, systems, language) needs to stay in place—and what can evolve?
- How are we preparing teams to carry the culture forward without constant intervention?

Plans and Visuals

To successfully evolve culture, clarity and consistency are essential. A simple, shareable plan helps everyone understand the direction of change, while distributing the responsibility for messaging ensures that language and tone remain aligned across the organization. This shared ownership reinforces the cultural driver of shared purpose, where many voices carry the same message with coherence and conviction.

At this stage, visual branding becomes a powerful tool. Imagery, frameworks, infographics, and storytelling through design help translate abstract ideas into something tangible. These visuals don't just enhance communication, they symbolize a new way forward. When integrated into customer-facing branding, they signal a dynamic cultural shift that supports talent attraction, retention, and engagement. This is when the cultural driver of generating energy comes alive and when visuals spark curiosity, emotional connection, and momentum.

But this is also a critical inflection point. Without intentional follow-through, even the most promising cultural initiative risks becoming just another forgotten program. True cultural evolution takes time because culture is made of people, each with their own pace of learning, readiness, and capacity for change. Reaching everyone in a meaningful way requires patience, empathy, and strategic repetition. It's not enough to launch a good idea; we must nurture it until it becomes part of how we think, speak, and act together.

This phase determines whether the work becomes embedded or evaporates. By aligning messaging, empowering others to carry it forward, and using visuals to reinforce meaning, we create the conditions for culture to evolve not just as a concept, but as a lived experience.

Feedback Loops

To stay on track and maintain momentum we must set up continuous feedback loops within our alliances to focus on listening to how the organization is operating and working with new knowledge and skills. What is working easily, where is the demand, what is the pull, what is popular? This means going beyond traditional Kirkpatrick four-part model (1994) evaluating the levels of behavioral change and using internal data insights to test appetite, to see who is opening emails/documents/event information, and look at open and click-through rates in the same way we observe customer/ marketing data.

Following are some feedback loops that advance sharing:

- **Peer-to-peer feedback:** Encourages open dialogue and shared learning, helping individuals align their perspectives with collective goals. Not always easy to implement as people are more nervous than ever to judge each other and offend; however, a strengths-based platform creates the easy ramp up to build trusted bonds between peers that can withstand more challenging feedback over time.
- **360-degree feedback:** Provides insights from multiple sources, reinforcing a holistic understanding of team dynamics and cultural expectations. Maintaining accountability for this feedback by ensuring it is open and honest but *not* anonymous makes impact of learning from feedback much richer and faster because individuals can explore more about the feedback context and question what they

could do differently. This way it is used to strengthen relationships and collaboration rather than cause issue with whispers behind closed doors.

- **Real-time performance feedback:** Uses digital tools to offer instant insights, ensuring alignment and adaptability in fast-changing environments. People love feedback on performance if stats and data are available. The quicker people can get that feedback, the quicker they can respond and step up or adapt.

- **Storytelling and narrative feedback:** Helps shape shared mindsets by reinforcing culture through experiences, case studies, and success stories. Influencers are best at doing this well in short time frames, cutting to the chase of the feedback issue and tying it directly to the culture.

- **Reflective feedback loops:** Encourages self-awareness and growth by prompting individuals to evaluate their own contributions to the collective mindset. We often spend so much time looking forward we often leave no time to reflect and maximize the learning from this critical form of self-focused feedback. Journaling in some way makes this easier, and new technology offers us an array of options for capturing it with reminders at exactly the right point in the day to do so!

These feedback mechanisms create alignment, trust, and adaptability, ensuring that shared mindsets evolve organically and sustainably.

In one organization we ask our graduates when they finish their graduate program to get together and work on a project that researches key organizational issues and asks them to make recommendations to improve on them (including what this group of people can do themselves). What's important is we don't stipulate what the issues might be; we let the teams decide on these. Not only does this encourage people who are new to the workplace to look at organizational issues but also it tells us what the issues are from this group's perspectives and how they could further build ownership. In the past couple of years we have had presentations on how we support neurodivergent people in the workplace, how we are looking at the environmental impact of artificial intelligence (AI), how we collaborate effectively to build brand awareness, and how we raise awareness of mental health. This is a vital feedback loop and always tells us where our culture is hitting the mark for this generation and where it isn't. We'd recommend this to organizations to diversify how they get information about the culture of their organization and what might need some further attention.

Listening: The Leadership Discipline That Sustains Cultural Evolution

Listening for leaders stewarding cultural evolution, it is nothing less than a strategic act—one that shapes what endures, what adapts, and what is left behind. It means that rather than simply creating tons of content to engage our people and risk overwhelming them, we meet them where they are.

Case Study: The Listening Loop: How One Organization Made Culture Stick

When HorizonTech (not its actual name), a mid-sized engineering firm, launched its "human-first" culture initiative, the early signs were promising. Leaders had cocreated new mindsets for empathy, collaboration, and psychological safety. Town halls buzzed with energy. Teams began experimenting with new rituals—weekly check-ins, gratitude circles, and cross-functional learning pods.

But six months in, the momentum began to fade.

Rather than doubling down on messaging or launching another campaign, the chief human resources officer, Maya, took a different route. She introduced a simple but radical practice: listening loops.

Every fortnight, a rotating group of employees—from interns to senior managers—joined a facilitated session where they shared what felt real, what felt performative, and what was quietly resisting change. No presentations. No defensiveness. Just stories, patterns, and presence.

One insight emerged early: While leaders spoke of psychological safety, many frontline staff still feared repercussions for speaking up. Another: The gratitude rituals felt forced in some teams, especially where burnout hadn't been addressed.

Maya didn't just collect this feedback, she acted on it. She worked with team leads to redesign rituals that felt authentic. She coached executives to model vulnerability. She embedded a culture pulse dashboard that tracked emotional energy, not just engagement scores.

Over time, the listening loops became a cultural ritual in themselves. They weren't just a feedback mechanism—they were a signal: We're still listening. We're still evolving. This culture belongs to all of us.

Two years later, HorizonTech's human-first culture wasn't a program—it was a practice. And it was sustained not by slogans, but by the quiet power of listening.

Moments That Matter

The skill of blending learning into life experience and moments that matter is critical if we are to keep evolving culture at pace. People are consuming learning content in new ways and more so outside of or on the fringe of work. For instance, someone may feel more able to go for a run at lunchtime to benefit their physical and mental health if they are also listening to a podcast that is work-related.

Because we now move across multiple channels, crossover messaging captures our attention more effectively especially when we experience follow-me omnichannel marketing, where the same theme appears consistently across different platforms. The impact of this repetition to an individual is that it can simply feel serendipitous but is a viable marketing approach that works. And this goes for who is doing the marketing, too. As mentioned, we are seeing more celebrities and actors crossing over into the realm of self-care and leadership learning. This changes how employees consume learning and creates different expectations of the experience of learning from their own organization. The production, the glamour, the entertainment factors matter. Compare the Drew Barrymore show with an interview feature about overcoming challenge and a resilience webinar based in PowerPoint slides, which is often how people currently receive information from their organizations. Branded, controlled chat functions, where only some people can ask questions at specific times, scripted with prequalified questions, and people being there but with their cameras off, results in limited interaction, and therefore limited humanness.

We need to target information to people to meet them where they are and where they need it with the timeliest approach. For example, if we are overloaded in our own lives with the normal life duties and rushing around doing chores and errands, a timely text message half an hour before an appointment with the location, time, room number, and any reference information is what creates brand loyalty, knowing that someone has thought about what matters in the moment and how this event might fit into your busy life. For cultural evolution initiatives, we must be clever and do this thinking, knowing how a new event, skill, and opportunity might benefit the individual but feel like another thing in the way of and in addition to their existing workload. AI can assist with applying this at scale, learning what works and when, and targeting messaging at exactly the right time for maximum attention.

Removing Blockages Quickly

When such a large change is unfolding across many teams, we need to be ready to remove blockages as soon as they appear. In a world where information is instantly accessible, people are far less willing to wait and they simply move on without engaging. This means that when events or opportunities are created, rapid responses and clear escalation routes become essential. Strong alliances across the organization make escalation far easier. Although we aim to empower everyone to contribute to cultural evolution, some barriers can only be removed through escalation and cutting through the tangle of rules and processes that slow progress. Because hierarchical structures often make escalation difficult to navigate, it helps to identify and legitimize escalation routes up front. That way, when issues arise, they aren't met with confusion or delay but are recognized and acted on quickly. Clear communication, shared terminology, and aligned expectations across those alliances enable leaders to respond decisively.

One example is finding a login error after a mass communication has gone out. Identifying the right person to resolve the issue within minutes is paramount to not lose user interest. Most users will try to log in again after a single error, but drop-off rates increase sharply after two failed attempts—often up to 50%. Clear error messages, easy password recovery, and a trusted brand can improve retry rates. Frustration builds fast, so making the login experience smooth, supportive, and low-friction is key to reducing abandonment and keeping users engaged. This prevents setbacks that require further reengagement.

Human Nature and Storytelling

How do we empower all leaders of change to embrace the human to human engagement of it? How do we get learn about what really matters to people to know what is an efficient and effective use of our time?

Storytelling, as we have seen all the way through this process, is a great way to do this. Stories help by identifying common experiences that people recognize and reflect their own personal understanding of change. This creates connection where people feel closer to the storyteller, who is validating their own experience by highlighting and sharing their vulnerabilities, drawing in the listeners to their world. This human essence and spirit is powerful and can emanate out and reach all areas of organizations. Podcasting shows how storytelling has become a major component for evolving culture at scale.

Setting Up the Infrastructure for the Future

Measuring cultural evolution requires more than tracking engagement; it demands a nuanced understanding of how people think, feel, and connect. A codesigned culture dashboard based on what you are actually trying to achieve is more insightful and offers a dynamic way to monitor progress by aligning metrics with the core cultural drivers. You can go back to the work when we were building awareness and repurpose this to help you track the right dashboard components. In the past we have tended to look imperfectly for quantitative measures we can monitor. But as technology advances, especially AI, we can broaden this scope. In particular, tracking colleague sentiment can be incredibly valuable, and AI is making this increasingly easier for organizations to do. The right prompt can mean that data that once would have taken experts and weeks to complete can be done in a matter of minutes. This means we can ask more open questions of people and stop treating every employee interaction like a data-gathering exercise.

This is a brilliant development for those interested in reculturing because culture doesn't live in spreadsheets, it lives in hallway conversations, rituals, resistance, and renewal. Qualitative research, that is, non-numerical data, listens for meaning, not just metrics. It's how leaders spot early signals, decode energy shifts, and track whether change is truly landing or just being performed. Qualitative research is uniquely suited to tracking culture because it captures the lived experience, emotional nuance, and social dynamics that quantitative metrics often miss. Unlike surveys or key performance indicators, which measure what's visible and countable, qualitative methods such as written or spoken interviews and narrative inquiry reveal how people feel, interpret, and respond to cultural shifts. This depth is essential for culture work, where change is rarely linear and often shaped by informal networks, unspoken assumptions, and symbolic acts. In short, qualitative research doesn't just track culture, it listens to it, interprets it, and makes its evolution visible.

Purpose alignment reveals whether individuals see their work as meaningful and connected to the organization's mission. Collective mindset indicators help assess shifts in thinking, openness to change, and shared beliefs across teams. Energy levels, captured through pulse surveys or relational energy mapping, show where momentum is building or fading, which is critical for sustaining engagement. And connection scores, which reflect trust, belonging, and psychological safety, illuminate the emotional fabric of the culture. Together, these measures offer a real-time view of how deeply the culture is evolving, enabling leaders to adapt, reinforce, and celebrate progress with clarity and intention.

How AI Can Help

AI can really enable organizations and teams to ensure we can continue to pay attention to our reculturing efforts, long after the acceleration phase. AI is revolutionizing the qualitative research we need as part of this skill by turning what was once manual and resource intensive into something fast, scalable, and deeply insightful. For organizations navigating culture, leadership, or customer experience, this shift is game changing. Here are some techniques we have seen innovative companies use:

- **Automated thematic analysis:** AI can scan thousands of open-ended responses, interviews, or transcripts in minutes identifying patterns, clustering themes, and surfacing emotional tone with remarkable precision. What used to take weeks of manual coding now happens in real time.
- **Sentiment and emotion detection:** Natural language processing tools can detect not just what people say, but *how* they feel—capturing nuance, tone, and emotional shifts across large datasets. This is vital for culture work, where emotion often signals alignment or resistance.
- **Conversational AI for data collection:** AI-powered chatbots and voice assistants can conduct interviews, adapt questions in real time, and engage participants at scale. This makes qualitative research more accessible, inclusive, and consistent, especially across global teams.
- **Visual and voice analysis:** Advanced tools now analyze facial expressions, body language, and vocal tone from video or audio recordings. This adds a rich layer of nonverbal insight, helping organizations understand how people *really* respond to change, leadership, or messaging.
- **Speed and scale without losing depth:** AI enables organizations to process qualitative data 20× faster than humans—without sacrificing nuance. This means leaders can act on insights while they're still relevant, not months later.

Here are some further examples of how AI can help:

Armoring: Prompt AI to find the best available up-to-date research and evidence of the cultural evolution required and summarize it into engaging and simple collateral in multiple accessible formats—interview scripts, articles, blogs, videos, infographics. Prompt AI to create the business case for your own organization to make this shift aligned to your business strategy with compelling arguments.

Awareness: Prompt AI to design question sets/discussion tools that help change agents explore new concepts with people in the organization without forcing them into a position on them. Build some of these questions into new pulse survey mechanisms through portals and internal communication channels and analyze available data to determine when the organization is ready for new phases on the maturity curve.

Alliances: Use AI to assist in scheduling across multiple stakeholder groups to coordinate opportunities for connection in all formats. Reach and create communities of refuge for alliances to be the bedrock of the cultural evolution.

Acceleration: Create AI interventions that are aligned in language and message, supporting collateral and content that is engaging for a wide range of audiences.

Attention: We can use AI to create tracking across large datasets, identify patterns in data, analyze this against indicators set, and target where further attention is required.

When leading large cultural evolutions and maintaining attention to keep them on track over time, we need both huge passion for enhancing organizational performance and high levels of emotional support to face the day-to-day resistance of a large organization.

How Attention Works in Practice

Let's be realistic: Maintaining momentum isn't always going to be positive. The skills we highlight don't stop. Our work on armoring and alliances help us manage the inevitable setbacks that occur, yet it is very likely we will have moments when things feel like they are going in reverse. Many of us have experienced big leadership changes in the middle of wider cultural evolution work, which can feel very threatening. Will the new leadership support the efforts? This can unfortunately be hard, time-consuming, and emotionally draining. Essentially, we know that any change requires cognitive effort as we learn new ways of working, and we can no longer drift into habits that allow us some brain downtime.

In this increasingly always-on culture, not just at work but through our personal pursuits and responsibilities, society seems to crave slower, more mindful opportunities to engage with our worlds and avoid the burnout behavior of constantly pushing ourselves on and on for more and more, faster and faster. The AI assistant approach to work and life is beginning to alleviate the brain drain for the early adopters who learn to work with AI in a way that feels more supportive of human sustainability.

If we are to actually evolve culture at scale and pace, then AI is going to be the enabler. We need to readdress the fear of AI taking over the world and our jobs and reinvigorate our workplaces by use of AI to release the human pressure we are facing at work. AI could be the key to human sustainability and is likely to be our best support for maintaining the culture change we have influenced. For the work we have been exploring here we can increase pace and scale with AI in numerous ways. We just need to ask ourselves continually if this is what we need to do—how AI could help us.

Attention may be the final skill in reculturing. It builds on the ones before it, but it is not any less important. In fact, it's a necessity. When leaders keep actively observing, listening, and responding to the emotional and behavioral shifts unfolding across their teams, they transform change from a strategic initiative into a lived experience. Attention reveals what's resonating, what's resisting, and what's quietly rewriting the culture. It ensures that transformation is not just launched but is a legacy. As research shows, organizations that fail to attend to culture risk losing relevance, trust, and momentum. By contrast, those that treat attention as a cultural practice build resilience, alignment, and a future-ready workforce. In short, attention is how change becomes culture.

Conclusion: Rapid Reculturing at Pace and Scale

Culture is no longer a backdrop in our workplaces; it's the battleground and the blueprint. It shapes every conversation, every decision, and every signal we send. In this book, we've named the urgency, mapped the terrain, and offered a new mandate: to reculture with intention, at pace and scale. Not as a side project or a leadership trend, but as the core work of organizational survival, relevance, and renewal.

We've faced the truth: The old era is gone. The tools that once promised engagement now feel like bandages on deeper wounds. The world has changed irreversibly with diversity, artificial intelligence (AI), and social media having reshaped how we connect, contribute, and lead. And yet, within this disruption lies a profound opportunity: to build cultures that are not just reactive, but regenerative. Cultures that don't just survive change but shape it.

Reculturing is not about tweaking values posters or launching another initiative. It's about letting go of old assumptions, rethinking what drives performance, and rehumanizing the workplace. It's about activating four essential drivers: purpose, collective mindsets, energy, and human connection, and embedding them in your teams through five transformative skills: armoring, awareness, alliances, acceleration, and attention.

This is not a linear journey. It's a dynamic, living process and one that requires emotional resilience, strategic clarity, and deep human courage. It asks leaders to become sense makers, not just managers. To build alliances that stretch across silos, generations, and power structures. To tune into energy, not just engagement. And to hold attention, not through control, but through care, storytelling, and trust.

Reculturing is how we move from lost to thriving. From cult-like rigidity to collective wisdom. From transactional contact to deep human connection. It's how we future-proof our organizations, not by resisting change, but by embracing it with clarity, compassion, and courage.

But let's be honest: This work is not easy. It will challenge your assumptions, stretch your leadership muscles, and ask you to show up differently. It will require you to suspend outdated beliefs, to listen more deeply than ever before, and to lead even when it's inconvenient. It will ask you to build alliances in places you've never looked, and to trust energy as a signal not just a sentiment.

And yet, this is the work that matters most.

We said at the beginning that the biggest organizational decision we make is the speed we move toward the culture that enables humans, the planet, and AI to thrive. Because culture is not what we say, it's what we choose, what we signal, and what we sustain. It's the invisible architecture of belonging, performance, and possibility. Strategy brings us the ideas of where to go, the North Star but it's culture that gives us the means to get there. And in a world that's accelerating, the organizations that thrive will be those that reculture with purpose, pace, and humanity.

So as we close this book, the real work begins.

Ask yourself:

- What am I willing to let go of?
- What am I ready to stand for?
- Who do I need to ally with?
- Where is the energy calling me?
- How will I pay attention to what matters most?

Because the future of culture is not for your communications function to write about, it's written in relationships, in rituals, in the small moments that shape meaning. It's written in how we show up when no one's watching, and how we lead when everyone is.

Reculturing is not a theory; it's a philosophy and science-backed practice. It's the courage to notice what's broken, the conviction to imagine what's possible, and the confidence and conversations to build back what's needed. It's the shift from managing change to embodying it. From reacting to redesigning. From surviving to shaping.

And it starts with us.

Whether we're a CEO, a team leader, a culture champion, or a curious reader, our role in reculturing matters. Because every conversation you host, every alliance you build, every signal you send is part of the cultural code. And when enough of us choose to reculture with intention, the system begins to shift.

So let this be your turning point.

- Not toward more control, but toward more connection
- Not toward more certainty, but toward more courage
- Not toward the culture you inherited, but the one you choose to cocreate

The future belongs to those who reculture with humility, with hope, and with humanity.

The future is not waiting.

It's listening.

It's watching.

And it's ready to be recultured.

References

Abramova, O., Gladkaya, M., and Krasnova, H. (2025). The differential effects of self-view in virtual meetings when speaking vs listening. *European Journal of Information Systems*, Vol 34, Issue 2, 230–248.

Alzahawi, S, Reit, E. S., and Flynn, F. J. (2024). A legend in one's own mind: The link between ambition and leadership evaluations. *PNAS Nexus*, Vol 3, Issue 8, 295. https://doi.org/10.1093/pnasnexus/pgae295

Andersen, E. (2013, May 31). *21 Quotes From Henry Ford on Business, Leadership and Life*. Retrieved from Forbes: https://www.forbes.com/sites/erikaandersen/2013/05/31/21-quotes-from-henry-ford-on-business-leadership-and-life/?sh=551de100293c

Baron, J. (2008, January). *Actively Open Minded Thinking*. Retrieved from Research Gate: https://www.researchgate.net/publication/285693848_Actively_open-minded_thinking

Bashford, S. (2025, August 1). *The Call Centre Engagement Report 2025*. Retrieved from Make a Difference: https://makeadifference.media/culture/40-of-call-centre-staff-plan-to-quit-on-wellbeing-grounds-despite-being-highly-engaged-at-work/

Bestvater, G.-W. O. (2023, June 29). *BlackLivesMatter Turns 10*. Retrieved from Pew Research Center: https://www.pewresearch.org/internet/2023/06/29/blacklivesmatter-turns-10/

Block, P. (2018). *Community: The Structure of Belonging*. Berrett-Koehler.

Booth, L. (2025, February 26). *Economic Update: Uncertain Times for Business*. Retrieved from Commons Library: https://commonslibrary.parliament.uk/economic-update-uncertain-times-for-business/

Botsman, R. (2024, September 12). *The Vital Role Trust Will Play*. Retrieved from Fast Company: https://www.fastcompany.com/91189037/the-vital-role-trust-will-play-in-the-ai-powered-future-of-work

Bottomley, H. F. (2025, July 9). *Gen P Populism and the Playlist Culture*. Retrieved from Odgers: https://www.odgers.com/insights/2025-annual-people-culture-dinner-gen-p-populism-and-the-playlist-culture/

Brown, B. (2010). *The Power of Vulnerability*. Ted Talk.

Buchanan, A. (2024, April 23). *Benefit Mindset*. Retrieved from Medium: https://medium.com/benefit-mindset/100-mindset-definitions-a-critical-review-c315a1c27ee0

Buckingham, M., and Coffman, C. (1999). *First, Break All the Rules: What the World's Greatest Managers Do Differently*. Simon and Schuster.

Bureau of Labor Statistics. (2024, September 26). *News Release*. Retrieved from Bureau of Labor Statistics US Department of Labor: https://www.bls.gov/news.release/pdf/tenure.pdf

Cable, D. (2018). *Alive at Work: The Neuroscience of Helping Your People Love What They Do*. Harvard Business Review Press.

Cameron, K. (2021). *Positively Energizing Leadership*. Berrett-Koehler.

Cappelli, P., and Nahmeh, R. (2025, August). *Hybrid still isn't working. Harvard Business Review*, https://hbr.org/2025/07/hybrid-still-isnt-working?giftToken=6021307661754397792736

Casse, P. (2012). *Challenging Leadership the Skolkovo Approach*. Xlibris.

Centers for Disease Control and Prevention. (2018). Suicide mortality in the United States, 1999–2017. National Center for Health Statistics Data Brief No. 330.

Clark, D. (2025, September 19). *Economy and Politics*. Retrieved from Statista: https://www.statista.com/statistics/1207746/coronavirus-working-location-trends-britain/

Clarkson, S. (2024, January 22). *Why Purpose Should Be a Top Priority for Founders and Entrepreneurs*. Retrieved from HSBC Innovation Banking: https://www.hsbcinnovationbanking.com/en-gb/insights/growing-a-business/why-purpose-should-be-a-top-priority-for-founders-and-entrepreneurs

Common Cause Foundation. (2016). *Perceptions Matter: The Common Cause UK Values Survey*. Author.

Csíkszentmihályi, M. (2022). *Flow: The Psychology of Happiness*. Rider.

Deloitte. (2025). *2025 Gen Z and Millennial Survey*. Retrieved from Deloitte: https://www.deloitte.com/global/en/issues/work/genz-millennial-survey.html

Dweck, C. S. (2006). *Mindset: The New Psychology of Success*. Random House.

Edelman. (2025, March 10). *The Unseen Impacts of COVID*. Retrieved from Edelman.com: https://www.edelman.com/trust/2025/trust-barometer/report-covid-flash-poll

Edmondson, A. (2018). *The Fearless Organization: Creating Psychological Safety in the Workplace for Learning, Innovation, and Growth*. Wiley.

Elkington, J. (2024). *Tickling Sharks*. Fast Company Press.

Eubanks, A. D., Reece, A., Liebscher, A., Meron Ruscio, A., Baumeister, R. F., and Seligman, M. (2023). Pragmatic prospection is linked with positive life and workplace outcomes. *The Journal of Positive Psychology*, Vol 19, Issue 3, 419–429. https://doi.org/10.1080/17439760.2023.2230479

Farghaly Abdelaliem, S. M., and Abou Zeid, M. A. G. (2023). The relationship between toxic leadership and organizational performance: The mediating effect of nurses' silence. *BMC Nursing*, Vol 22, Issue 4. https://doi.org/10.1186/s12912-022-01167-8

Faster Capital. (2025, April 15). *Performance Metrics: Employee Engagement Scores*. Retrieved from Faster Capital: https://www.fastercapital.com/content/Performance-Metrics-Employee-Engagement-Scores-Fostering-a-Dynamic-Workplace-with-Employee-Engagement-Scores.html#:~:text=In%20the%20realm%20of%20performance%20metrics%2C%20the,as%20a%20pivotal%20indicator%20of%20or

Flade, P., Asplund, J., and Elliot, G. (2015, October 8). *Employees Who Use Their Strengths Outperform Those Who Don't*. Retrieved from https://www.gallup.com/workplace/236561/employees-strengths-outperform-don.aspx

Foreman, L. (2023, January). *An Exploration of the Thoughts and Emotions Associated with Goal Attainment*. Retrieved from Oxford Brookes Business School: https://radar.brookes.ac.uk/radar/file/235f7830-b303-41dd-b063-9fd91e8455a3/1/Foreman2023GoalAttainment.pdf

Frankl, V. E. (1946/2004). *Man's Search for Meaning*. Rider.

Gallup. (2025). *State of the Global Workplace 2025*. Retrieved from Gallup: https://gallup.com/workplace/349484/state-of-the-global-workplace.aspx

Gartenberg, C., and Serafeim, G. (2019). *Corporate Purpose and Financial Performance*. Organization Science.

Gladwell, M. (2002). *The Tipping Point: How Little Things Can Make a Big Difference*. Abacus.

Gladwell, M. (2024). *Revenge of the Tipping Point: Overstories, Superspreaders, and the Rise of Social Engineering*. Little, Brown.

Glick, S. (2023, September 27). *How Gen Zers are Reshaping the Healthcare Industry*. Retrieved from Oliver Wyman: https://www.oliverwymanforum.com/gen-z/2023/sep/how-gen-zers-are-reshaping-the-healthcare-industry.html

Global Wellness Institute. (2023). *Wellness Economy Statistics and Facts*. Retrieved from Global Wellness Institute: https://globalwellnessinstitute.org/press-room/statistics-and-facts/

Goffee, R., and Jones, G. (2006). *Why Should Anyone Be Led by You?* Harvard Business Review Press.

Goleman, D. (1996). *Emotional Intelligence*. Bloomsbury.

Goleman, D. (2007). *Social Intelligence: The New Science of Human Relationships*. Arrow.

Gomes, J. (2022). *Leading in a Non-Linear World: Building Wellbeing, Strategic and Innovation Mindsets for the Future*. Wiley.

Grant, A. (2014). *Give and Take*. Penguin Books.

Greenberg, E., Schaefer, E., and Weddle, B. (2024, April 9). *Tradespeople wanted: The need for critical trade skills in the US*. Retrieved from McKinsey: https://www.mckinsey.com/capabilities/people-and-organizational-performance/our-insights/tradespeople-wanted-the-need-for-critical-trade-skills-in-the-us

Greenleaf, R. (1998). *The Power of Servant Leadership*. Berrett-Koehler.

Gurdjian, H. L. (2014, January 1). *Featured Insights Why Leadership Development Programs Fail*. Retrieved from McKinsey: https://www.mckinsey.com/featured-insights/leadership/why-leadership-development-programs-fail

Han, H. (2014). *How Organizations Develop Activists: Civic Associations and Leadership in the 21st Century*. Oxford University Press.

Harrison, S., and Sluss, D. (2017). Newcomer idea emergence: An inductive study of sharing outsider ideas while becoming an insider. *Academy of Management*, Vol 2015, Issue 1, 12855.

Hayes, S. C., and Brownstein, A. J. (1986). Mentalism, behavior-behavior relations, and a behavior-analytic view of the purposes of science. *The Behavior Analyst*, Vol 9, 175–190.

Hayes, S., Strosahl, K., and Wilson, K. (1999). *Acceptance and Commitment Therapy: An Experiential Approach to Behavior Change*. Guilford Press.

Hogan, K. (2022, September 15). *Why Leaders Can't Ignore the Human Energy Crisis*. Retrieved from https://www.linkedin.com/pulse/why-leaders-cant-ignore-human-energy-crisis-kathleen-hogan/

Holt-Lunstad, J., Smith, T., and Bradley Layton, J. (2010). Social relationships and mortality risk: A meta-analytic review. *PLOS Medicine*, Vol. 7, Issue 7, e1000316.

Ipsos. (2024, September 23). *Wellbeing That Works: Tackling Burnout Through Leader-Led Change*. Retrieved from Ipsos Karian and Box: https://ipsoskarianandbox.com/insight/72/wellbeing-that-works-tackling-burnout-through-leader-led-change

Ipsos Global Trends. (2024). *Splintered Societies*. Retrieved from Ipsos Global Trends: https://www.ipsos.com/en/global-trends-2024/splintered-societies

Jones, R. (2025, July 23). *One in Three Young People Say They Feel Lonely at Least Once a Week*. Retrieved from Ipsos: https://www.ipsos.com/en-uk/one-three-young-people-say-they-feel-lonely-least-once-week-despite-three-quarters-saying-they-have

Kadence. (2025). *Why Data Storytelling is Essential*. Retrieved from Kadence: https://kadence.com/en-us/why-data-storytelling-is-essential/#:~:text=Memorability,after%20the%20presentation%20is%20over

Kantar, R. M. (2004). *Confidence: How Winning Streaks and Losing Streaks Begin and End*. Crown.

Karakulak, A., Başkurt, A., Koseoglu, G., and Aycan, Z. (2022). Worrying about leadership: Is it a liability or an advantage for leadership of women and men? *Psychology/Organizational Psychology*, Vol 13, 675522.

Keller, S. (2019, July 10). *A Better Way to Lead Large Scale Change*. Retrieved from McKinsey People and Organizational Performance: https://www.mckinsey.com/capabilities/people-and-organizational-performance/our-insights/a-better-way-to-lead-large-scale-change

Kellerman, G. R., and Seligman, M. (2023). *Tomorrow Mind: Thrive at Work with Resilience, Creativity and Connection*. John Murray Business.

Kelly, Z. R. (2025, April 7). *Grow or Go Why CEOs Must Act Now*. Retrieved from McKinsey: Our Insights: https://www.mckinsey.com/capabilities/growth-marketing-and-sales/our-insights/next-in-growth/grow-or-go-why-ceos-must-act-now

Kirkpatrick, D. L. (1994). *Evaluating Training Programs: The Four Levels*. Berrett-Koehler.

Klein, N. (2002). *Time to Think*. Cassell.

Kleine, A.-K., Rudolph, C. W., and Zacher, H. (2019). Thriving at work: A meta-analysis. *Journal of Organizational Behaviour*, Vol 40, Issue 9–10, 973–999.

Klinghoffer, D., and McCune, E. (2022, June 24). Why Microsoft measures employee thriving, not engagement. *Harvard Business Review*.

Kotter, J. (2012). *Leading Change*. Harvard Business Review Press.

Kübler-Ross, E. (2014). *On Death and Dying: What the Dying Have to Teach Doctors, Nurses, Clery and Their Own Families* (50th Anniversary Edition). Scribner Book.

Lavrusheva, O. (2020). The concept of vitality, review of the vitality related research domain. *New Ideas in Psychology*, Vol 56, 100752.

Lewin, K. (1947). Frontiers in group dynamics: Concept, method and reality in social science; social equilibria and social change. *Human Relations*, http://hum.sagepub.com/content/1/1/5

Lewis, S. L., and Maslin, M. A. (2018). *The Human Planet: How We Created the Anthropocene*. Penguin Books.

Lysova, E. I., Allan, B. A., Dik, B. J., Duffy, R. D., and Steger, M. F. (2018). Fostering meaningful work in organizations. *Journal of Organizational Behavior*, Vol 110, 374–389.

MacLeod, D., and Clarke, N. (2009). *Engaging for Success: Enhancing Performance Through Employee Engagement*. Retrieved from Dera IOE: https://dera.ioe.ac.uk/id/eprint/1810/1/file52215.pdf

Macy, J., and Johnstone, C. (2012). *Active Hope: How to Face the Mess We're in Without Going Crazy*. New World Library.

Malnight, T., Buche, I., and Dhanaraj, C. (2017). Competing on social purpose. *Harvard Business Review*.

Mankins, M., and Garton, E. (2015). Engaging your employees is good, but don't stop there. *Harvard Business Review*.

Maor, K. S. (2024, June 17). *People and Organizational Performance*. Retrieved from McKinsey: https://www.mckinsey.com/capabilities/people-and-organizational-performance/our-insights/the-inside-out-leadership-journey-how-personal-growth-creates-the-path-to-success

Mayer, H., Yee, L., Chui, M., and Roberts, R. (2025, January 28). *Superagency in the Workplace: Empowering People to Unlock AI's Full Potential*. Retrieved from McKinsey Insights: https://www.mckinsey.com/capabilities/mckinsey-digital/our-insights/superagency-in-the-workplace-empowering-people-to-unlock-ais-full-potential-at-work

McCrae, N., Gettings, S., and Purssell, E. (2017). Social media and depressive symptoms in childhood and adolescence: A systematic review. *Adolescent Research and Review*, Vol 2, 315–330.

McKinsey. (2020, April 22). *McKinsey Quarterly Purpose: Shifting from Why to How*. Retrieved from McKinsey: people and organizational performance: https://www.mckinsey.com/capabilities/people-and-organizational-performance/our-insights/purpose-shifting-from-why-to-how

Medlama, M., Vianney, L. S., Piring, R., Sentosa, I., and Annamalah, S. (2025). The impact of artificial intelligence on leadership decision-making: Opportunities and challenges. *Communications on Applied Nonlinear Analysis*, Vol 32, Issue 9s, 1878.

Ministry of Justice. (2025, March 13). *Statistics*. Retrieved from Gov.uk: https://www.gov.uk/government/statistics/tribunals-statistics-quarterly-october-to-december-2024/tribunal-statistics-quarterly-october-to-december-2024

Miron, O., Yu, K. H., Wilf-Miron, R., and Kohane, I. S. (2019). Suicide rates among adolescents and young adults in the United States, 2000–2017. *JAMA*, Vol 321, Issue 23, 2362–2364.

Moon, H. (2022). *Coaching A-Z: The Extraordinary Power of Ordinary Words*. Page Two Books.

Mojtabai, R., Olfson, M., and Han, B. (2016). National trends in the prevalence and treatment of depression in adolescents and young adults. *Pediatrics*, Vol 138, Issue 6, e20161878.

Morgenstern, J. (1998). *Organizing from the Inside Out*. Henry Holt and Company.

Murray, B. (2025, April 11). *Business. Forbes*. https://www.forbes.com/sites/conormurray/2025/04/11/ibm-reportedly-walks-back-diversity-policies-citing-inherent-tensions-here-are-all-the-companies-rolling-back-dei-programs/

Norris, J. (2025, July 23). *Aligned for Transformation: Collaborative Approaches to Change Management in Alliances*. Retrieved from https://josephcnorris.com/aligned-for-transformation/

Onyemelukwe, I. C., Ferreira, J. A. V., and Ramos, A. L. (2023). Human energy management in industry: A systematic review of organizational strategies to reinforce workforce energy. *Sustainability*, Vol 15, Issue 17, 13202.

Owolabi, G. (2018). Overcoming the human energy crisis. *People First Magazine*, Vol 7, 40–43.

Obama, M. (2018). *Becoming*. Crown.

Patterson, K., Grenny, J., McMillan, R., and Switzler, A. (2002). *Crucial Conversations: Tools for Talking When Stakes Are High*. McGraw-Hill.

People Insight. (2025). *Organisational Change: Why Do So Many People Hate It?* Retrieved from https://peopleinsight.co.uk/why-organisational-change-so-hard/

Pink, D. H. (2009). *Drive: The Surprising Truth About What Motivates Us*. Riverhead Books.

Qualtrics. (2025). *What Are Organisational Core Values?* Retrieved from Qualtrics Employee Experience: https://www.qualtrics.com/en-gb/experience-management/employee/organisational-core-values/#:~:text=What%20are%20organisational%20core%20values,customers%2C%20partnerships%2C%20and%20stakeholders

Ratner, K., Hill, P., and Bronk, K. (2022). Purpose-driven prospection: The role of purpose in future-oriented thinking and planning. *Journal of Positive Psychology*, Vol 17, Issue 5, 631–643.

Robert Walters. (2024, September 23). *News Blog*. Retrieved from Robert Walters: https://www.robertwalters.co.uk/insights/news/blog/conscious-unbossing.html

Rosenberg, L., Schumann, H., Dishop, C., Willcox, G., Woolley, A., and Mani, G. (2025). Large-Scale Group Brainstorming and Deliberation Using Swarm Intelligence and Generative AI. *27th International Conference on Enterprise Information Systems*. Science and Technology Publications.

Sayed, N. (2022, June 26). *A Quarterly Review of Socialist Theory*. Retrieved from International Socialism Journal: https://isj.org.uk/what-did-blm-achieve/

Scanlon, K. (2024). *In this Economy: How Money and Markets Really Work*. Ebury Edge.

Scharmer, C. O. (2016). *Theory U*. Berrett-Koehler.

Scharmer, C. O., and Kaufer, K. (2007). *Presencing: 7 Practices for Transforming Self, Society, and Business*. Berrett-Koehler.

Schein, E. (2016). *Organizational Culture and Leadership* (5th Edition). Wiley.

Schippers, M. C., and Hogenes, R. (2011). Energy management of people in organizations: A review and research agenda. *Journal of Business Psychology*, Vol 26, 193–203.

Schwartz, T. C. M. (2007, October). Manage your energy, not your time. *Harvard Business Review*.

Seligman, M. E. P. (2011). *Flourish: A Visionary New Understanding of Happiness and Well-Being*. Free Press.

Seligman, M. E. P., Railton, P., Baumeister, R. F., and Sripada, C. (2016). *Homo Prospectus*. Oxford University Press.

Senge, P. (2006). *The Fifth Discipline: The Art and Practice of the Learning Organization* (2nd Edition). Random House Business.

Sinek, S. (2011). *Start with Why: How Great Leaders Inspire Everyone to Take Action*. Penguin.

Statista. (2025). *Daily Time Spent on Social Networking by Internet Users Worldwide from 2012 to 2025*. Retrieved from https://Statista.com/statistics/433871/daily-social-media-usage-worldwide/

Training Industry. (2024). *Training Industry.com Learning Services and Outsourcing*. Retrieved from Training Industry: https://trainingindustry.com/wiki/learning-services-and-outsourcing/size-of-training-industry/

Twenge, J. M., Joiner, T. E., Rogers, M. L., and Martin, G. N. (2018). Increases in depressive symptoms, suicide-related outcomes, and suicide rates among U.S. adolescents after 2010 and links to increased new media screen time. *Clinical Psychological Science*, Vol 6, Issue 1, 3–17.

Tyler, E. B. (1871). *Primitive Culture*. Cambridge University Press.

UKG. (2023). *Navigating the Human Energy Crisis; Optimizing Organizational Plasticity; and the Gen X Effect*. Author.

USA News Independent. (2025, January 2). *Why It Seems Like All of America's Chains Are Closing*. Retrieved from USA News Independent: https://www.usanewsindependent.com/business/why-it-seems-like-all-of-americas-chains-are-closing-2188/

Vaknin, S. (2025, February 5). *How Self Mediates External and Internal Realities*. Retrieved from https://vaknin-talks.com/transcripts/How_Self_Mediates_External_and_Internal_Realities/

Vilhauer, M. (2025, June 26). Building self-awareness: Why it's more than looking inward. *Psychology Today*. https://www.psychologytoday.com/us/blog/everyday-resilience/202506/building-self-awareness-why-its-more-than-looking-inward

Vitasek, K. (2022, March 10). Why collaboration yields improved productivity (and the science behind it). *Forbes*. https://www.forbes.com/sites/katevitasek/2022/03/08/why-collaboration-yields-improved-productivity-and-the-science-behind-it/

Vogel, B., Raes, A. M. L., and Bruch, H. (2022). Mapping and managing productive organizational energy over time: The Energy Pattern Explorer tool. *Long Range Planning*, Vol 55, Issue 6, 102213.

Watson Jr., T. J. (1962). *IBM History Business Beliefs*. Retrieved from IBM. com: https://www.ibm.com/downloads/documents/us-en/10c31775c6d400e8

Walker, B., and Soule, S. (2017). *Changing Company Culture Requires a Movement, Not a Mandate*. Harvard Business Review Press.

Wellness Creative Company. (2025). *Latest Health and Wellness Industry Stats*. Retrieved from Wellness Creatives: https://www.wellnesscreatives.com/wellness-industry-statistics/#:~:text=Let's%20start%20by%20looking%20at,%5BWellness%20Creative%20Co.%5D

Wheatley, M. (2006). *Leadership and the New Science: Discovering Order in a Chaotic World* (3rd Edition). Berrett-Koehler.

Wheatley, M. (2023, November 27). Who Do We Choose to Be with Margaret Wheatley. (I. Delio, Interviewer)

Wheatley, M. (2024). *Restoring Sanity*. Berrett-Koehler.

Yang, A. (2013). *Academia, Review of Tuckman's Model*. Retrieved from https://doi.org/10.1080/13678861003589099

Zao-Sanders, M. (2025, April 9). How people are really using gen AI in 2025. *Harvard Business Review*.

Acknowledgments

This work reflects the cumulative insight, dedication, and support of many individuals, and we are pleased to acknowledge their contributions. Although responsibility for the final text rests with us, the ideas presented here have been distilled from nearly 50 years of shared professional experience gained from organizations in all industries, public and private sector, across more than 100 countries of the world. The lessons captured in these pages are the product of long practice, sustained reflection, and the steady accumulation of insight gained through real work in real settings.

We are especially grateful to the colleagues, our teams, collaborators, and partners who have walked alongside us over the decades. Their willingness to engage deeply, challenge our assumptions, and explore emerging ideas in the midst of practical demands has shaped our thinking in profound ways. The concepts we developed here owe much to those who modeled integrity, curiosity, and commitment in the environments where we worked together.

We also wish to express our appreciation to the many practitioners and leaders who allowed us to learn from their day-to-day realities. Their openness in sharing both successes and setbacks provided essential grounding for the themes explored in this work. The insights we have drawn from these experiences are rooted not in theory but in the hard-won lessons of practice and daily responsibility for making it happen.

To the friends, colleagues, and mentors who have offered steady encouragement throughout this long journey, we extend our sincere thanks. Their perspective, patience, and confidence have supported us through periods of transition, challenge, and renewal.

To the professional bodies that have embraced us: the Chartered Institute of Personnel Development, Association of Business Psychology, British Psychological Society, Institute of Directors in the United Kingdom, International Positive Psychology Association, WeConnect International, The Lodis Forum, Wellbeing at Work, HR Leaders, British American Business Council, and in Texas: HR Leaders Network Houston, American Leadership Forum, HR Houston, and Texas Economic Development Council.

To Wiley and the editorial team for believing in this work and its "right for right now" feel and the professional contributions to its success—may this be the start of a long and fruitful collaboration.

Finally, we acknowledge the many individuals whose influence may not be visible on the page but has been no less significant. Each conversation, book circle, breakfast club, collaboration, and gesture of support has contributed to the development of this work. We are grateful for the collective effort that made its completion possible.

We hope this book leads a conversation that is so desperately needed in our businesses and we acknowledge what is yet to come.

About the Authors

Alex Bailey is CEO and founder of Bailey & French a global consulting firm. She is an organizational/industrial psychologist and a global expert in humanizing the workplace, having pioneered the application of early scientific research in positive psychology at scale worldwide. A dynamic public speaker, she moderates key conversations on international stages and hosts monthly live events streamed to thousands, tackling workplace mega trends. She also writes for publications including *Dynamic Women in Business Magazine, Management Today*, and *HR Magazine*, sharing insights on purpose, performance, human sustainability, and human connection.

With over 25 years of experience working with and within large global organizations, Alex blends cutting-edge research with people-focused strategies to drive cultural evolution and create environments where individuals and teams thrive. Her innovative approach highlights human differentiators that set us apart from artificial intelligence (AI), empowering organizations to face the future with confidence.

Under Alex's leadership, Bailey & French has grown to 160 team members based out of Brighton, United Kingdom, and Houston, Texas, United States, and has expanded reach from across Europe and firms spanning North America to over 155 countries worldwide working with hundreds of thousands of leaders. Alex personally supports exec/board/ C-suite teams of blue-chip companies and government bodies through major transformation focusing on strategic human engagement. Her visionary leadership is redefining purpose-driven businesses by embedding human connection and sustainability into organizational success worldwide.

She has supported the International Positive Psychology Association as a division advisor, is an enterprise ambassador for the University of Brighton, and was an original volunteer for Action for Happiness, growing its membership base from a small UK initiative to a global movement.

Bailey & French recently won "Company of the Year" and Alex was a finalist for "Businesswoman of the Year 2022" in the Dynamic Business Awards (Platinum Media). She's also received the BHABA Award for Innovation in 2019 and was a Sussex Business Awards finalist for Large Business of the Year, 2021.

Alex has lived between the United Kingdom and the United States all her life and currently splits her time with her family between Sussex and Texas.

Kerri O'Neill is a renowned human resources and organizational change strategist. She is currently the chief people officer at Ipsos in the United Kingdom and Ireland and its global AI workplace transformation lead. Ipsos is a global leader in market research and insight operating in over 90 countries. With more than two decades of experience in strategic human resources (HR) and organizational transformation, Kerri has built a reputation for whip-smart thinking and rewriting the people strategies that enable businesses to thrive in complex, fast-changing environments.

Recognized as part of the CIPD HR30, Kerri is a multi-award-winning leader, a trusted voice in the HR community, a regular keynote speaker, and a strategic advisor for boards and leaders seeking to transform their organizations. As a member of UK CIPD AI Advisory Board she champions ethical innovation, proving that technology and humanity can—and must—coexist.

Kerri has been at the heart of some of the most defining shifts of our recent times delivering commercial solutions that have made a measurable difference. From helping to steer a global insurer through the financial crisis, to leading the people strategy to accelerate a major retailer shift to online commerce to ensuring a regulator could build its online safety capabilities in record time and now leading the AI transformation of the workforce,

Her global journey includes working in Singapore for four years, where she designed and implemented strategies that influenced decisions across continents and cultures.

Kerri's impact extends beyond the corporate sphere into the boardroom. As a trustee on the board of directors at Oxfam GB, she helps ensure the governance and strategic direction of one of the world's leading international nongovernmental organizations. She has also served on the board of an arts-based organization and has acted as an ambassador for girls' education globally. A qualified executive coach, passionate mentor, and community builder, she champions emerging leaders, sharing insights and building the next generation of talent. Her mission is clear: to create thriving organizations ready to succeed in the years ahead.

Kerri lives in Farnham, Surrey (United Kingdom), with her husband and daughter.

Index